SING THE BELOVED COUNTRY

SING THE BELOVED COUNTRY

THE STRUGGLE FOR THE NEW SOUTH AFRICA

Peter Hain

Pluto Press
LONDON • CHICAGO, IL.

First published 1996 by Pluto Press
345 Archway Road, London N6 5AA
and 1436 West Randolph, Chicago,
Illinois 60607, USA

British Library Cataloguing in Publication Data
A catalogue record for this book is available from the British Library

ISBN 0 7453 0996 8   hardback

Library of Congress Cataloging in Publication Data
Hain, Peter, 1950–
Sing the beloved country : the struggle for the new South Africa /
Peter Hain.
     p.   cm.
Includes bibliographical references and index.
ISBN 0–7453–0996–8 (hardback)
1. Hain, Peter, 1950–   . 2. South Africa—Politics and
government—1948–   3. South Africa—Race relations.
4. Revolutionaries—South Africa—Biography. I. Title.
DT1945.H35   1996
968.08—dc20   96–26350
                                                              CIP
Printing history: 01 00 99 98 97 96   5   4   3   2   1

Designed, typeset and produced for Pluto Press by
Chase Production Services, Chipping Norton, OX7 5QR
Printed in the EC by J. W. Arrowsmith Ltd, Bristol

For Sam and Jake: these are your roots

CONTENTS

LIST OF MAPS

FOREWORD

The African National Congress has created a remarkable spirit of national reconciliation by being generous in victory and forgiving in government. We have only been able to do so because of our people's wonderful tolerance and absence of any desire for revenge.

But forgiving is not the same as forgetting. We must never forget that the ANC leadership would have remained in our cells, and our people would have remained in the prison of apartheid, without the support of the many millions who struggled across the world to defeat the Old South Africa.

Peter Hain does not allow us to forget. His story of that struggle is very much to be welcomed. I remember how, with Nelson Mandela and our comrades on Robben Island, we heard with great joy of the demonstrations he led to stop the 1969–70 Springbok rugby and cricket tours. In the decades that followed, our spirits were also lifted by the unstinting campaigning of the Anti-Apartheid Movement.

We remember, too, how his parents joined many thousands of other South Africans, black and white, in the internal resistance – and we salute their courage. If others had done the same, much suffering, much pain and much killing could have been avoided.

Of course we shake hands with our old enemies, both inside our country and abroad. But our hearts remain with all those who supported us when it really mattered. Let this book be a testament to the courage and sacrifices of all anti-apartheid campaigners the world over.

Let me also make a fresh appeal: those who boycotted South African goods should now buy them. To create the jobs, the houses, the schools and the hospitals that our people cry out for, we must have the support of a new international solidarity movement. Foreign investment, fair trade agreements, international aid and assistance – all are needed. We have defeated apartheid. Let us now complete the job of building our new non-racial democracy.

Walter Sisulu
Orlando East,
Johannesburg,
July 1996

ACKNOWLEDGEMENTS

I am grateful to my parents, Adelaine and Walter Hain, who throughout my life have unstintingly given me love and support. To the extent that I have been able to help bring about political change, they have been indispensable. Both helped with this book, my father with extensive research and drafts of some chapters, my mother with advice and typing; my sister Sally also helped with typing. I am grateful to my wife Pat for so supportively continuing to put up with my hyperactivity. My thanks also to Anne Beech, Ethel de Keyser, Jill Hays, Isobel Larkin and Donald Woods for their comments on the manuscript.

Peter Hain,
Resolven, Neath
July 1996

*Do not deceive yourself into thinking
that racialism is just another
tyranny, like political tyranny, or
religious tyranny. I know many people
who have changed their religion, and
many who have changed their politics.
But I know of nobody who has ever
changed their race. And that is the
way to Armageddon. For racialism is
the only absolute tyranny.*

Albert Luthuli,
ANC President 1952–67

PROLOGUE

Nelson Mandela paused and looked up. Stretched out in front of him was Pretoria, the old capital of apartheid. Below, the huge multi-racial crowd waited expectantly. Many could hardly credit they were actually witnessing his installation as the new President of South Africa.

Was this for real? The man who had been locked up for 10,000 days? The long-time hated 'terrorist' of white folklore? Now about to assume the highest office in the land as a revered figure after a magnificent election victory? Would they wake up and find it was all a dream?

Hours before, tens of thousands of blacks had poured onto the carefully manicured green lawns stretching below the Union Buildings, the fine old colonial seat of government. They had done so with some trepidation. Not simply because they feared Mandela's induction might be snatched away at the last moment. Not simply because they were still in a state of suspended disbelief at the democratic transformation of the country. But because in the old days, blacks – except for nannies in charge of white children – were not even allowed to step onto the grass they now carpeted so joyously: like many of the country's fine parks, it had always been reserved for whites.

The symbols of change were everywhere. On top of one of the much feared Casspirs – armoured vehicles which had terrorised the townships – the new national flag fluttered languidly in the sunshine. Overhead a flock of jets shot by to salute the new President. Alongside, police officers and soldiers relaxed with the crowd which only a few years before they would have harassed and intimidated.

No, the people didn't have to pinch themselves. Nor did the hundreds of millions across the world who watched live coverage on television. It was no mirage. The date was 10 May 1994, the African National Congress had been elected by a landslide and Nelson Mandela was about to take the oath of office. For the first time in modern history a highly privileged elite – perhaps the most privileged of all – had given up power voluntarily. Not after a violent putsch but – even if reluctantly – relatively peacefully and democratically. The people were correct: it was indeed a miracle.

This is a story of that miracle. It is not *the* story. Millions took part in the struggle against apartheid. Some played an absolutely decisive role, many a significant one. But most, including my family, were foot soldiers in the rise and fall of apartheid. Partly by intent and partly by chance we happened to be involved almost from the beginning to the end, living first inside South Africa and then – after being forced into exile – outside.

Our particular experience is a convenient vehicle for telling the story in a way that is intended to be popular and readable. We make no claims to special importance. Yes, my parents were among the leaders of the struggle in Pretoria in the early 1960s. Yes, they were jailed, banned and eventually denied a livelihood. Yes, I led the campaign against apartheid sports tours from 1969–70. Yes, I faced attacks – one near fatal – from the South African security services, while living in London. But our role was modest. And our sacrifices were infinitesimal compared with those of countless others so brutally killed, maimed, jailed for life or who suffered terrible poverty and privation. This book is their testimony. Their sacrifices were not in vain.

MAP 1 SOUTHERN AFRICA

1 ROOTS

Some time between midnight and the early morning, a hand shook me awake. 'Peter, your parents have been put in jail.' I was eleven years old. It reminded me vaguely of the previous year when I had also woken in the early hours, this time with strangers in the bedroom of our Pretoria home. Except that then it had seemed incongruous: Security Police were searching through my motor car scrapbooks for incriminating evidence which of course wasn't there. Now it seemed much more for real.

None of my white cousins or schoolfriends would have experienced anything like this, for they were 'normal' English-speaking whites. So by origin were my parents. I was born in 1950: my mother was descended from the English 1820 settlers and my father from Glaswegian immigrants after the 1914–18 World War. Our lifestyle, at least to begin with, was conventional: father out at work, mother running the home, a brother and two sisters, all living in a comfortable rented detached house set in ample grounds with a black servant living in a separate room next to the garage.

Until I was about eight my parents' social circle was typical. We were far from affluent, but it was a happy, carefree and secure childhood, with the weather and the space for outdoor activities. Pretoria in those days was very easy going and we were able to roam without restriction on our bicycles and in our soapbox cars. And every December the two rear bench seats of our Volkswagen minibus were turned into a bed for the 700-mile overnight trip to my maternal grandparents' home on the banks of the Kowie River, at the little seaside town of Port Alfred in the Eastern Cape. There we spent our Christmas holidays, fishing off the jetty or spending long lazy days on the broad sandy Indian Ocean beaches.

The process of making South Africa such a very pleasant place in which a white boy could grow up had begun some 300 years earlier. In 1652, the first permanent settlers from the Netherlands landed at the Cape of Good Hope on the south-western tip of Africa. In 1688, Huguenot refugees arrived from France to be joined later by German immigrants; the Afrikaner people derived mainly from these three ethnic groups. The land of the indigenous nomadic herdsmen, the Khoikhoi (Hottentots), was progressively expropriated and eventually they, together with Malay slaves from the Dutch East Indies and the offspring of mixed race marriages, became the Cape Coloured people (or 'Coloureds'). The other indigenous inhabitants, the San hunter-gatherers (Bushmen), were virtually eliminated by hunting down and killing. Additionally Indian indentured labour was imported from 1860 to work the sugar cane plantations in Natal, and formed another significant racial group.

After Britain annexed the Cape in 1806, British settlement increased. In the 1820s some 5000 immigrants (including my mother's ancestors) were settled along the 'white' side of the Fish River, about 500 miles east of the Cape, as a bulwark against the black tribes that occupied most of the remaining area of the country. By the 1830s many Afrikaners (Boers) had become dissatisfied with British rule in the Cape. A major reason was the abolition of slavery, which for generations had provided the economic basis for Boer agriculture, together with the low compensation paid by the British upon emancipation. So, in what became known as 'The Great Trek', they moved north-eastward into black territory, using the advantage conferred by their guns and horses to subdue any black tribes that resisted them and eventually establishing their own independent Boer states. Ultimately almost the whole of the land of what is now known as South Africa had been expropriated and was under white dominance.

By the beginning of the second of the Anglo-Boer Wars in 1899, South Africa consisted of the Cape and Natal (both British colonies) and the independent Boer Republics of the Orange Free State and the Transvaal. This war, which resulted from Britain's wish to gain control of the Transvaal goldmines (under the pretext of obtaining the vote for the foreigners who had flocked in to work them), ended with the defeat of the Boers in 1902. It also saw the first concentra-

tion camps, when the British moved Boer families off the
farms which provided bases for the marauding Boer guerrillas, crowding them into camps where sanitary conditions
were primitive and disease rife. Some 26,000 Afrikaner
women and children died, leaving a scar on the Afrikaner
psyche which still endures.

However Britain could not extinguish Afrikaner national-
ism: the treaty which ended the war led to negotiations, and
the eventual granting of South Africa's independence in
1910. Under the Act of Union political equality was given to
all whites but restrictions on the rights of blacks, Indians
and Coloureds continued. So the conquest of the country
ended with whites occupying 88 per cent of the land they
had chosen to farm and settle (and which just happened to
contain all the country's known natural resources). The main
black tribes were shouldered aside into scattered pockets of
land away from the 'white' areas, called Native Reserves. The
1913 Natives Land Act, a cornerstone of South Africa's racist
legislation, prevented blacks from acquiring land in 'white'
areas (i.e. all but 12 per cent of the country). The Act also
enabled the eviction of 'surplus natives' who had lived on
'white' farms before their acquisition by the white owner. As
a result thousands of black families were driven off farms, to
wander homeless and starving; or to live in squalid townships called 'locations' outside the urban areas. The main
body of Indian people was in Natal and most Coloureds were
in the Cape.

Until the age of 19, my mother lived on the outskirts of Port
Alfred, close to a Coloured family and with Africans of the
Xhosa tribe passing her door en route to the town. Her father
was prominent in the Eastern Cape branch of the mainly English speaking United Party which was led by Jan Smuts, and
she sometimes accompanied him to public meetings. She was
the more politically aware of the two when she married my
father in 1948. Although he had been brought up to question
everything, and although his parents had been socialists in
their youth in Glasgow, they did not become involved in the
party politics of their adopted country; like most British immigrants they went along with the status quo.

Most white South Africans continued to live a life thriv-
ing off apartheid but curiously insulated from its terrible consequences. Current affairs was not being taught in schools
and my parents had little knowledge of the mesh of repressive laws that stultified black life. They knew little of the

African National Congress (ANC) or of its new emerging
leaders in the late 1940s: Oliver Tambo, Walter Sisulu and
Nelson Mandela; but, unusually for whites, they did share a
regard for, and tolerance towards, blacks.

In the 1948 general election there was a decisive result.
Jan Smuts' United Party (UP) had taken South Africa into
the Second World War on the Allies' side by a mere 13 votes
(there was significant pro-Nazi sympathy among Afrikaners,
some of whose leaders, including a later Prime Minister John
Vorster, were interned). The UP, which had governed the
country throughout the war, was unexpectedly defeated. The
winning Afrikaner Nationalist coalition offered the whites-
only electorate a much more fundamentalist ideological commitment to rigid separation of the races than the more pragmatic UP. The new Prime Minister, Daniel Francois Malan,
took office fully prepared with a strong and united party that
was in complete control of the Afrikaner people socially, economically, religiously and educationally.

The Nationalist Government reformulated the country's
traditional racial divisions with a policy termed 'apartheid'
(meaning 'separateness'). Its legislative cornerstone was the
Population Registration Act, a later amendment to which
statutorily defined 'whiteness' in terms which perfectly captured the Orwellian character of apartheid:

A white person means a person who:
(a) in appearance is obviously a white person and who is
    not generally accepted as a Coloured person; or
(b) is generally accepted as a white person and is not in
    appearance obviously not a white person.

Under this Act all South Africans were processed by Race
Classification Boards into their racial groups. This determined the form of obligatory identity document with which
they would be issued. If they were judged white or Coloured
(Indians and Chinese were included with Coloureds) this
would consist of an identity card containing a photograph,
signature, identity number and racial group. If judged to be
black ('Bantu' in the official jargon) and over the age of 16,
the document would be a reference book which would also
specify in which particular urban area he or she had permission to be, whether permission had been granted to work
there and for whom. The book would have to be signed by
the employer every month and had to include tax receipts.
The Reference Book – commonly known as a 'pass' – had to

be kept on the bearer's person 24 hours a day and failure to produce it to the police on demand rendered blacks liable to arrest under the Pass Laws.

On the basis of race the Group Areas Act set out where the individual could live and with whom. If the person was judged white, this would not be of undue concern, since white areas comprised 88 per cent of the country and included all the industrial and business areas, all the urban areas with their garden suburbs and swimming pools, and all the popular beauty spots and holiday resorts. If the person was judged Coloured, living would be restricted to designated residential areas outside the towns, and commercial activities would be confined to these areas, although employment could be sought in the towns. Coloureds could also find, as Indian shopkeepers in the Transvaal did, that they were uprooted from premises which they and their families had occupied for half a century, then banished miles away to the bare *veld*.

If they were judged black, they would find themselves further classified into a particular tribal group. The latter classification would determine – subject to the permission of the local chief – in which tribal reserve they would have residential rights. To live outside this reserve (which they might never have seen or have any knowledge of, and which could be as much as a thousand miles away) required the permission of a white official, entered in the pass. This permission, which was not automatically granted and could be withdrawn at any time, would be for a specified area only, usually a town. Furthermore, blacks could not remain in any area other than the one for which they had specific permission for more than 72 hours without another permit.

With the exception of domestic servants who were allowed to 'live in', all blacks residing in an urban area were obliged to live in segregated municipal townships, usually separated from the town proper by a buffer strip of open country. A permit was required to live in these townships, which were under the control of a white superintendent; no white could enter them without a permit. Children over the age of 18 could not live with their parents in these townships without a permit, and in the larger townships, which were segregated on tribal lines, a wife of a different tribe required a permit to live with her husband. Every urban area had a curfew – from 11 p.m. in the larger towns and 9.30 p.m. in the smaller ones – after which no black could be on the streets without a special pass signed by a white.

It was also important to control dissent, including among whites. Under the 1950 Suppression of Communism Act, as the former British Lord Chancellor Lord Gardiner pointed out, you were a 'communist' if the Minister of Justice said so. The Communist Party of South Africa – which had been founded in 1921 and was the only white group to work with blacks without any sense of a colour bar – was forced to dissolve itself. The Act signalled the beginning of the end of the rule of law in South Africa, since it enabled the Minister of Justice to restrict the liberty of individuals without trial or charge. The minister could issue banning orders against anybody who was deemed to be engaged in any activity that was 'furthering the achievement of the objects of communism'. The minister was not obliged to give reasons for bannings and the victim had neither right of appeal nor recourse to the courts.

A banning order was in force for five years and, among other things, restricted banned people to a specified magisterial district and within that district prohibited them from entering certain areas such as areas reserved for different racial groups, educational premises and courts of law. The ban, as our family was also to discover, prohibited banned persons from communicating with one another. They could not be publicly quoted, were prohibited from participating in the preparation of any published matter and from giving educational instruction to anyone except their own children. They could not belong to any organisation which discussed the policies of the Government, were prohibited from attending gatherings of more than two people and were required to report to the police once a week. A more extreme form of banning was 'house arrest' under which, in addition to the restrictions mentioned above, victims were prohibited from leaving their dwellings between 6 p.m. and 6 a.m. on weekdays and from midday on Saturdays until 6 a.m. on Mondays. They could only be visited at home by individuals named in the ban, and could be required to report to the police every day: in effect they became non-persons.

After my father completed his university architectural degree in 1949 he got a job in Kenya, where I was born, in Nairobi in February 1950. In 1951 my parents decided to return to South Africa. The more relaxed racial structure in Kenya had been an eye-opener, as was the heart of black Africa they observed and experienced in an eventful 3000-mile drive back home. After a stay at Port Alfred, we moved to Natal, living first in Pietermaritzburg and then Ladysmith, where my brother Tom was born. Then, in 1953, my parents received a letter from Peter Brown, Secretary of the newly formed non-racial Liberal Party of South Africa, saying that he had been given their names by a mutual friend from Kenya, Jock Barnes, also now back in South Africa, as people who might be interested in joining the Liberal Party. Their experiences in Kenya and on their trip, together with the thrust of the Nationalist Government's policies since 1948, encouraged a positive response. A branch was started in Ladysmith, and the inaugural meeting took place in our house and was addressed by Alan Paton. Among those who joined was Elliot Mngadi, a Zulu who was later to become the National Treasurer of the party and a much loved Liberal; he remarked: 'This is the first time I've ever come through the front door of a white man's house.'

Despite their involvement with the Liberal Party, my parents had remained surprisingly ill-informed of significant events on the non-white side of South African political life. They had little knowledge, for example, of the 1952 Defiance Campaign of civil disobedience mounted by the African National Congress, in which over 8000 volunteers committed technical offences such as contraventions of Pass Laws, apartheid regulations and curfew regulations. Many, including Nelson Mandela, were jailed.

Nor did my parents know of the banning in 1953 of about 100 ANC and trade union leaders, including the ANC President Albert Luthuli and Nelson Mandela. And they were only vaguely aware of the Congress of the People that the ANC organised at Kliptown near Johannesburg in 1955, attended by 3000 delegates of all races at which the Freedom Charter calling for equal rights for all South Africans was adopted. In the Congress Alliance the ANC was joined by the SA Indian Congress (which had been formed by Gandhi in 1894), the SA Congress of Trade Unions (SACTU), the newly formed Coloured Peoples' Organisation and the Congress of Democrats (COD) which had been formed in 1953, mainly from ex-members of the Communist Party. That these important developments passed my parents by, illustrates how even politically aware whites were insulated from the pulse of the black majority and its growing resistance to the growth of apartheid.

The African National Congress – originally called the South African Native National Congress – had been established in

January 1912. It rejected tribal divisions and demanded equal rights and justice for blacks. The first gathering opened with a hymn 'Nkosi Sikelel' iAfrika' (God bless Africa), which became the ANC's national anthem. The ANC flag, adopted in 1925, was black for the people, green for the land and gold for the resources. For decades the organisation had conducted a dignified, peaceful campaign for justice. But this had achieved little, and in 1944 a group of young radicals, led by Walter Sisulu, Oliver Tambo and Nelson Mandela, formed a Youth League to galvanise the ANC. Mandela became President of the League, which had prepared a Programme of Action aimed at organising the ANC into a militant mass movement to stimulate the development of a powerful national liberation force. After the ANC elections in 1949, in which the League-supported candidate Dr Moroka became President, Sisulu was appointed Secretary-General, Mandela was elected to the National Executive and the Programme of Action was adopted. It rejected apartheid, advocated the use of boycotts, strikes, civil disobedience and non-cooperation and called for a national stoppage of work to be organised as a day of protest against the government's reactionary policy.

So the ANC was launched on a wholly new strategy based on mass direct action. But before the protest could be organised on May Day 1950, an ad hoc grouping of the Transvaal ANC, Communists and the Indian Congress called for a stoppage on the same day in the Johannesburg area to protest against the banning orders placed on several prominent activists. Despite the furious opposition of the Youth League and a government ban on demonstrations, over half the workforce stayed at home. This grassroots backing for the strike was an eye-opener to the young intellectuals in the League. Mandela said the day was a turning point in his life, as he witnessed both the ruthlessness of the police (18 killed and over 30 injured) and the support given by black workers. He met and became friends with two of the stoppage organisers, Paul Joseph (whom we later met in England) and Ahmed Kathrada (later an ANC MP in the Government of National Unity).

Later in 1950 Mandela and Sisulu discussed the next stage of the Programme: the call for civil disobedience. Sisulu thought all races should be invited to take part in the campaign. Mandela, though initially resistant, remembered the May Day demonstration when the people had supported something he had opposed. From then on he accepted cooperation from all races, as well as from Communists. In 1952 Chief Albert Luthuli was elected ANC National President, with Mandela elevated as his deputy. Luthuli remained in post until 1967 when, banned to his home in Groutville, Natal and in failing health, he was knocked down by a train and killed. (He was succeeded by Oliver Tambo, then in exile in Lusaka, who remained President until his own death in 1993.)

In 1954 we moved to Pretoria, where my parents had married and where my sister Jo-anne was born that October. The move temporarily loosened their connection with the Liberal Party when they were unable to make contact with any local members. Later, when my aunt Jo was living in London, as they had always wanted to visit Britain, they decided they had better do so before their children were old enough to incur substantial travel costs and while she was still living there. They sold their car to pay for the fare, my father arranged for a job in London, and we embarked at Cape Town at the beginning of 1956. In England, we lived in London at first, where I began school in Ealing, and then moved to an empty cowman's cottage on a friend's farm in Ruckinge overlooking Romney Marsh in Kent. My sister Sally was born there that Christmas.

Soon after they had arrived my parents discovered the *Manchester Guardian* (after discarding *The Times* and *Daily Telegraph*, which they thought no political improvement on the Johannesburg *Star*) and the *Observer*. Through both papers they gained an understanding of world affairs which would not have been possible through the parochial and conservative South African press. Great events occurred in 1956: Suez, when the British, French and Israelis attacked Egypt, and the Soviet invasion of Hungary – they strongly opposed both.

They also read of the tumult in their home country. In August 1956 10,000 women of all races gathered at the seat of government, the Union Buildings in Pretoria, in protest against the extension of the Pass Laws to women and left a petition with 7000 signatures at the Prime Minister's office. Then in December 156 people – 105 blacks, 23 whites, 21 Indians and 7 Coloureds – including Luthuli, Sisulu, Mandela and Tambo, were arrested on charges under the Suppression of Communism Act and high treason.

In 1957 the Immorality Act, outlawing sexual intercourse between whites and members of any other racial group, was introduced. That year also saw the successful bus boycotts against a rise in fares in Alexandra township outside Johannesburg and in Lady Selborne in Pretoria, and large scale unrest in the Western Transvaal as women protested against passes. Large numbers were arrested and 500 people took refuge across the border in Botswana.

My parents had followed all these events avidly, and were becoming concerned and restive. Late in 1957 when my father's old firm in Pretoria telephoned and asked him to return, they decided to do so. He flew out early in December and Mom followed by sea with us on a Union Castle liner (the normal way in those days). There was a hum of excited anticipation as the ship pulled into Port Elizabeth docks in the hot summer sunshine. For a little boy it seemed an enormous drop from the deck to the quay below where Dad, whom we had not seen for six long weeks, waited with both sets of grandparents. I could also see hammerhead sharks circling the hull.

2 REPRESSION

The local Liberal Party had become active by the time we returned to Pretoria in 1958 and, after being contacted by its Chairman, John Brink, my parents rejoined. Their introduction to the branch's activities was dramatic. A peaceful women's demonstration against passes in the nearby black township of Lady Selborne was broken up by baton-wielding police; many were injured and feelings ran high. John Brink had driven in to try to restrain the police and when he failed to return my Dad drove out to look for him and was met by John returning in a windowless car. The township was in an uproar, his car had been stoned and he'd only managed to get out when the local ANC organiser, Peter Magano, jumped onto the bonnet.

Later my parents were to become so well known in Selborne that they could come and go at all times with impunity. They were soon on the Pretoria Liberals' Committee and my mother became Branch secretary, a position she held until she was banned in 1963. The Liberal Party's appeal was based on membership open to all racial groups on an equal basis, while other SA political organisations, including the ANC and the Congress of Democrats, were racially exclusive. It was therefore the only party that all South Africans could join, where they could formulate party policies, participate in elections and serve as officers. Unlike the parties represented in Parliament (including Helen Suzman's Progressives formed in 1959), it was committed to universal franchise. Although it contained a range of opinion from socialists to classical liberals, both its unity and its radicalism sprang from an uncompromising support for human rights and a fierce anti-racism.

The Pretoria party's main activities were in Lady Selborne, the freehold township where the majority of its black members lived, and in the Cape Reserve/Asiatic Bazaar, where there was a substantial Coloured and Asian membership. Entrance to Pretoria's African townships of Atteridgeville and Mamelodi was controlled by police posts on the main gates, restricting access for whites. But a black member had shown us an unmarked back entry into Atteridgeville, enabling clandestine visits there when required. In Lady Selborne, the Cape Reserve/Asiatic Bazaar areas and Eastwood, the party was able to organise because these areas were open to all races. Lady Selborne, cheek-by-jowl with white suburbs, was not even separated by the usual buffer-zone of *veld* from the outlying white suburbs.

On 1 August 1958, the Treason Trial opened in the Old Synagogue courtroom in Pretoria. At lunchtime, many of the accused went outside for a meal provided in turn by the local Indian community and by sympathisers. The Liberals also helped and it was then that my parents first met and talked to Walter Sisulu and Nelson Mandela (whom they remember as 'a large, imposing, smiling man').

Charges were dropped against 65 of the accused (including Luthuli and Tambo) and the remaining 91 (including Mandela and Sisulu) were charged with treason. To support the Treason Trial defendants and their families, the British Defence and Aid Fund for Southern Africa (BDAF) had been founded in London in 1956 by Canon John Collins and raised £250,000, with the money distributed by a local Defence and Aid Fund. The BDAF arose out of an earlier initiative in 1953 when Trevor Huddleston, then a young priest in South Africa, wrote to Canon Collins to ask if his Christian Action agency could support the families of people imprisoned in the Defiance Campaign, and Collins raised £800. So began a fundraising campaign which, over the next 40 years, sent more than £100 million to defend opponents of apartheid and support their families.

In 1958, a Liberal Party member, Patrick Duncan, launched a weekly news and comment magazine, *Contact*, covering the anti-apartheid struggle. My parents subscribed and Mom later became its Pretoria correspondent, covering Nelson Mandela's trial and other trials until she was banned. But many whites in Pretoria, a bastion of Afrikanerdom, remained bitterly opposed to the very existence of the Liberal Party. Students at the local university, an Afrikaans-speaking institution, were militantly pro-apartheid and would line up outside party meetings, shouting slogans and abuse. By contrast my parents became close friends with many blacks, like David Rathswaffo, who lived in Lady Selborne and was a Clerk at the Supreme Court in Pretoria, where all the major political trials took place. In 1959 the Government decided that blacks should not carry out such responsible tasks, so David was replaced by a white man – whom he had to train for the job – and made redundant. He was later engaged as the branch's organiser, operating mainly in Lady Selborne and the townships.

Meanwhile the noose of apartheid tightened remorselessly. Having taken over from Prime Minister Malan in 1954, J.G. Strijdom died in 1958 and was succeeded by Hendrik Verwoerd, a more intellectual leader who had an absolute belief in apartheid. In 1959, in order to complete the educational separation of the races, Verwoerd introduced the Extension of University Education Act, which ended the attendance of blacks at the white universities and set up black colleges in the rural areas of the Northern Transvaal and Zululand. Several years earlier, he had complained that the pre-apartheid system of schooling had misled blacks by showing them 'the green pastures of white society in which they are not allowed to graze'. The 1953 Bantu Education Act, Verwoerd said, was to train blacks for their station in life: 'What is the use of teaching a Bantu child mathematics when it cannot use it in practice?'

In 1959 a prominent Pretoria Liberal and local doctor, Colin Lang, contested the Pretoria East by-election to the Provincial Council as the Nationalists' only opponent. He turned in a creditable performance, with 24 per cent of the vote, saving his deposit. Our home was the campaign headquarters. This was my parents' first experience of electioneering and canvassing for a non-racial party among the overwhelmingly racist white electorate. I remember, aged nine, leafleting in the white suburbs, set among Jacaranda trees. Party members came across from Johannesburg to help – one of whom was Ernie Wentzel, a young advocate who subsequently became a great friend. He addressed open air public meetings from the back of a flat-bed lorry, silencing the hostile audience's shouts of 'Would you like your sister to marry a Kaffir?' (a common challenge to Liberals at the time) with the response (in a heavy Afrikaans accent): 'Christ man, you should see my sister!'

The by-election acted as a spur to the Pretoria branch and

for a year a monthly newsletter was distributed in Brooklyn
and Waterkloof, the two suburbs in which canvassing had
taken place. As it had been the suggestion of a branch activist, Maritz van den Berg, and of my parents, they were
deputed to produce it. Called *Libertas*, it had an editorial in
both English and Afrikaans, with articles in both languages
and later often in Sotho as well.

Around this time, a strong Africanist group broke from the
ANC, alleging the latter's domination by its white partner in
the Congress Alliance, the Congress of Democrats, which they
also criticised for being communist. Under the slogan 'Africa
for the Africans' they formed the Pan-Africanist Congress
(PAC), lead by Robert Sobukwe, a lecturer in African languages
at Witwatersrand University. The formation of the PAC
seemed significant and as the credo of blacks going it alone was
at odds with the Liberal Party's non-racial spirit, Sobukwe was
invited to address a branch meeting to put the PAC case. He
appeared with sundry blanketed henchmen and my parents
found him an imposing and engaging personality. But they
were not impressed by the fundamentalist utterances of some
of his colleagues nor by his failure to explain satisfactorily how,
once apartheid was abolished, he proposed to re-unite all the
races that it was PAC policy to divide.

However they were heartened by another prominent personality, the British Labour MP Barbara Castle, who was on a visit
to South Africa. With her vibrant, red-headed presence she
took everyone by storm – scandalising whites and boosting the
whole anti-apartheid struggle by refusing, for example, to use
whites-only lifts in Pretoria and insisting upon using the goods
lift specified for blacks.

In February 1960 the British Prime Minister Harold Macmil-
lan addressed the South African Parliament. *Libertas*, among
many others, had urged him to warn the Government of
where its policies were leading, so the Pretoria branch was
thrilled when he did just that in his famous 'winds of
change' speech. It was a shot in the arm to the anti-apartheid forces and a great embarrassment to Verwoerd and the
Nationalists. The psychological value of such interventions
could hardly be exaggerated, because there were so few
means of fighting the authorities in a police state.

The speech engendered hope among blacks burdened by
anger, poverty and frustration. The ANC leader, Albert
Luthuli, called for an economic boycott, and protests against
the Pass Laws increased. The ANC planned a major

campaign urging the abolition of passes on 31 March, leading up to mass demonstrations. The PAC also planned a campaign against the Pass Laws to begin on 21 March, when members were to leave their passes at home and surrender for arrest; the action was to be non-violent, they would disperse peacefully if ordered to do so and the police were informed. Although the ANC considered the campaign was insufficiently prepared and refused to cooperate, the PAC went ahead. At Sharpeville township near Vereeniging, south of Johannesburg, PAC members surrendered themselves at the police station and a peaceful crowd of residents, curious to see what was happening, pressed against the surrounding wire fence. Suddenly policemen standing on armoured vehicles inside the wire opened fire, using over 700 rounds and killing 69 men, women and children and wounding over 180 others. Most were shot in the back while running away. A few hours later at Langa, outside Cape Town, 2 were killed and 49 injured at a demonstration.

For days afterwards the police laid siege to Sharpeville: food was running short and my mother loaded our minibus with provisions, donated through the Liberals by all sorts of people. Stopping for petrol in Pretoria, she asked a black attendant to check the tyre pressures because 'we are heavily loaded with food for Sharpeville'. The van was instantly surrounded by black attendants, checking the tyres, cleaning the windscreen and then escorting them onto the highway, with encouraging shouts and whistles.

The killings reverberated around the world and riots swept the country. The Treason Trial was proceeding in Pretoria and Chief Luthuli, who was staying at John Brink's house while giving evidence, publicly burned his pass on 26 March and called on others to follow suit. His action coincided with the Government's suspension of the Pass Laws, which my parents heard about with great excitement at the Transvaal Provincial Congress of the Liberal Party. Luthuli was arrested, tried and later fined. My mother had the privilege of being sent to pay the fine and transport him back to the Brinks' home where I remember meeting him.

All political meetings had been prohibited immediately after the Sharpeville killings. Then on 30 March a state of emergency was declared and soon afterwards 2000 activists were detained (including all the Treason Trialists, Luthuli and other defence witnesses), plus 10,000 others. On 30 March a peaceful column of 30,000 blacks marched from the townships to Cape Town, led by a young PAC organiser from Lady Selborne,

Philip Kgosana. But it dispersed peacefully after police assurances to Kgosana that the Prime Minister would meet him to discuss black grievances. When he returned for this meeting, he was promptly arrested.

The relaxation of the Pass Laws gave false hope that they were to be abolished. For a short period there was a feeling throughout the country that apartheid was teetering: white political, commercial, financial and religious organisations called for an inquiry into the causes of the disturbances and a reassessment of policy. Then, as continuing strikes and protest marches rocked the country, the UN Security Council passed a resolution blaming the government for the shootings (Britain and France abstaining). An economic panic ensued. Foreign investment halted and there was a sharp outflow of capital, the share market slumped and the country's reserves fell.

Nevertheless the Pass Laws were reinstated on 7 April and the next day the ANC and PAC were declared unlawful organisations. The bannings were a heavy blow, particularly to the ANC, which for nearly half a century had struggled peacefully against discriminatory laws which in Europe would long before have led to bloody insurrection. Mandela and his colleagues (in prison at the time during the Treason Trial), decided they had no alternative but to reorganise the ANC to enable it to function underground. The PAC adopted the same course. Its leader Robert Sobukwe was imprisoned for three years for organising the Pass Law protests, followed by two further periods on Robben Island. (In 1969, suffering from cancer, he was released, banned and sent to Kimberley where he died in 1978.)

On 9 April Dr Verwoerd was shot in the head by a deranged white farmer while attending the Rand Easter Show and for a moment Nationalist resolve faltered; the acting Prime Minister, Mr P.O. Sauer, said in an astonishing speech on 21 May: 'The old book of South African history was closed a month ago and, for the immediate future, South Africa will reconsider in earnest and honesty her whole approach to the Native question.' However, Verwoerd recovered and resumed the reins of power more determined than ever to press ahead with his policies.

This period in 1960 was a tense time for our family. Along with some 2000 anti-apartheid activists, many prominent Liberals were detained throughout the country, including the National Chairman, Peter Brown. In Pretoria John Brink, Colin Lang and Reverend Mark Nye were arrested and

Maritz van den Berg took over as Chairman. For the first time our phone was tapped, our mail intercepted and our house in Arcadia Street regularly observed by the Security Police, but somehow my parents managed to preserve family life amid all the political pressures.

Then in June Mom was advised that her name had been seen on a list of people to be arrested and she should leave immediately. We arrived home from school to be told we were going on holiday. It was a nice surprise, though when I (as the oldest) was told the real reason my excitement was tempered with worry that we might be caught. As we headed for our grandparents' home in Port Alfred, it was a relief to see that we were not being followed.

My Dad managed to hitch a lift and joined us later. Since it was a criminal offence to divulge information on detainees and there was difficulty communicating between areas, he had been asked to check on the state of the party in the Eastern Province and Natal. We drove there before returning to Pretoria and I remember Alan Paton's house, The Long View, high up over-looking the hills outside Durban. He was kindly, though a little gruff, to a ten-year-old boy only half aware of his inter-national reputation. 'I'm not an all-or-nothing person, Peter. I'm an all-or-something person', he told me.

We returned after the emergency was lifted at the end of August and the remaining detainees were released. But soon afterwards our home at 1127 Arcadia Street was raided by the Security Police for the first time. Statements by people wounded at Sharpeville taken at Baragwanath Hospital the day after the shootings were seized and never seen again.

During the emergency the branch's white members contrib-uted food parcels for the families of ANC or PAC detainees and I sometimes helped my parents deliver these in our minibus to Lady Selborne, Atteridgeville and Eastwood. By now Mom had become known in Pretoria as the person to contact whenever anyone fell foul of the police, on one occasion helping bail a group of women from Soweto, including Walter Sisulu's mother. With the ANC and PAC now illegal, black member-ship in the Pretoria branch of the Liberal Party – by this time the only legal anti-apartheid group in the city – boomed. Branch meetings were held in our living room with my father and others collecting members from Lady Selborne and the Cape Reserve and taking them home afterwards.

In October 1960, Verwoerd called a whites-only referendum to decide whether South Africa should become a republic. The

Liberal Party called for a 'No' vote, not because it opposed a
republican state but because it saw this as heralding further
apartheid restrictions and my parents put up large 'NO' posters
after dark. The result was quite close: 850,000 voted Yes with
776,000 No and so, after 150 years, the country's links with
the British Crown came to an end. Eight months later Verwoerd attended the Commonwealth Prime Ministers' Conference in London and applied for South Africa's continued membership as a republic. But criticism of apartheid's treatment of
blacks was so strong that he was obliged to withdraw his appli-
cation and on 31 May 1961, the 51st anniversary of the Union, South Africa officially became a republic outside the Commonwealth – thus making anti-apartheid activists like us feel
even more isolated.

At the beginning of 1961, under its policy of eliminating
so-called 'blackspots' (black areas close to white towns), the
Government began the process of removing Lady Selborne
residents to Ga-Rankua, a rural area many miles away from
Pretoria. After repeated appeals had failed, the Pretoria
branch collected over 5000 signatures house to house in
Selborne for an appeal to be sent to the United Nations
asking the UN to intercede. But this too failed. Soon afterwards I woke one morning in the small hours to find the
Security Police searching my bedroom and going through my
motorcar files. They upset the cage of my pet white mouse
which escaped only to be pounced on and killed by our cat.
    That March the Treason Trial ended with the acquittal of
all defendants and Oliver Tambo left the country to ensure
that the ANC organisation survived outside South Africa.
Mandela went underground before he could be rearrested,
and became leader of the ANC armed wing, Umkhonto we
Sizwe (Spear of the Nation), which he said would perform
sabotage with strict instructions not to kill. I recall intense
discussions with my father who was totally opposed to violence, saying it always breeds more violence. He also warned
however that the longer apartheid continued the more violent
things would inevitably become.
    With the collapse of the Treason Trial, the Government
rushed through new powers to contain unrest, including
detention without trial for 12 days, which was passed in May
1961. Though still underground, Mandela called for a three-
day 'stay-at-home' from 29 to 31 May to protest against all
racial laws. My parents realised that it was merely a matter
of time before they would be detained. They told us of the

likelihood, and arranged for our grandparents to move in to look after us should it happen – which it did, in late May. With fellow party activists Maritz van den Berg and Colyn van Reenen they were putting up posters about the 'stay-at-home' one night in Lady Selborne (a perfectly legal activity) when the Security Police turned up and detained them. It didn't seem shocking to me; after all we had been through, it seemed almost normal and I recall being concerned rather than upset. My mother kept the letter I wrote to her. 'We are missing you a lot', it said in the clear, careful writing of an eleven-year-old.

After being held for the statutory 48 hours in Pretoria Central police station they were detained under the 12-day law – the first people to be so. The three men were taken off to a cell in Pretoria local jail: their conditions were not bad and they had each other's company. But my mother was locked up by herself in a large echoing hall in Pretoria Central Prison in which the white women detainees had been held during the 1960 emergency. She could hear the screams of black women prisoners being assaulted reverberating up the stairwell. She also found the wardresses, who came to watch her in the bath, flesh-creeping and intimidating. The four were in prison during the 31 May Republican Celebrations which took place in Pretoria and were pleased that it rained heavily throughout. After 12 days, they were all released on bail and ordered to appear later on some vague charge under the Suppression of Communism Act. I vividly remember walking home from school with Tom and Jo-anne and seeing my Dad, with Sally on his shoulders, strolling down the road to meet us. The police were naturally unable to produce any incriminating evidence and after a second court appearance the charge was withdrawn and they were released unconditionally.

The end of May stay-at-home had been a great success on the first day. But it fizzled out after misleading newspaper accounts on the extent of support together with massive police raids (some 10,000 blacks were detained), intimidation and opposition by the PAC (who objected to cooperating with other races). The last disciplined, mass non-violent demonstration to be held in South Africa was over.

By this time relations with our relatives had become increasingly strained. Although our wider family was quite close, none of them was at all politically involved. My uncle Hugh was by then the millionaire owner of a construction company and did not want his business affected. My aunt Marie ran a travel agency in Pretoria and felt obliged to place an advert in the *Pretoria News* saying that her company had nothing to do with the Mrs Hain of the Liberal Party who happened to be her sister-in-law. Despite the absence of any personal hostility between us, a barrier grew as we moved in different worlds. Later when life became extremely difficult and my father was out of a job, our well-off relatives could have helped; they chose not to do so. They remained in all other respects friendly towards us and (within the white framework) decent, caring citizens. It was simply that they were not 'political' and we were an embarrassment.

In June 1961 John and Meg Brink, who had been the driving force in the Pretoria branch for so long, left with their family for Australia. In such an authoritarian society, anti-apartheid activity made family life very difficult, and was not conducive to professional advancement. My father had been regularly warned about his Liberal Party activities and during his detention he received a letter of dismissal from the Transvaal Works Department. Losing his job was a big financial blow and we were helped by a donation from an anonymous party member. I remember shopping 'on tick' and being very aware that none of my schoolfriends were in a similar predicament.

In July 1961 Balthazaar Johannes ('John') Vorster was appointed Minister of Justice and in December the ANC leader Chief Albert Luthuli was awarded the Nobel Peace Prize. In the same month Umkhonto, directed by Nelson Mandela, began a campaign of placing incendiary bombs in government offices, post offices and electrical substations and carried out 200 attacks in the following 18 months. My parents were amazed that some of these bombs were placed in Pretoria offices where all Government workers, down to the cleaners, were white – until their ANC friend from Lady Selborne, Peter Magano, said, 'Don't forget the messenger "boys" are still black!' The term 'boy' was patronisingly applied by whites to all black men and from an early age I remember castigating friends when they called out to their gardeners in this way. The spectacle of bumptious young whites casually talking down to greying black grandfathers epitomised for me the daily indignity of apartheid.

With Mandela still underground a small farm was rented on Umkhonto's behalf at Rivonia on the outskirts of Johannesburg, and he spent some time there with his wife Winnie and their two daughters. Then in 1962 he left the country to visit

North, East and West Africa and London, where he met the
Labour and Liberal Party leaders and was photographed outside
Parliament. Rivonia, as it was to become known, became the
headquarters for Umkhonto and its ANC advisers.

During 1962 the Pretoria Liberal Party branch opened an
office at the north end of Prinsloo Street. Although very basic
(there was no electricity), David Rathswaffo as organiser and
my mother as secretary could be contacted there and branch
meetings took place there too. My father took over as chair and
so my parents occupied what were effectively the two top positions in Pretoria's legal anti-apartheid forces. As such they
became even more prominent targets in this, the citadel of
Afrikanerdom. They seemed to be permanently in the *Pretoria
News*. Late in 1962 my father began to write frequent leader
page articles for the *Rand Daily Mail*, the country's main liberal
newspaper. The same year the Sabotage Act was introduced.
Under it Helen Joseph, one of the original Treason Trial
accused whom my parents knew, became the first person to be
house arrested and confined at home between 6 p.m. and
6 a.m. and during weekends.

Then on 5 August, having been 17 months on the run,
Nelson Mandela was finally captured near Howick Falls in
Natal, after an informer had tipped off police. Mostly disguised as a chauffeur, he had evaded the authorities and
travelled throughout the country organising the ANC underground, with the media dubbing him the 'Black Pimpernel'.

Mandela's trial opened at the Old Synagogue in Pretoria
on 22 October and my mother covered it for the Liberal
magazine *Contact*. She was often the only one in the white
section of the public gallery when Mandela entered each day;
after raising his fist in the *Amandla!* salute to the packed
black section he would turn and do the same to her. She
found this acknowledgement very moving. Nearly 30 years
later when she and I met him in the House of Commons
she said, 'I don't suppose you remember me.' To which he
replied, giving her a great hug, 'How could I forget!' Mandela's magnetic personality dominated the courtroom but did
not prevent him being sentenced to five years' hard labour,
initially in Pretoria Central Prison before being transferred to
Robben Island. Winnie Mandela attended the trial each day,
often looking magnificent in tribal dress. Once, my sisters
went with Mom and Winnie bent down and kissed the two
little blonde girls, to the evident outrage of the onlooking
white policemen.

By now the world was beginning to mobilise against apartheid. On 6 November 1962 the General Assembly of the United Nations voted for sanctions against South Africa. My parents had become friendly with sympathetic people in two of the Foreign Embassies based in Pretoria, the administrative capital: Coen Stork from the Netherlands and Rudi Ernst from West Germany. Both mentioned the difficulty of meeting non-whites socially and suggested that the Liberal Party host a gathering to remedy this. The occasion of the Transvaal Congress of the Party early in 1963 was used to hold the first such gathering at our house with Alan Paton, Peter Brown and prominent Johannesburg members attending in addition to Pretoria people. It was a great success and many guests went on to a public meeting in the Asiatic Bazaar addressed by Brown and Paton. This was the forerunner of what became known amongst Liberals as our 'diplomatic parties'.

In January 1963 my mother was summoned before the Chief Magistrate of Pretoria and warned to desist from engaging in activities 'calculated to further the aims of Communism'. He was unable to specify which of her activities fell within this definition and advised her to write to John Vorster, Minister of Justice, for clarification. The reply from his Private Secretary merely repeated the phrase and then stated 'Should you so wish, you are of course at liberty to ignore the warning and, if as a result thereof, it is found necessary to take further action against you, you will only have yourself to blame.' Around this time a newspaper cartoon appeared which had Vorster saying 'Go and find Adelaine Hain, see what she is doing and tell her she mustn't.'

Meanwhile an offshoot of PAC, POQO (meaning 'we alone'), had been formed in 1962 in cells throughout urban and rural areas. They had the avowed intention of attacking white communities and murdering informers. In November two whites and five blacks were killed in the Cape, and in February 1963 five whites were killed in the Transkei. A POQO cell was formed in Pretoria and members in Atteridgeville combed the adjoining army firing range and recovered unexploded shells for sabotage use. But before they could take any action there were widespread arrests throughout the country, many of them secondary school children. Black parents suddenly found that their teenage children had disappeared. The detainees were held at police stations in and near Pretoria. Relatives were not informed, it was illegal to publicise arrests, and so it was almost impossible to find the detainees until they were produced in court.

My mother spent hours haunting the courts – sometimes dashing from one building to another when 'grapevine' information told of another group being produced. She waited for the detainees to appear so that she could find out their names, inform the parents and get legal representation for them if necessary. Most had been assaulted and tortured and she recalls one with a perforated eardrum and suffering from electric shock torture who had gone completely out of his mind and sat staring vacantly into space.

By 1963, with Liberal activists like my parents proving increasingly troublesome to both the Security Police and ministers, the Government set about the systematic destruction of the Party. In Parliament the Minister of Justice, John Vorster, accused Liberals and Communists of 'creating POQO'. The Liberals were smeared by the Nationalists and their press, who falsely suggested that the Party had been implicated in the Cape and Transkei killings. Government ministers stated in Parliament 'we will have to restrict the Liberal Party'. A cartoon in the English-language *Pretoria News* of 11 March 1963, titled 'the Scapegoat', had a goat marked 'Liberal Party' being dragged by a knife-wielding Vorster up a hill towards a sacrificial pyre at the summit, with Verwoerd and other government luminaries forming an applauding procession behind him. So, during 1963, many prominent members throughout the country were banned. The fear of repression increased almost daily, and I remember my parents warning us that life was going to get much more difficult. On 1 May 1963 a beleaguered Government extended its police state by introducing the notorious 90-day law which increased the existing 12 days for which people could be held without charge (and under which my parents were held in 1961) to 90 days.

In April, Walter Sisulu went underground while on bail pending an appeal against a six-year sentence for furthering the aims of the ANC and inciting the 1961 stay-at-home. On 12 July he and eight others, including Govan Mbeki, a prominent ANC leader from the Eastern Cape, were captured at the Rivonia farm. Many incriminating documents were found and three others were subsequently arrested. All disappeared into 90-day detention. Nelson Mandela was brought back from Robben Island to the Pretoria prison and what was to become known as The Rivonia Trial commenced at the Palace of Justice in Church Square, Pretoria. Then, on 9 October, the judge quashed the indictment. But although this demonstrated there was still some semblance of independence in the judiciary, the accused were immediately rearrested in the courtroom on a charge of sabotage.

A fresh trial began at the end of February 1964 and lasted over three months. The defence began with a four-hour-long statement from the dock by Accused No 1, Nelson Mandela, which he concluded with the now famous words: 'During my lifetime I have dedicated myself to this struggle of the African people. I have fought against white domination, and I have fought against black domination. I have cherished the ideal of a democratic and free society in which all persons live together in harmony and with equal opportunities. It is an ideal which I hope to live for and to achieve. But if needs be it is an ideal for which I am prepared to die.' These powerful words were a great inspiration to all involved in the struggle. But the trial was literally a matter of life and death because all those found guilty faced the death penalty.

There were world-wide pleas on their behalf. The UN called for their unconditional release and for that of all political prisoners in South Africa by 106 votes to 1 (the sole dissenter being the South African representative). Alan Paton – by now an internationally known author, especially for his masterpiece *Cry the Beloved Country* – praised their sincerity and courage and appealed for clemency 'because of the future of this country'. On 12 June they were all sentenced to life imprisonment. Dennis Goldberg was gaoled in Pretoria; Mandela, Sisulu, Mbeki, Mhlaba, Motsoaledi, Mlangeni and Kathrada were sent to Robben Island. The ANC's entire leadership had been sliced off and the scope for internal resistance was now paper thin.

With the lease of our house in Arcadia Street coming to an end, we moved home in July 1963 to a smallholding at The Willows, to the east of Pretoria and not far from Mamelodi. The rented house consisted of two large thatched *rondavels* (circular dwellings) on a terrace well back from the road and at the foot of a *kopje* (small hill). With a small, leaky swimming pool and space to play football and cricket, it was wonderful for children. It also had the added advantage of being in the catchment area for Pretoria Boys High, a state school which my father had attended.

Our move to The Willows seemed to take the Security Police by surprise. It was some weeks before they traced us, during which we escaped their attention for the first time for years. Our telephone had not yet been connected and they were unable to trace us that way. Then one day our maid

Eva Matjeka answered the door to a man who asked her the name of her 'baas'. Eva did her 'dumb kaffir' routine (with white strangers she always pretended to know nothing and understand less) and he was turning away when my mother went to see what was happening. He saw her, turned back and said that he was looking for a house that he'd heard was for sale. Eva was furious with my Mom for appearing. 'He's Special Branch', she said, 'now they'll know where we live'. She was right. Thereafter we had the usual Security Police cars parked on the road outside, our phone was speedily connected and tapping resumed.

In September 1963 there was a knock at the door which I answered, joined by my Mom. We were confronted by the same two large Security Police officers who had arrested my parents in 1961 – Sergeants Viktor and van Zyl (referred to as 'banana fingers' because of his huge hands). They handed Mom an envelope containing her banning order. This ran for five years and limited her to being in the company of not more than one person at a time, restricted her movements to the Pretoria magisterial district, prohibited her from entering certain specified places such as factories, non-white communities, school or university areas and Courts of Law. It also required her to report five miles away to Arcadia police station every Wednesday. The ban effectively ended her work as Secretary of the Pretoria Liberal Party and stopped any overt political activity whatsoever. It was also unique: for the first time in any banning order she was prohibited entrance to courts. The conclusion was that her practice of haunting the courts to gain representation for political prisoners, particularly during the POQO trials, was the main reason for her ban.

It was hardly unexpected; we had all discussed the possibility for months. But it left her feeling angry and frustrated. She was not even allowed to come into our schools and discuss our progress with teachers: that had to be done standing outside on the pavement. She effectively ceased to be a public person and could not be quoted by the media. The restriction on meeting more than one person at a time was a near fatal blow against political action.

Gradually however, she adjusted and worked out ways of acting as a contact for political prisoners whose relatives continued to approach her for assistance when they had problems. She seemed to me to be just as active and, although she could no longer participate overtly in the life of the Liberal Party, she was kept in touch daily with events by David Rathswaffo who took over the secretaryship. He would

telephone from a callbox near the party office and she would
then drive in to a prearranged rendezvous.

We began holding our 'diplomatic' parties again, with the
Security Police loitering around the gate taking down the car
registration numbers. The parties were usually timed to co-
incide with major Liberal Party events in Johannesburg, so
that party luminaries such as Alan Paton, Peter Brown and
Ernie Wentzel could attend in addition to our Pretoria members. My Mom's ban prevented her from taking part, so she
would sit in the kitchen and be visited by the guests one at
a time. Tom and I used to serve drinks under the guidance
of a Coloured member, Alban Thumbran (who had been a
waiter) while Jo-anne and Sally helped with the snacks.

On one occasion I heard a noise just outside. Peering
through the window in the dark I caught a glimpse of someone lurking on the side of the *kopje*, and called out to my
Dad 'Special Branch, Special Branch'. As we ran out there
was a commotion and a figure began charging noisily up
through the bushes and stony layers of the *kopje*. By now
the partygoers began to spill out. My Dad, running after his
quarry, shouted 'Peter – bring the gun!' Although I knew this
was a ruse the man ahead must have panicked. He picked
up a rock and threw it towards my Dad. It glanced off a tree
right in front of his face, and the man made off into the
night. The next morning we went up to have a look and
found a large gash on the branch; it brought home to us that
what had seemed like an exciting incident could have ended
in a family tragedy.

Two friends, Dr Fabian Ribeiro, a black doctor from Mamelodi, and his wife Florence, a sister-in-law of the PAC leader
Robert Sobukwe, used to drop in regularly at The Willows.
Unusually for blacks, they were financially well off. But
apartheid drastically restricted the way they could spend their
money. They could not own a house in their township, send
their children to the school of their choice, or take their
family on holiday since there were no resorts for blacks. So
they drove a Mercedes and dressed very well, Florence at the
height of fashion. In those days non-whites were not permitted to try on clothes before purchasing, so special arrangements had to be made for Florence to go in to Hamiltons,
Pretoria's top clothes shop, after hours so that she could try
on her choices without upsetting white customers.

Because of his political activities, my father's work opportunities were restricted to a limited number of private employers

who would take him on. We found increasing difficulty in making ends meet, so reluctantly we decided we could no longer afford our maid, Eva Matjeka. To everyone's regret, Eva, who had become one of the family, had to go. Her departure had only one positive effect: the servant's room was vacant when someone else had most need of it.

One morning my mother received a fraught telephone call from David Rathswaffo. Jimmy Makoejane had escaped from court and come to him for help. Aware that our phone was tapped, she cut him short by saying she would come into town right away. Jimmy was one of our PAC friends from Lady Selborne, who had been involved in the POQO campaign in 1963 and had managed to flee. But he had been kidnapped from a train on the Rhodesian border by the Security Police and returned for trial before managing to escape again during a recess. Jimmy was dropped off late that night near our house, where Dad secretly collected him and installed him in Eva's empty room.

The next day, with Jimmy lying down on the back seat of a friend's car and covered by a rug, Dad drove him out, attracting no interest from the Security Police who were watching for our cars. Jimmy got clean away, eventually ending up in Tanzania. My brother Tom and I knew something was happening that night, but we had learnt not to ask too many questions – I only heard the full story long afterwards in London. But when the Security Police played back their phone tap tapes, they arrested David who said that Jimmy had told him he'd been acquitted, had 'borrowed ten bob' and disappeared. They held David for a few days, taking away his epilepsy pills, but, fortunately for my parents, he told them nothing more.

Throughout these years I remained keen on sport and personally experienced the extent to which apartheid infected it. We used to swim regularly at the town's international standard swimming pool at Hillcrest. In 1962 South Africa was involved in lucrative trade deals with Japan and visiting Japanese businessmen were granted 'honorary white' status, allowing them to stay in hotels and enjoy privileges usually confined to whites alone. A Japanese swimming team came over too and, after initially refusing it access to the pool, Pretoria City Council relented: business apparently triumphing over racism. But the decision caused such uproar that the pool was drained after the team departed so that white customers could relax in fresh water.

We also used to watch our home football team, Arcadia, at the Caledonian stadium. (I played in its youth side.) Partitioned off on the other side of the stadium from us whites were non-white spectators, some personal friends. We used to mingle before the match and then separate. As with other sports events, we could not stand together or use the same entrances, toilets or facilities. Although Arcadia was an all-white team playing in an all-white league, black spectators were among the noisiest and most partisan supporters. Then the Government introduced proclamations banning non-whites from such major sports events. Our friends could no longer attend. The carnival atmosphere at Arcadia's home matches disappeared, but crowds of blacks still gathered outside, listening to the match. Some of the keenest shinned up to watch from trees adjoining the ground. But this so angered white neighbours that, as I watched in anger and frustration, police dogs were used to drive them from these vantage points.

In 1964 the Bantu Laws Amendment Act was passed. Another draconian piece of legislation, it removed the right which some blacks had to reside in urban areas and empowered the Government to 'endorse out' any black if it decided that the area's labour requirements had been satisfied, or deemed the black person to be 'undesirable' or 'idle'. Whichever way we turned, apartheid's vice-like grip was tightening remorselessly.

3 EXPLOSION

Over five days in July 1964 many members of the African Resistance Movement (ARM) were arrested. Some were friends in the Liberal Party who felt that non-violent means had reached the end of the road and that the sabotage of installations such as power pylons was the only way forward. Others were from the ANC Youth League and the Congress of Democrats. Those involved included socialists and independently-minded radicals. They were mostly young white idealists frustrated by the denial of legal and peaceful channels for change.

The ARM's first act of sabotage had taken place nearly three years earlier and my parents knew some of those who were discussing this route and had themselves been sounded out. Apart from the moral questions raised by violence, my parents considered such action naive and counter-productive as it would simply invite even greater police state repression without achieving anything tangible. For obvious reasons those undertaking the sabotage did not resign from the Liberal Party as its rules obliged them to do, and this occasioned considerable acrimony when their activities were eventually revealed. My parents had serious discussions with close friends and I often talked to my father about his views. The trouble with violence, he insisted with passion, was that it tended to develop a life of its own. Whatever the intention, once started it spread automatically. There was no way of containing it either: even blowing up a remote pylon risked killing an innocent person who might have been passing by.

The round-up of ARM members came after the police discovered documents on the movement at the Cape Town

flat of a regional organiser, Adrian Leftwich, a prominent
Liberal Party member, who turned state witness and was
later paraded around the country giving evidence against his
former comrades. Among those arrested was a Liberal Party
member and good friend of ours from Johannesburg, Hugh
Lewin, who later wrote *Bandiet*, a memorable book on his
time in prison. Another Liberal friend, Randolph Vigne, got
news that Leftwich was talking and immediately left on a
Norwegian cargo ship from Cape Town on a borrowed passport.

By now our family, which had always managed to live
something akin to a normal life, was beginning to feel
severely hemmed in. Then came a shattering event. On 24
July 1964 a bomb exploded on the concourse of the Johannesburg station, mortally injuring an old lady and severely
maiming a young girl. Shocked at hearing the news on my
bedroom radio, I sought reassurance from my parents, not
really thinking that they would be involved, but needing to
hear them say so. They were both very upset, my father
sounding off against the 'idiots who did that sort of mindless
thing'. Whoever was responsible had better not come to him
for help, he told me grimly.

That weekend Ann Harris and her six-week-old son David
turned up unexpectedly at our home in The Willows, telling
us that her husband John had been arrested and was being
held in Pretoria Local Prison. My parents had met John and
Ann a few years earlier when they were new Johannesburg
Liberal Party members. Both were teachers. John shared my
Dad's interest in sport, cars and motor racing (rather uncom-
mon interests among the politically involved), so they got on
very well, as did Ann and my Mom. They visited us in
Pretoria and John went with us to several motor races. We
used to go regularly to Grand Prix and major sports car races
at Kyalami, near Johannesburg, where our minibus would be
parked at Clubhouse Corner and the whole family would
watch from its roof.

Distraught, Ann explained how she had been refused permission to see John in Pretoria Local Prison. But she had
been told that she could bring food for him each day and
collect his laundry. Could my parents put him on their list
for food parcels? However, as she could not drive and was
dependent upon others bringing her the 40 miles from
Johannesburg for prison visits, Mom and Dad suggested she
stayed with us until his release. They assumed that John,
who had been banned in January that year and therefore

would have been watched, could not be involved and would be released in a week or so. So the girls gave up their bedroom for the adjoining playroom and Ann and little David moved in. But instead of a short stay, they were to be with us for nearly 18 months and became part of the family.

Thus began a daily trek to the jail for my mother and Ann, taking food to John, Hugh Lewin and others who were all held incommunicado under the 90-day law. The extra housework occasioned by a tiny baby, coupled with the daily 25-mile round trip to the jail, transporting children to and from school and my father to and from work, meant that it became difficult to cope without help. Mom contacted Eva who was without a job and she took up residence with us again.

Ann's arrival at our house changed our lives forever. The station bomb had thrown the white community into a frenzy: never before had whites been struck in this way. The security services were quick to exploit the resulting panic, and we received extra attention.

After a while, when all the other ARM detainees had been visited by relatives, and Ann still had heard nothing, my parents began to realise that there was something seriously amiss. Then they noticed a blood stain on a shirt in John's laundry. After his lawyer made enquiries a member of the Security Police turned up with a letter for Ann – frightening ten-year-old Jo-anne who came running in saying through her tears 'I didn't cry in front of him.' The letter was the first direct communication Ann or the lawyers had received from John. He wanted to reassure her that he had cut himself shaving – and he joked that he was unused to wet shaving as he'd had to hand in his electric shaver. In reality, of course, he was still bleeding from the horrendous beatings which caused a broken jaw and damaged testicles.

As his detention continued it became apparent that John must have had some connection with the station bomb. But we remained unaware of the extent of his involvement until over a month after the explosion, when the old lady, Mrs Ethel Rhys, tragically died (her 12-year-old granddaughter, Glynnis Burleigh, was maimed for life) and John was charged with murder. Ruth Hayman, a Liberal Party friend and John's lawyer, was then able to see him for the first time. Ruth was terribly upset at the state she found him in; he had only been charged after his jaw, which had been wired up, had mended enough for him to appear in court.

By now Ann had admitted John's responsibility for the

bombing to my parents and, once he was charged on 14 September, they told us. There was no question but that we should do what we could to help. Although condemning without qualification what he had done, my parents remain convinced John never intended to harm anybody. He had meant it as a spectacular demonstration of resistance to tightening police state oppression. Indeed he had telephoned a warning to both the station police and two newspapers, urging that the station concourse be cleared. This was not done and the result was devastation on the station and the pretext for the Government to enforce an even more oppressive regime. We suspected at the time that ignoring John's warning was deliberate, and this was confirmed years later. A former security informer, Gordon Winter, stated in his book *Inside Boss* that the decision not to use the station loudspeaker system to clear travellers from the concourse had been passed on through the head of the Security Police, H.J. van den Bergh, to the Justice Minister, John Vorster.

My parents' support for Ann and help for John inevitably made them even more direct targets. The harassment became vitriolic: our house was now under continual surveillance, with Security Police cars parked on the road outside 24 hours a day, and as we left we would be tailed – on one occasion even when Tom and I rode down to the nearest shops on our bikes. Raids were also more regular; once I cycled home from school to find their cars in the driveway and Security Police searching through my books and papers. In encounters like this, they were the enemy and I glared at them, refusing to be intimidated. A young officer discovered a list of names which constituted my own chosen 'World XI' cricket team. It had stars like Gary Sobers, Wes Hall, Richie Benaud and even South Africa's Graeme Pollock, like me a left-handed batsman and my idol. But the names were listed at random and I had attached numbers indicating positions in the batting order. The officer thought he'd found a coded list and rushed excitedly to show it to his superior, Captain Celliers, who, after a quick glance, told him not to be a damned fool. One up to us: the kind of small victory which kept our spirits up whenever we recounted the story.

Meanwhile Maritz van den Berg had been detained under the 90-day law on 29 July and held in Pretoria Local Prison for a month before being unconditionally released. It was soon obvious that he had spoken freely because others were immediately pulled in for questioning. One of them, Alban Thumbran, was released again almost at once and

telephoned to warn us 'Maritz is talking'. This was to be
the signal for messages to be relayed, by various means, to
as many people as my parents thought might need to
know. One party colleague, Derek Cohen, was only contacted after Mom had thrown off pursuing Security Police
vehicles in an exciting chase with all of us children in the
car. Shortly after he left by plane for London the Security
Police called round looking for him.

In September 1964, my father was visited at his office and
handed a banning order with a special clause attached to it.
The same day I opened our front door to a burly figure who
handed my mother an addendum to her ban, personally signed
by the Minister of Justice, John Vorster. It contained a similar
new clause giving them special permission to talk to each
other. This was exceptional: as they were the first married
couple to be banned, they had to be given an Orwellian exemp-
tion from the normal stipulation that banned persons were not
allowed to communicate. From then on, aged 14, I became
increasingly active in a liaison role, taking and passing
messages to individuals with whom they were prevented from
communicating, such as journalists and other banned people.
Thus they were able to continue much of their political work
behind the scenes.

Their bans meant that neither of my parents was able to
attend John Harris' trial in Pretoria, which began on 21 September – though they gave as much support as they could
from the outside. To their shock, his co-conspirator, John
Lloyd, another Liberal Party member, was to be the main
prosecution witness and it became vital to get news to Lloyd
that if he gave evidence John Harris would be sentenced to
death. Mom, who knew Lloyd's girlfriend, was able to smuggle such a message in to him and established from her that
he had received it.

However, Lloyd ignored this warning. At the trial he did not
merely give evidence in corroboration of John's own confession
(which would have carried a life sentence for manslaughter),
but went further. He insisted that John had said that it would
be tactically advisable for a few lives to be taken because it
would save many lives in the future. John consistently denied
this and police testimony in court confirmed that he had indeed telephoned a warning to the railway police and urged
them to clear the concourse, in order to avoid injuring anyone.
Nevertheless the judge accepted Lloyd's version and in his
judgement stated that this helped prove John had 'an intention

to kill' and so was guilty of murder. John was accordingly sentenced to death on 6 November, with Lloyd's the key evidence which supported the 'intention to kill' necessary to sustain a capital offence.

From the outset Lloyd was kept away from the others. When they were all transferred to Pretoria Local Prison at the end of July, he was housed on his own at a Pretoria police station, allowed frequent visits from his mother in his cell and given proper bedding with sheets. Evidence at the trial showed that Harris and Lloyd had been the only ones in their ARM cell still at liberty after the main arrests. The two had discussed a number of projects to 'make a big splash' to show that the organisation had not been destroyed, as the Justice Minister, John Vorster, had boasted on the radio. Among these were a bomb at Johannesburg station, a bomb in an underground car park and bombs in the private post boxes at Pretoria Post Office, all to be carried out on 24 July. John Harris was to carry out the first and Lloyd the other two. However, Lloyd (the flatmate of Hugh Lewin who had been arrested on 9 July) was himself detained on 23 July, the day *before* John carried out his part of their project. It was not established whether the security services thereby had had advance notice of the station bomb, but Lloyd's initial statement to the police mentioning John Harris, and the latter's proposal to plant a bomb at a station, was taken at 12.45 p.m. on 24 July, nearly four hours before the explosion (this statement only became available in 1995).

When John Harris was sentenced to hang, Mom came home as quickly as possible to speak to us ahead of anyone else. My brother Tom went completely white with shock, but I had been expecting it and during the next five months the shadow of the hanging was over us. Meanwhile our efforts were directed at attempts to save John's life. First there was an appeal on 1 March. When that failed, because no additional evidence was forthcoming, there were many clemency appeals which my parents helped organise. Ann flew down with John's father to Cape Town for an interview with the Minister of Justice, John Vorster. Clemency petitions from a range of public figures were presented and the matter was raised in the British House of Commons.

A week after John's sentence four more ARM members stood trial in Pretoria: our friend Hugh Lewin, Baruch Hirson, Raymond Eisenstein and Fred Prager (whom my parents knew from the Johannesburg Liberal Party). Fred was acquitted, and the other three were found guilty. Hugh was given a seven-year sentence, Raymond five and Baruch nine. My mother used to stand behind the court building each day to catch a glimpse of Hugh being driven in, and they would exchange waves. Again – and although he had promised not to give evidence against him – the main prosecution witness in Hugh's case was John Lloyd, his flatmate, whom Hugh had actually recruited to the ARM. Other ARM trials were held in Cape Town and Pietermaritzburg.

After giving evidence against Hugh, Lloyd was released in exchange for turning state witness and soon afterwards left with his mother for Britain, where a job awaited him. Ensconced safely there he was approached and asked to assist in John Harris' appeal by retracting his 'intention to kill' evidence, which lawyers considered to have been crucial to John's conviction. Hugh Lewin's girlfriend Jill Chisholm (whom Lloyd knew well) met him in Bristol and asked him to retract. But he refused and, when she persisted in trying to persuade him he threatened to tell the South African Security Police that she was trying to get him to perjure himself.

So another approach was tried. Ruth Hayman, John Harris' lawyer and a prominent member of the Johannesburg Liberal Party, also well known to him, flew over. At great professional and personal risk she approached Lloyd who agreed to a draft affidavit retracting his evidence and left promising to return in the morning to sign it. But he failed to do so. (Ruth was banned and house arrested after her return to South Africa.) Randolph Vigne, another ARM member who had escaped to Britain, then tried a third time. He met Lloyd who initially agreed to sign an affidavit saying that he no longer believed what he had said in evidence was the truth – then reneged and eventually signed only a watered down, anodyne statement which was forwarded to the State President through the Embassy – but it was too little and too late. Lloyd even ignored Ann's final desperate cable – 'I plead for life with the conviction that I and your friends would have done it for you.'

While John Harris was held on death row he managed to convey a message to Ann that he had been approached by a warder who wanted to help him escape. At great personal risk, and from the outset suspicious of a set-up, my parents decided to help Ann. But, after weeks of tense and contorted dealings with the warder, including paying him over £1000 – Mom insisting that Ann had elastoplast stuck discreetly over her fingertips so as to cover her prints – the plot collapsed. It had been a Security Police trap from the beginning.

John was hanged at dawn on 1 April 1965 and I remember waking, unusually early, as the moment arrived. Immediately our phone rang and the caller asked to speak to Ann. My mother refused, recognising the voice of a Security Police officer who went on to say mockingly, 'Your John is dead.' My memory is of being overwhelmed by a sort of blank hopelessness. For days beforehand I had found myself imagining acquiring a helicopter to get him out somehow. Like my parents I hadn't condoned what he had done; on the contrary we had bitterly condemned it both before and after we knew he was responsible. But under any civilised system, he would have continued to devote his life to teaching children and would never have been involved in subversion which ended in his being hanged by the neck.

My father and our barrister friend, Ernie Wentzel, had previously asked permission from the prison Kommandant, Brigadier Aucamp, for the body to be released for cremation. This was not a normal procedure and, to everyone's surprise, it was granted and a service was arranged at the Pretoria crematorium for 7.30 a.m. that same day. (Ernie thought that the permission was given so the Security Police could monitor who would attend.) As banned persons my parents required permission to go and this was duly given, but my father's request to read the address was refused the evening before and I offered to take over. It was too late to ask anyone else and there would not have been many people willing or able to undertake a task that invited notoriety.

So, at the age of 15, dressed in my school uniform, I found myself standing at the lectern before the assembled congregation. The ceremony had been carefully prepared and all I had to do was read the address. As I began, my voice cracked and I wondered whether I could carry it off; but fortunately the moment passed. We were all moved by the number and variety of people, apart from relatives, who attended the funeral. The chapel was full and when I looked down from the raised lectern I saw many friends – Liberal Party members from both Pretoria and Johannesburg, people from the townships and even members of the diplomatic corps. All had made a stand by attending, all knew that their names would be diligently recorded by the Security Police officers outside. The proximity of the coffin a yard to my left containing the body of a friend hanged only two hours earlier made the experience especially unsettling. It had been explained to me how I needed to press the button to take the coffin away, but in the middle of the service I realised that I

hadn't been told when to do it. The last thing I wanted was
to get this wrong. But then, while singing the Freedom
Rider's song 'We Shall Overcome', I thought this must be it:
what seemed a totally irrevocable step as the coffin moved
eerily away out of sight. An hour later I was back at school,
having missed the first lesson. Though the school had been
warned I would be late, none of my classmates knew the
reason until a report with my photograph appeared in the
papers the following day.

The station bomb became a pivotal event. It was exploited
both to increase repression and to systematically discredit
and destroy the Liberal Party. In 1965 the period for which
people could be held without charge was extended from 90 to
180 days; two years later it was to become indefinite. The
Liberals' magazine, *Contact*, closed after its fifth editor was
banned and Alban Thumbran, the Cape Reserve member to
whom my parents were especially close, was banned. Ruth
Hayman, the Johannesburg member and John Harris' lawyer
who was my parents' friend and legal mainstay was banned
and house arrested. Our battered old Volkswagen minibus,
for years effectively the Pretoria Liberals' main transportation,
was stolen in circumstances which pointed to Security Police
responsibility; it was eventually found months later in Harte-
beespoort Dam some 35 miles west of Pretoria after the
water level had fallen drastically in a drought.

By now my father's continued employment as an architect
who specialised in hospital design was threatened. He had
been out of work for two months after his arrest in 1961.
Then he had had a temporary job in Johannesburg before
being taken on by a Pretoria firm, which among other commissions, carried out the design of hospitals for the Transvaal Works Department (TWD) – the employer who had
sacked him on his arrest. When told of his political problems, the head of the firm said that these were of no interest
to him provided they didn't interfere with the work. Until
his banning in September 1964 my father worked for them,
mainly on hospitals for the TWD, which meant liaising with
his former colleagues there.

Soon after his ban a workmate told him that the firm had
received a letter from the TWD informing them that if they
continued to employ him they would no longer receive TWD
work. He felt obliged to resign. Although his resignation was
reluctantly accepted, an agreement was reached that he
would open his own office and they would quietly continue

to feed him the work. The arrangement worked successfully until late 1965, when a slump led to the cancellation of many TWD projects and a consequent drying up of the work passed on to him. He had a few commissions of his own for projects outside the Pretoria magisterial district (to which his ban confined him), but permission to leave Pretoria to inspect and survey the sites was refused by the Minister of Justice, despite the intervention of the South African Institute of Architects on his behalf. He had had great difficulty in obtaining work after his imprisonment in 1961 and it was now clear that, confined to Pretoria with its much more restrictive political climate, and with word out in the profession that private architectural firms would get no work if they employed him, his prospects of getting a job were virtually nil.

So, with great sadness and even greater reluctance, my parents, who had no private means, decided they had no alternative but to leave their country for one in which Dad could obtain work. He wrote to the London firm that had employed him in 1956 and was immediately offered a job. We then accepted a friend's generous offer of rented accommodation in Gwendolen Avenue, Putney. Meanwhile Ann Harris and David were to leave us in January 1966, first to stay with relatives in Johannesburg, then moving on to London to the flat above ours.

It was a traumatic decision for all of us. My father, then aged 41, knew that his already badly disrupted architectural career would be further undermined. Both my parents were leaving the country of their birth for which they had sacrificed many of the comforts and privileges of white life. My brother and sisters and I were leaving our friends for a future unknown. We resisted the idea until we realised it was inevitable. One small consolation was that my brother and I discovered that Stamford Bridge, the stadium of Chelsea, the English football club which we supported, was near our new home. I was able to book tickets for the World Cup football finals, so there was something else exciting to look forward to. We also talked of seeing cricket at Lord's and motor races at Silverstone and Brands Hatch – places of awe to young 'colonial' boys.

Friends raised the finance for our passages on a Union Castle liner from Cape Town. Dad was eligible for a British passport because his father had been born in Glasgow and my mother was eligible as she had married him before 1951. I was British, having been born in Kenya, and my sister Sally had been born in Britain. This left Tom and Jo-anne, and the British Embassy helpfully registered them, so that we all had British documents. However, the Security Police were unaware of all this and when my parents applied for permission to leave the Pretoria area they were obstructive, until it was pointed out that we had British passports and had in error already been issued with departure permits. The latter were then withdrawn and replaced with one-way exit permits which prohibited my parents from returning to South Africa and withdrew their citizenship. In the typically bloody-minded manner of the local bureaucracy, permission to leave Pretoria was then delayed until the last moment – at one point it looked as though we would have to postpone our departure.

We children went to a farewell party in the Liberal Party offices, representing our parents whose ban prevented them from attending. Then, on 14 March 1966, many of our friends, together with my father's parents and party stalwarts (including the banned Alban Thumbran lurking alone at the end of the platform), came to Pretoria railway station to see us off on the first leg of our journey to Cape Town, 1000 miles away. Tears were plentiful. Waiting on the platform at Johannesburg station there were more party members to say farewell and shower us with parting gifts. On both occasions there was talk that we would be back one day to savour the freedom of a new South Africa, but we had no illusions: these were only ritual exchanges. The apartheid state seemed immortal. We were going for good.

We steamed out of the old docks into the heaving Cape rollers past Robben Island, grim behind the spray, where Nelson Mandela and his colleagues were incarcerated, leaving behind a South Africa in which the powers of darkness were very much in the ascendant. The principal liberation movement, the ANC, was outlawed and in disarray; its leaders were in jail; its military wing Umkhonto seemingly crushed. The PAC was in a similar state. The most militant white organisation, the Congress of Democrats, which had worked closely with the ANC, had suffered the same removal of its upper echelons and had been banned in 1962. The non-racial Liberal Party was badly damaged by the banning of over 50 of its activists and by defections to the ARM (two years later the Prohibition of Political Interference Act forced it to disband). The Progressive Party, ostensibly non-racial, but with franchise qualifications and other elitist restrictions that effectively resulted in a white party with a few token affluent blacks, was the only opposition untouched, its stalwart Helen Suzman the sole voice of sanity in Parliament.

So my parents departed with heavy hearts. There was no glory in going into exile: they felt intensely guilty at leaving friends and colleagues behind, though simultaneously relieved at the easing of the all-consuming pressure under which they had been living for the previous three years. They wrote a press release issued in my name saying they were only leaving because my father could no longer obtain employment and how much they regretted having to go – something which their bans still prevented them from saying themselves.

But, as it transpired, they left to join others in exile in what was to become a decisive era of international struggle against apartheid. As our beloved South African coast disappeared from sight, we had no idea that we would find ourselves playing a role in that struggle.

4 PROTEST

We arrived in Britain the day after Labour's huge general election victory in April 1966 and election posters were still on display. But, aged 16, I was more struck by watching television for the first time and looking forward to our first opportunity of going to see Chelsea play at home. The idea of joining international protest campaigns against apartheid was farthest from my mind.

We concentrated upon building a new life on the assumption that we were never going back. As we were to discover, many South African exiles in Britain then lived a kind of limbo existence – waiting to return: that was their choice. But my parents were determined to put down roots, to get involved in the community and to make Britain our home. Although they joined the Anti-Apartheid Movement almost immediately – I followed about a year later – and naturally took a keen interest in South African affairs, meeting other exiles including old friends, it was nearly three years before we were thrust into hyperactivism again.

Our arrival also followed a general election in South Africa which gave the National Party an overall majority of votes for the first time in a 17 per cent swing. Then, in September 1966, Dr Verwoerd, the fundamentalist apartheid Prime Minister, was assassinated by a white parliamentary messenger. But it was the one-off act of a deranged loner. Verwoerd was succeeded by John Vorster, then Minister of Justice, who had personally signed my parents' banning orders and who ushered in a new era in which the security services were to gain much more powerful leverage over the direction of government.

Just as resistance appeared to be diminishing inside South Africa, so it opened up on another front outside. The British Anti-Apartheid Movement (AAM) had been formed in 1959, in response to a call from ANC President Albert Luthuli for an international boycott movement which gathered momentum after the Sharpeville massacre the following year. The growing awareness of events in South Africa had been sparked off by Alan Paton's *Cry the Beloved Country* and Bishop Trevor Huddleston's *Naught for Your Comfort*, both searing indictments of apartheid published in the 1950s.

The AAM quickly began to attract broad support in the churches, trade unions, Parliament, on the left and amongst liberal opinion. With increasing numbers forced into exile, it quickly became the focus for something more than a solidarity group. South Africans of high calibre – Abdul Minty, Ethel de Keyser, Vella Pillay and Ruth First to mention just a few – became the driving force in the movement. It gained influence in both diplomatic circles and on the streets during an era in which demonstrations mushroomed. The AAM was informally but closely aligned to the ANC which had an office just down the road in London's West End.

Among progressive people, boycotts of South African fruit and other products were common. This was a period of relative trade union strength and most unions adopted firm solidarity policies. The AAM extended this boycott strategy with well-researched campaigns demanding economic sanctions and an end to British military cooperation with South Africa, including withdrawal from a naval base on the Cape peninsula in Simonstown. In countries like Australia, New Zealand, Sweden and Holland, anti-apartheid forces also began to be active, often involving exiles who had settled there.

An important focus of the boycott action was sport. South African teams had always been all-white and the whole sports system was riddled with apartheid. Teams were selected on the basis of race, not merit. Apartheid laws barred mixed clubs, mixed school sport, and teams from one racial group playing in an area designated for another. Even black-only teams playing away required special permission to be entered in their pass books.

In the early 1960s, sport might have appeared an unusual choice for political protest, at best peripheral, at worst eccentric. But this was misunderstanding the whole white South African psyche. Whites were sports mad. Afrikaners were especially fanatical about rugby. Whether it was participation in the Olympics or a rugby or cricket tour, international sport gripped the white nation as nothing else did – and more important granted them the international respectability and legitimacy they increasingly craved as the evil reality of apartheid began to be exposed by horrors such as Sharpeville. Moreover it was easier to achieve success through practical protest against sports links than it was to take on the might of either international capital or military alliances.

In 1958 the Campaign Against Race Discrimination in Sport was formed in Britain by Trevor Huddleston and backed by a number of public figures, church groups and organisations. It immediately challenged South Africa's participation in the 1958 Empire and Commonwealth Games in Cardiff and began to lobby the International Olympic Committee and British sports authorities. In 1960 the Campaign called for a boycott of the South African cricket tour to Britain and, in an unprecedented stand, the England Test cricketer David Sheppard (later to play a leading anti-apartheid role when he became a bishop) refused to play. The same year the annual meeting of cricket's ruling body, the MCC, heard in icy silence a demand that links with racialist cricket should be abandoned from Roland Bowen, the editor of the *Cricket Quarterly* and a cricket historian. In New Zealand, Maoris had been consistently excluded from the 'All Blacks' (New Zealand rugby teams) touring South Africa on many occasions. This had provoked little public opposition. But when the same practice was announced in 1959 for a tour the following year, there was widespread pressure for its cancellation. In 1965 the British Anti-Apartheid Movement organised placard-carrying pickets outside each ground on the South African cricket tour.

Meanwhile, the South African Non-Racial Olympic Committee (SAN-ROC) had been forced into exile. It had been formed in 1962 to lobby for the country's expulsion from the Olympics by the anti-apartheid South African Sports Association. (The latter had been launched four years earlier to co-ordinate the battle for non-racial sport and represented some 70,000 sportsmen and women; its patron was Alan Paton and its secretary Dennis Brutus.) SAN-ROC's leaders were banned and harassed to such an extent that, like the ANC, it could no longer operate legally inside the country; the fact that sports officials too were victims of the police state gave the lie to the cry that sport should be divorced from politics.

SAN-ROC's effective leader at the time, Dennis Brutus, was successively banned, house arrested, and finally sen-

tenced to hard labour on Robben island. Trying to escape his
ban and attend an International Olympic Committee (IOC)
meeting in Europe in 1963, he was arrested on the Mozam-
bique-Swaziland border and taken back to Johannesburg
police headquarters. Trying to escape again, he was shot in
the stomach. An ambulance for whites arrived, found he was
a Coloured and drove off; he waited bleeding on the pavement for a vehicle that could take non-whites. The same
year John Harris, who succeeded Dennis Brutus as SAN-ROC
Chairman, had his passport confiscated as he tried to fly out
to an IOC conference, and was later banned. Nevertheless
SAN-ROC was successful in getting South Africa suspended
from the Olympics for the first time in 1964.

Victories in sport were crucial during a period when internal resistance was being smashed and external successes
were hard to come by. The New Zealand Rugby Union
finally bowed to public pressure and called off their planned
tour in 1967 after it became clear that the South African
Government would not accept the selection of any Maoris.
Much the same occurred a year later when the 1968 English
cricket tour was cancelled after Pretoria's refusal to accept
the selection of Basil D'Oliveira, a Cape Coloured who for
several years had been a regular English Test player. 'It's not
the England team. It's the team of the anti-apartheid movement', blustered Prime Minister Vorster. That this was an
issue absolutely central to the ideology of white domination
was demonstrated with devastating clarity in the National
Party organ *Die Transvaler* on 7 September 1965. Pointing
out that 'the white race has hitherto maintained itself in the
southern part of Africa' because 'there has been no miscege-
nation', its editorial continued:

> The absence of miscegenation was because there was no
> social mixing between white and non-white ... In South
> Africa the races do not mix on the sports field. If they
> mix on the sports field then the road to other forms of
> social mixing is wide open ... With an eye to upholding
> the white race and its civilisation, not one single compro-
> mise can be entered into – not even when it comes to a
> visiting rugby team.

Countless statements could be quoted by top rugby,
cricket, sports or government figures justifying racism in
sport on the most spurious and blatant basis. Some resorted
to extraordinary sophistry, almost word for word the kind of

thing which Hitler and his fellow Nazis used to exclude Jews from pre-war German teams. Others resorted to plain fantasy. Attempting to justify the omission of blacks, a white Olympics swimming official said in 1968: 'Some sports the African is not suited for. In swimming the water closes their pores and they cannot get rid of carbon dioxide, so they tire quickly.' Those who claimed that, over the South African issue, sport and politics should not mix, were either ignorant, naive or hypocritical. Sport was intrinsic to the very fabric of apartheid and its maintenance on a racist basis was therefore important to the continuation of apartheid.

In late 1967 and early 1968, I was still at school in London, in my final year doing science A-levels. Gradually I became increasingly politically involved, reading my parents' *Guardian*, following current debates and avidly discussing topical issues like the Vietnam War with my father. In Britain there had been huge anti-bomb marches in the late 1950s and early 1960s organised by the Campaign for Nuclear Disarmament, and direct action tactics were adopted by its militant offshoot, the Committee of 100. When we arrived, similar protests were beginning to grow against the Vietnam War. Direct action was the order of the day, especially following the wave of protest and civil rights demonstrations in America. I was angry about the failure of Harold Wilson's Labour Government to deal firmly with the illegal rebellion by the white minority in Rhodesia who had made a Unilateral Declaration of Independence (UDI) to maintain their racist rule.

The campaign against UDI was being organised by the Anti-Apartheid Movement and I began to attend its meetings more regularly. Partly because of the Labour Government's timidity on Rhodesia and Vietnam, partly because of our connection to the South African Liberal Party and partly because the British Young Liberals were then a vibrant, irreverent force for radicalism, I decided to join them. It quickly led me into an exciting culture of left-wing ideas. The Young Liberals – whose leaders, in a neat publicity manoeuvre, appropriated the term 'Red Guards' from Mao in China and called for a 'cultural revolution' in Britain – provided an ideal crash course in political education. I started reading voraciously, was taught how to draft press releases, deal with the media and how to organise. The prevailing ideology was not 'liberal' at all but explicitly socialist. We called ourselves 'libertarian socialists', with a strong emphasis upon militant, though non-violent, direct action where necessary.

As apartheid moved up the political agenda, a number of leading Young Liberals formed a 'Southern Africa Commission' (SAC) early in 1968. This brought together members with an interest in the area and, although I had only joined the YLs in Putney a few months before, I quickly came into contact with its national leaders. I was the only ex-South African involved, which was to bring me into close contact with individuals who wanted to be active, including non-Young Liberals, in the wider anti-apartheid movement. I was later introduced to Chris de Broglio and then Dennis Brutus who were in exile, running SAN-ROC from Chris' London hotel. In October I was elected to the National Committee of the Anti-Apartheid Movement.

The outrage at the South African Government's refusal in September 1968 to accept Basil D'Oliveira's inclusion in the England cricket team – and the subsequent cancellation of the tour – proved to be a watershed. It followed weeks of seedy manoeuvring and high drama. D'Oliveira – by then an established Test player – was first offered £40,000 to declare himself unavailable by a South African-based representative of the cigarette company Rothmans. Then, to everyone's astonishment, he was left out of the touring party. The distinguished cricket journalist, John Arlott, wrote: 'No one of open mind will believe that he was left out for valid cricketing reasons.' Finally, D'Oliveira was included when the Warwickshire all-rounder Tom Cartwright withdrew with a shoulder injury.*

After all this, the English cricket authorities announced in January 1969 that they would proceed with the scheduled 1970 cricket tour by a white South African team. Just before the decision I had drafted a motion which SAC approved in January 1969 pledging 'ourselves to take direct action to prevent scheduled matches from taking place unless the 1970 tour is cancelled'. The motion got a small mention in The

---

* Ironically, Tom Cartwright became one of my constituents when I was elected MP for Neath in 1991 and my teenage son Jake was coached under his supervision. We became friends and in 1995 he told me that he had always been unhappy about the idea of going on tour, that pressure had been put on him to accept despite the fact that it was known to Lord's he was injured, and that he withdrew out of conviction – not simply for the publicly quoted explanation.

Times and it was sent to the cricket authorities. (I had not tried to get it through the AAM National Committee as it was cautious and conservative on the question of direct action, in retrospect understandably so since this might have jeopardised its broader following.)

When the go-ahead for the tour was announced, with the dust hardly having settled on the D'Oliveira affair, there was uproar. In May 1969 SAN-ROC held a public meeting in London and, among others, I raised from the floor the question of direct action to stop the tour. Dennis Brutus was in the chair and very supportive. Sports apartheid protests in Britain up until that time had been *symbolic*: holding up banners outside sports grounds and the like. These had been impressive and vital stages in the process of mobilising awareness. Indeed they still had an important role to play. But the new dimension was *direct action*: physically disrupting the very events themselves and thereby posing both a threat and a challenge which could not be ignored by the sports elites who had been impervious to moral appeals and symbolic protest. Besides being novel and having a huge potential for impact, it also had the advantage of being highly newsworthy with strong visual images in the new television age. It was the product of that unique late 1960s era of student sit-ins, Vietnam demos, the Paris 1968 revolt, the American anti-war and civil rights movements: we merely applied similar direct action techniques to the world of sport.

A new more militant movement gathered momentum alongside the AAM which maintained the discreet, sometimes uneasy, distance necessary to its more conventional role. A private tour by an all-white South African club side sponsored by a wealthy businessman, Wilf Isaacs, experienced the first ever taste of direct action against cricket in Britain, and almost certainly throughout the world. At the opening match in Basildon in July 1969, a group of Young Liberals walked on to the pitch. Play was interrupted for over ten minutes until police dragged us, limp, off the field. At subsequent matches in Oxford and the Oval, south London, there were even greater and more successful disruptions which were independently organised by local anti-apartheid groups. The same month, on the opening day of a Davis Cup tennis match in Bristol between South Africa and Britain, I travelled down with two fellow Putney Young Liberals and we ran onto the court, on this occasion disrupting play for the first time in an international event in front of live television coverage. Later in the three-day tournament, play was further

disrupted by an invasion and flour bombs were thrown onto
the court in protests organised by the Bristol Anti-Apartheid
group.

The publicity for each direct action protest encouraged
others. The fact that the events were taking place across the
country and action could be taken locally meant the movement was characterised by considerable local autonomy and
spontaneity. A network fell into place. With the active en-
couragement of Dennis Brutus and SAN-ROC, the Stop The
Seventy Tour Committee (STST) was launched at a press
conference in September 1969. It had broad support from the
AAM and the United Nations Youth to the National Union
of Students, Christian groups, young Communists, Trotsky-
ists and Liberals. A Reading University student, Hugh Geach,
was secretary and at the age of 19 I was pressed by Dennis
Brutus and others into a leadership role and found myself
acting as Press Officer and convenor of the Committee (later
assuming the Chair), pledging 'mass demonstrations and disruptions throughout the 1970 tour'. We also promised demonstrations against the Springbok rugby tour which, rather
belatedly, we had realised was due to start in six weeks' time
and had determined would be a dummy run for stopping the
following summer's cricket tour.

Ever since my involvement first surfaced in the media in
the summer, the South African press had begun to take an
increasing interest. They rapidly elevated me to the status of
a 'hate' figure. The fact that 'one of their own' had turned
against them was clearly disconcerting and there were all
sorts of angles about my 'taking revenge' for the treatment of
my parents and so on. The STST campaign had hardly been
publicly launched when I received a welcome indication of
its potential impact. In early October, a registered letter postmarked Pretoria arrived from the South African Minister for
the Interior. It informed me that my right as a British citizen
to enter the country without an 'alien's temporary permit' or
visa had been withdrawn. (In fact I had no intention of
returning nor had I indicated any desire to do so.)

On the back of growing excitement and publicity, the campaign simply took off. Our modest flat in Gwendolen Avenue,
Putney, became the headquarters' address and 'office'. Mom
quickly assumed the crucial role of unofficial dogsbody, fielding
phone calls, coordinating information and helping with cor-
respondence. Dad wrote leaflets and background briefs. Suddenly, in a reversal of roles from our life in South Africa, I had
become the front person; but I could not have done this with-

out their constant support in the background. My public threats of direct action against the rugby tour and confident predictions that we could stop the cricket tour generated widespread publicity. I found myself being interviewed on television and radio for the first time, and using the guidance and experience I had gained through the Young Liberals, dealt with the press on a daily basis. This coincided with the start of my mechanical engineering course at Imperial College, London University. I used to spend lunch breaks with homemade sandwiches in a phone box talking to journalists and local organisers through messages relayed from my mother at home where the phone rang incessantly.

A mass movement was snowballing, locally based, spontaneous, independently organised, usually focused around student unions, though involving trade unions, local AAM groups, socialists, liberals, independents and the churches. It was predominantly, though by no means exclusively, young and soon took the rugby tour by storm.

The opening match, against Oxford University, was switched after strong opposition from both the college authorities and student activists who sprayed weedkiller on the ground and threatened to wreck the match. The venue was kept secret to avoid demonstrations, but a friendly sports journalist had promised to phone us as soon as the press were informed. At 9.30 p.m. the night before, our phone rang and a familiar voice said 'Twickenham, 3 p.m.' News was immediately relayed to the Oxford Committee Against Apartheid and around the country where coaches of demonstrators waited: over 1000 rushed to the ground and the match took place under siege. Sensationally, the mighty Springboks lost, clearly unnerved by the atmosphere.

The tour organisers could not have played more into our hands. Switching the first fixture from Oxford at the last minute attracted front page lead stories on the morning of the match and set the scene for the remaining games of the 25-match tour. Local organisers suddenly realised they were part of a mass national movement. Each of the matches saw demonstrations of varying sizes. There were big set piece confrontations at the home of the English Rugby Union, Twickenham. As it lay within easy reach of central London, we were able to get 2000 inside – some 'disguised' by cutting their hair or wearing Springbok rosettes – and a similar number outside for the first scheduled match in late November. I was one of over 100 demonstrators who managed to climb over the fence surrounding the pitch and outwit the police. Play was stopped for more than ten minutes until we were carried off and ejected from the stadium.

The week before, in Swansea, there had been the most brutal confrontation of the entire tour. A 'Wales Rejects Apartheid' Committee had been formed with widespread support from all walks of life. But in South Wales – a socialist stronghold with an honourable tradition of international solidarity going back at least to the Spanish Civil War and which had a relatively strong Anti-Apartheid Movement – rugby fanaticism came first. At Swansea, there were ugly scenes as police threw 100 peacefully invading demonstrators back from the pitch and into the clutches of 'stewards' who promptly handed out a beating. One demonstrator's jaw was broken and he nearly lost an eye. Others, including women, were savagely assaulted. Journalists from papers like *The Times* which were not supportive of the demonstrations condemned the 'viciousness' of the police and stewards.*

By now the white South African establishment was apoplectic. An Afrikaans Government-supporting paper, *Die Beeld*, stated in an editorial: 'We have become accustomed to Britain becoming a haven for all sorts of undesirables from other countries. Nevertheless, it is degrading to see how a nation can allow itself to be dictated to by this bunch of left-wing, workshy, refugee, long hairs who in a society of any other country would be rejects.'

The police and rugby authorities got wise to our tactics. In Northern Ireland (itself in turmoil following civil rights protests) the match was cancelled for security reasons. Elsewhere matches were made all-ticket and security inside massively increased so that police stood shoulder to shoulder around the pitch facing spectators. In Cardiff all pretence of a normal rugby match was abandoned as barbed wire was put up around the field. Even in conservative Bournemouth the match was abandoned because the open ground there could not be defended.

---

* Twenty years later when I became Labour MP for Neath, a noted South Wales rugby stronghold barely ten miles from Swansea, constituents regularly claimed to have 'carried me off the ground' that afternoon. In fact I wasn't there, but the claim was made so often I stopped denying it: why spoil a bit of local folklore?

Our tactics changed as well. We knew that the STST campaign had by now been infiltrated (including at a national level). My home telephone number was tapped – a familiar though uncomfortable experience we thought had been left behind in Pretoria. So an 'inner group' of trusted activists was established to work on special projects. It booked a young woman into the team's Park Lane Hotel. She gummed up the players' doorlocks with solidifying agent to delay them getting out on the morning of the pre-Christmas match at Twickenham. A 'Mata Hari' was deputed to chat up the players. She struck up a friendship with one Springbok in Bristol and back in London they met again. He and some colleagues agreed to go with her to a reception party we had organised. But when she went to collect them after the post-match reception, she found her man was completely drunk and interested only in groping her at the hotel. One STST activist chained himself into the driver's seat of the team's coach waiting outside a London hotel, while others evaded the heavy police cordon at Twickenham and chained themselves to the goalposts until they were cut free. Orange smoke pellets were thrown among the players, which, as well as interrupting play, produced dramatic television and newspaper pictures. Wherever it went, the team was under siege; resting, training or playing. Over Christmas, two months into the tour, the players took a step inconceivable in the annals of Springbok history and voted to go home. But the management, under political pressure, ordered them to stay.

The tour finally staggered to an end, with the players bitter and unsettled. For the vice-captain, Tommy Bedford, it proved a cathartic experience. Within a year he publicly stated I should be listened to, not vilified, and praised our objectives. Although his response was a relatively isolated one in South Africa, it signalled the huge and destabilising impact of our campaign. For the first time the Springboks, accustomed to being lionised as perhaps the leading rugby nation in the world, had instead been treated as pariahs. They were no longer faced merely with the moral splutterings of people they could dismiss as 'misguided liberals and leftists' while they retreated into the warm hospitality of their host rugby supporters. This was something of quite a different order. Anti-apartheid opponents now had the physical capacity to threaten their ability to tour in the old way. For the more perceptive amongst them – such as their rugby supremo Danie Craven who had vowed before the tour never to have a black in a Springbok team but who was nevertheless a worldly individual – the lessons were ominous.

The reaction among the black majority in South Africa was however diametrically different. After their release years later, both Nelson Mandela and Govan Mbeki told me that on Robben Island news of the demonstrations had given all the political prisoners there an enormous morale boost; Mbeki said it had also brought a smile to their faces when they learnt that 'the son of the Hains' was leading the campaign. Hugh Lewin was then in the fifth of his seven years in Pretoria Central with a news black-out imposed. He described how reports had leaked through his warders, Afrikaner rugby fanatics to a man. First they started swearing to each other about the 'betogers' (demonstrators). Hugh was initially confused. Then he began to piece it together and realised something big was getting to them. Gradually the truth seeped out. He and his fellow 'politicals' were thrilled. For him the *coup de grace* came when the warders began moaning about 'that bastard Peter Hain' – though he found it difficult to match his recollection of a boy in his early teens with the ogre apparently responsible for these dreadful events. Hugh claimed to have detected in the quality of their soup served up on a Saturday evening how successful the demonstrators had been in disrupting that afternoon's game.

The role of the campaign illustrates the importance of successful international protest in supporting the internal resistance to apartheid which had been all but crushed over the previous decade. One of the few journalists who took the trouble to assess the impact amongst blacks was Jonathan Steele who wrote in the *Guardian* on 5 March 1970:

> It is not hard to find South Africans who are delighted by the demonstrations against the Springboks. Go into Soweto, or any other township, and just start talking to people. When they hear an English accent, and if you are not accompanied by a white South African, the masks fall. Eagerly, they want the news confirmed: 'Is it true that they are having to use a thousand police to hold back the demonstrators today? Is there really that much feeling against South Africa?' ... Their views on the Springbok tour were straightforward. They were against it. And so were their neighbours, and anyone else you talked to.

The saturation coverage given to the campaign in the South African media reached parts of South African life that no other boycott campaign was able to, because it was *sport* being hit. White South African men read and cared about the sports pages first. The fact that their beloved rugby was being disrupted was a huge psychological and physical blow. The extent of the impact is illustrated by the front page attention given to a sports tour that was *not* disrupted. Banner headlines greeted the return home of a Springbok canoeing team a week after the rugby tour had ended. The Johannesburg *Star* reported triumphantly that the team 'did not have to face a single demonstration' and quoted the captain as saying: 'Most demonstrators are hippies and hippies don't like water – that's why we weren't worried by them.' An obscure sport like canoeing would probably not have attracted large protest but, as it happens, none of us – hippie or otherwise – knew the team was visiting. Nobody even mentioned it in the British media: it came and went in secrecy, yet its audacity in 'outwitting' the awful demonstrators meant returning canoeists were welcomed as national heroes.

The rugby tour had provided the movement with a perfect springboard from which to work for the stopping of the cricket tour, due to start at the beginning of May. The fact that the Springboks had gone through to the bitter end meant the whole movement had been consolidated throughout the country. But opposition, coordinated by the AAM, went much wider. The churches, led by the former England cricket captain and Bishop of Woolwich, David Sheppard, urged cancellation. We realised that the Commonwealth Games, due to take place in Edinburgh that summer, could become an important lever. SAN-ROC's international expertise and contacts were put to good use as it was privately pointed out to African and Asian countries that they would be in an intolerable position by participating in the Games at the same time as an apartheid cricket tour was under siege elsewhere in Britain.

While all this was going on, a carefully timed bombshell exploded. Late in the night of 19 January, demonstrators simultaneously raided 14 of the 17 county cricket club grounds. All were daubed with paint slogans. In addition a small patch in the outfield of Glamorgan's Cardiff ground was dug up and weedkiller was sprayed on Warwickshire's Birmingham ground. Telephone reports from each group of demonstrators poured in throughout the night to the Press Association news agency and to the STST office, my home. In the morning the coordinated protest dominated the radio bulletins and there were screaming headlines in the evening papers, television programmes and the following day's news-papers.

The impact of the protests was principally psychological. Everyone had been caught by surprise and the widespread strength of the movement had been starkly revealed in an operation carried out with almost military precision. More than this, the fear at the back of the cricket authorities' minds – and probably shared by most others – had suddenly been realised: the spectre of a cricket tour collapsing amid damaged pitches and weedkiller was conjured up and began to crystallise. Speculation was rife, especially as it was not clear who had organised the operation. People inevitably accused STST – as it alone had the organisational capacity necessary to mount the raids – but I said that the STST national committee had not authorised the action and did not support it. The Anti-Apartheid Movement similarly denied all knowledge. The only national figure to give the raids full backing was the Young Liberal Chairman, Louis Eaks, who attracted headlines when he said 'some Young Liberals had been involved'.

Within weeks, 300 reels of barbed wire arrived at Lord's and most county grounds introduced guard dogs and security. The pressure on the cricket authorities grew. West Indies' cricket leaders angrily denounced the tour. There was specu-lation that African, Asian and Caribbean countries would withdraw from the Edinburgh Commonwealth Games. One by one, a range of public bodies came out against the tour and there was talk of trade unions taking industrial action. Labour MPs, including the AAM's Vice-Chairman, Peter Jackson, said they would join sit-down pitch invasions. The Chairman of the Government sponsored Community Rela-tions Commission, Frank Cousins, told the Home Secretary that the tour would do 'untold damage' to race relations.

On the 12 February the governing body, the Cricket Council, met at Lord's. It was a snowy night and the pitch was eerily surrounded by barbed wire, silhouetted against the whiteness. Lord's, the magisterial home of international cricket, looked for all the world like a concentration camp, symbolising the torment which had torn asunder this most dignified and graceful of games. After their meeting the Cricket Council issued a sombre statement explaining that the tour had been cut drastically to 12 matches from its original schedule of 28. Further it was to be played on just 8 grounds instead of the original 22 and artificial all-weather pitches would be installed as an additional security precaution. It was an astonishing decision, on the one hand indicative of the bunker-like obstinacy of Lord's and the reactionary ideology which prevailed there; on the other hand testimony to the growing power of the campaign.

The decision also propelled the campaign straight into party politics. The opposition Conservative Shadow Attorney General, Sir Peter Rawlinson, criticised the Labour Home Secretary, James Callaghan, for remaining 'neutral' and 'acknowledging the licence to riot'. Rawlinson also called for an injunction to be taken out against me because my public statements threatening to stop the tour constituted a 'direct threat to illegal action'. I was privately warned around this time by a friendly solicitor that my open advocacy of disruptive protests made me extremely vulnerable to a charge of conspiring unlawfully because the then conspiracy laws provided a catch-all basis for curbing radical political action. I noted the warning but felt I had no alternative but to press on regardless of the personal risk of a prosecution and likely prison sentence. Our whole strategy was predicated upon being open about our disruptive plans because it was public knowledge of our planned direct action which constituted our prime tactical weapon. The *threat* of direct action held the key to our strategy to get the tour stopped.

During February and March the campaign mushroomed. Committees and action groups to complement those established during the rugby tour sprang up throughout the country. The AAM was deluged with offers of help. About 100 enquiries a day by phone and mail poured into our home which was still the STST headquarters; my mother was almost permanently on the phone and the family flat was filled with volunteers and callers. The Prime Minister, Harold Wilson, publicly opposed the tour for the first time. The West Indian Campaign Against Apartheid Cricket was launched after the leading black activist, Jeff Crawford, contacted me; this introduced an important extra dimension which fused the battle against racism in British society with our campaign.

Meanwhile SAN-ROC, through the Supreme Council for Sport in Africa, consolidated the basis for a Commonwealth Games boycott. Trade unions came out against the tour: television workers and journalists threatened a media blackout, and radio's 'voice of cricket', John Arlott, announced he would not do the ball-by-ball commentaries for which he was internationally renowned. The top cricketer, Mike Brearley (later to become one of England's most successful captains) took the courageous step of speaking at the STST's national conference. Opposition was by now reaching right into the establishment. Leading public figures, including David Sheppard, formed the 'Fair Cricket Campaign' whose Vice-Chairman was the former Conservative Shadow Education Secretary, Sir Edward Boyle. Though explicitly committed to peaceful means and publicly distant from STST, the FCC was privately friendly and I had cordial discussions with its leaders.

By April, the campaign's momentum was still accelerating. Harold Wilson said that people 'should feel free to demonstrate against the tour', though he specifically criticised disruptive protests. The British Council of Churches also called for peaceful demonstrations. The Queen announced that neither she nor any member of the Royal family would make the traditional visit to the Lord's Test match, and the South Africans would not receive the traditional invitation to Buckingham Palace. Then, with the tour just six weeks away, the Supreme Council for Sport in Africa announced that 13 African countries would definitely boycott the Commonwealth games if the tour went ahead; Asian and Caribbean countries soon followed, raising the prospect of a whites-only Games running alongside a whites-only cricket tour. Sparked off by local direct action, the campaign had provoked an international diplomatic and political furore.

The Anti-Apartheid Movement played a crucial organisational role, both as a participant in STST and in its own right. Its indefatigable Executive Secretary, Ethel de Keyser, worked herself into the ground. An AAM poster caught the public's imagination and was widely published in the press. Under the caption 'If you could see their national sport you might be less keen to see their cricket', it showed a policeman beating defenceless blacks in Cato Manor township outside Durban. There was an ideal spectrum of protest from the lobbying activity of David Sheppard's Fair Cricket Campaign with its links into establishment opinion, through SAN-ROC with its expert international contacts, to the AAM with its conventional pressure group profile and its very effective links into the labour movement, and STST with its militant strategy. Although STST's direct action powered the whole campaign, it could have been isolated without a great hinterland of broad public support.

Meanwhile our organisational preparations proceeded.

Plans went ahead to blockade the team at Heathrow airport. Thousands of tickets were being bought up by local groups (the Games had been made all-ticket). The STST Special Action group ingeniously discovered the existence of an old tube train tunnel running right underneath Lord's with an air shaft which could facilitate a dramatic entry to the ground. But, although such activity was coordinated by STST from the centre, local groups operated quite independently. There was also a considerable degree of individualistic autonomy in the campaign. People were quite literally doing their own thing. I opened our front door one day to be faced by two youths who were model aeroplane fans. They told me how they intended to buzz the pitch during play from their aunt's flat which overlooked Lord's. There were reports from all over the country of other novel protest methods. Some individuals were breeding armies of locusts which they planned to let free on the turf. Others acquired small mirrors with which they intended to blind the batsmen.

Despite all this pressure the cricket establishment held firm. In mid-May, with the first match just three weeks away, they were invited to meet the Home Secretary, James Callaghan, who was by now very concerned at the likely threat to public order. After an unfruitful exchange in which he urged cancellation, he said he 'detected a lurking belief that they are a lonely band of heroes standing out against the darkening tide of lawlessness'. Certainly, the Cricket Council's members reflected old-worldly, far right political beliefs. But immediately after the meeting there came a decisive and unexpected boost to anti-apartheid forces. SAN-ROC's patient work paid off and South Africa was finally expelled from the Olympics.

The following week events scrambled to a climax. It became clear that the Prime Minister was about to call a general election. There was a notable shift in opinion. For the first time two highly influential individuals in the cricket world urged cancellation: E.W Swanton, cricket correspondent of the *Daily Telegraph* and Ted Dexter, the former England captain. The Cricket Council met in emergency session and – against all predictions – remained defiant, though effectively conceding our case for the first time by stating that there would be no future tours until South African teams were selected on a multi-racial basis. Still the drama was not over. The Home Secretary asked to see them again and formally requested cancellation. Another hurried meeting was arranged at Lord's and, on this occasion, the decision was final. The tour was off.

A campaign whose nine-month gestation was in the minds of a few people had now won with mass support. STST had emerged as one of the very few British protest groups – if not the only one – to have achieved its objectives completely. From the Cape Reserve in our home town of Pretoria came a simple but moving cable from the activist friends Poen Ah Dong, Alban Thumbran and Aubrey Apples who had waved us good-bye in 1966: 'And so say all of us.' (To have said anything more explicit would have invited police attention.) Messages of congratulation poured in. There were ecstatic celebrations as disbelieving supporters absorbed the full extent of their achievement. My own exhilaration was tempered by pure relief that what would certainly have become an ugly series of skirmishes had thankfully been avoided. We wound up STST and channelled action into the Anti-Apartheid Movement whose membership had more than doubled during the campaign.

For the first time in ten long bitter years since Sharpeville, black South Africans and whites involved in the resistance had something to cheer about. There were people abroad prepared to risk a great deal in standing up for *their* rights. This was a clarion call in the wilderness, a flash of light in the dark.

The boost to morale also stiffened internal resistance. Black attendance (now permitted for certain sports events after the earlier ban had reduced gate receipts) at white soc-cer matches fell appreciably. Previously unheard-of incidents occurred, such as a white referee being chased from the field of an all-black football match in February 1970. In June thousands of black spectators streamed on to the pitch in Kimberley and tried to carry off shoulder-high the black rugby star Bryan Williams after a match with the visiting New Zealand team. There was an ugly race riot as resentful white spectators started throwing bottles from the stands and baton-waving police had to restore order. Despite this, how-ever, even 'liberal' whites with an honourable record like Helen Suzman, the Progressive Party MP, remained critical. I had a confrontation with her on television and, after the STST campaign, my parents offered her a lift back from a party in London. She was critical of all boycotts, suggesting that people like us were 'out of touch'. The journey ended in icy silence.

It has always been the contention of apologists for sports links that maintaining contact provided a channel for

encouraging whites to see how the rest of the world lived
and so breed more liberal attitudes. This is pure fantasy.
Like other white South Africans, sports tourists could even
mix racially abroad whilst still seeing 'their' blacks at home
as totally different. During all the decades of so-called
'bridge-building', apartheid in sport had actually become more
entrenched. I was always convinced that an effective imposition of a sports boycott would be a decisive blow. And so it
proved to be: hardly had the cricket tour been stopped than
top South African cricketers, one after the other, tumbled out
to condemn apartheid in sport. Never before had they spoken
out like this. Peter Pollock, the fast bowler who had been
due to tour and who hadn't previously opposed apartheid in
sport, was forthright. A week after the tour cancellation he
told the Johannesburg *Sunday Times*: 'Sports isolation stares
South Africa in the face, and to creep back into the *laager* is
no answer. Sportsmen who genuinely feel there should be
multi-racial sport should say so.' Twenty five years later, the
captain of the ill-fated tour, Ali Bacher, told me: 'There is no
doubt the cancellation forced us to change. We wouldn't
have done so otherwise. It was the turning point. There was
no way back for us. You were right – we were wrong.'

Another welcome consequence was the increase in standing of the predominantly black sports groups committed to
non-racism. These had originally been grouped under the
umbrella of the South African Sports Association in the late
1950s. In each sport they existed as an alternative to the
dominant white body. They had been allied to the African
National Congress and, with the ANC banned and other
political action suppressed, non-racial sports groups became
an increasing focus for resistance against apartheid. In September 1970, a national conference of non-racial sports
groups in Durban signalled a new momentum and confidence in internal resistance to sports apartheid.

Nineteen-seventy was a cathartic year. Apart from STST's
success, and the Olympics expulsion, South Africa was expelled from Davis Cup tennis, international athletics, swimming, cycling, wrestling and gymnastics. This followed an
expulsion from boxing in 1968 and judo, pentathlon and
weightlifting in 1969. One by one, they got the push in team
sports. Only individual sports such as golf and tennis still
permitted white South African participation; by and large
anti-apartheid campaigners decided it was tactically unwise to
target individuals, even though they were undoubtedly the

privileged products of a racist sports system. Our attention focused on whites-only *team* sports since these reflected the apartheid system.

Most international sports bodies reflected the power relationships of the old days of empire, but by the late 1960s were becoming progressively more democratic as Third World countries asserted themselves. Consequently black nations became more influential and it was easier to win international sport to an isolationist stance. But, despite the 1969-70 tour, international rugby remained resistant to pressure, perhaps because it was overwhelmingly white-controlled.

From 1960 onward in New Zealand there had been growing pressure to cut rugby links. South Africa's refusal to allow Maoris to tour in New Zealand teams turned the argument back into New Zealand society where it became a huge issue. The Citizen's Association for Race Equality (CARE) coordinated the boycott movement. As a result of the pressure, in 1967 the Prime Minister, Keith Holyoake, virtually instructed the New Zealand Rugby Board to cancel a planned tour. The following year, the South Africans reluctantly accepted the inclusion of Maoris who would be given 'honorary white status', and a tour was arranged for June–September 1970. The Halt All Racialist Tours (HART), a more radical group led by Trevor Richards, was formed to campaign against the tour. It was helped by a notorious statement by a former South African Cabinet Minister, Albert Hertzog, who denounced the admission of Maoris: they 'will sit at the table with our young men and girls and they will dance with our girls', he protested. Following STST, direct action tactics were used for the first time as training sessions were disrupted and the team harassed all the way to its departure. In Haarlem, Holland, a badminton match was disrupted and two days later play was held up for half an hour after demonstrators dropped smoke bombs onto the court.

In mid-1970 militant protests were staged in Australia under the auspices of the Campaign Against Racialism in Sport (CARIS) which had been formed the previous year under the leadership of Peter McGregor. Black dye was thrown into the pool in a protest at the Australian swimming championships and a basketball game in Sydney was disrupted. Encouraged by STST's success, CARIS now focused upon the mid-1971 Springbok rugby tour to Australia and – in a virtual repeat – a cricket tour due to start in October.

I was invited to support the campaign and left for Sydney

on a 31-hour flight after sitting my first year exams at Queen Mary College, London University. (I had switched degrees from engineering to economics and political science.) My plane arrived two days before the Springboks, on 24 June and for the next two weeks I had a vigorous schedule of media appearances, speaking engagements and private tactical briefings. In Brisbane I was taken to the field where the match was due to be played. It was completely open, with no visible defences. In a television interview which was repeated for days afterwards, I said that it 'would be a piece of cake' to stop the match. Later the game was switched to a more secure venue.

The Springboks began in conservative Perth where the match was interrupted and there were 20 arrests. Already their difficulties were mounting. With the unions promising to boycott the servicing of planes, both the major domestic airlines decided they would not carry the Springboks. So the team had to fly 1700 tiring miles to Adelaide cramped into chartered light aircraft, the seven-hour flight nearly three times longer than that of the regular jet. I flew in on a scheduled flight from Brisbane to speak at a huge meeting in the Central Methodist Church. Over 1000 demonstrators besieged the match, there were interruptions to play, smoke flares were let off under the floodlights and the police and stewards lashed out indiscriminately, even arresting the mild-mannered Australia correspondent of *The Times*.

The campaign gathered pace. In Melbourne armed guards with dogs patrolled the venue. At a rally attended by 5000, I was greeted enthusiastically, saying that the campaign was 'well on the way to emulating the success that we achieved in Britain'. I went on: 'We are seeing a concentration camp type atmosphere building up and I welcome that. It strips this tour of all its pretensions.' The demonstrators then set off to march to the ground where 650 policemen with truncheons and horses started to wade into the march. The *Sydney Morning Herald* reported the next day: 'Many Victorian policemen took the law into their own hands.' The resulting violence was sickening. Even after the match as we walked peacefully away, police on horseback charged us – my most frightening experience in years of demonstrating.

On 8 September 1970, one month after the battered Springboks had departed, the legendary cricketer Sir Donald Bradman announced as Chairman of the Australian Cricket Board of Control, that 'with great regret' the tour had been cancelled. This was another decisive blow. Apartheid sports' days were now numbered and I was invited to New York to give evidence to the United Nations Special Committee Against Apartheid.

Rugby, however, remained a difficult nut to crack. We were able to stop tours coming abroad, but it was very difficult to prevent teams from visiting South Africa.

Despite opposition England went ahead with their tour in 1972. By this time we had formed the Stop All Racist Tours campaign (SART) of which I was Chair. A group of demonstrators disrupted the England training session in Twickenham. We also arranged for the team coach to be hemmed in at their hotel in Richmond prior to their departure for London's Heathrow airport. Just before the coach was due to leave, we called the fire brigade, which descended on the hotel in force. Additionally we requested several skips to be brought, ostensibly to take away rubbish, but in fact to block in the team. We were unable to stop this tour, nor the one by the British Lions in 1974. Prior to the latter's departure I was one of a dozen people who broke through security and staged a rooftop occupation of the Rugby Football Union's offices at Twickenham. However the Labour Foreign Minister, Joan Lestor, a stalwart of the Anti-Apartheid Movement, instructed the British Embassy to withdraw the usual courtesy facilities for a visiting national side like the Lions. We also greeted their return at a Heathrow airport hotel with pickets and my sister Sally threw a flour bag at the former Conservative Prime Minister Edward Heath, who was there to greet the team.

In 1973 we had occupied the reception area of the West End hotel in which the visiting New Zealand rugby team were staying in a protest against the Springbok tour scheduled for New Zealand later in the year. The disruption to customers so upset the hotel management that they forced the team's officials to meet and talk with us. In 1974 I was asked to visit France for several days to join the campaign there against a visiting South African rugby side. Although the protests were relatively muted, they were an important first in taking the battle into France where the campaign against apartheid was much weaker.

Meanwhile in New Zealand the campaign was more vigorous and created more internal political impact than anywhere else in the world. Society was split down the middle and the issue became central to the country's politics. The Springboks were due to tour in 1973 and the campaign of opposition coordinated by HART was relentlessly effective. Even the smallest South African sports link was a target for protests. The unexpected victory for the Labour Party in the November 1972 general election meant that there was now a government sympathetic to the anti-apartheid cause. But HART's leader, Trevor Richards, had no doubt that, like STST, it was the threat of direct action which would be decisive. He stepped up threats to disrupt the tour, provoking a frenzied debate about law and order and inviting charges from right-wingers that he was 'running the country'. It was all too reminiscent of my own experience three years before. As the pressure increased, the Minister of Defence was advised that up to 1000 soldiers would be needed to bolster the police and protect the tour from demonstrations; he said he would 'not commit New Zealand soldiers to bash other New Zealanders at rugby fields or anywhere else'.

As the year wore on, the political pressure for the cancellation became immense. As in Britain three years before, the Commonwealth Games, due in Christchurch the following year, were in jeopardy, with black countries refusing to attend if the tour proceeded. Finally, on 10 April, the Labour Prime Minister, Norman Kirk, announced that the tour was to be 'postponed until the South African team was chosen on the basis of genuine merit'. This historic announcement heralded the decisive breakthrough in New Zealand – but again it occurred because of the threat of direct action and in the face of bitter opposition from the rugby authorities who still had not accepted the argument.

Three years before, the *Financial Times* had reported the success achieved by STST, 'Is it purely coincidental that the stepping up of the anti-apartheid campaign in Britain and America during the past year or so has been accompanied by a sharp falling off in the inflow of capital into the country? Those who follow these matters are convinced it is not.' Our sports campaign had achieved a much wider impact by focusing public attention on apartheid as a whole.

With the 1970 cricket tour stopped there was still an important role for imaginative direct action tactics. Those centrally involved in STST launched the 'Action Committee Against Racialism' specifically to apply its direct action strategy elsewhere. We discovered that a South African Trade Centre was scheduled to open in central London's St Martin's Lane. We also discovered it was financed by the South African Government and wrote to the estate agents warning that the premises would become the target 'for an intensive campaign of demonstrations'. The threat received extensive publicity and we copied the letter to surrounding shops and offices, provoking paranoia through the building. We followed this up with a noisy picket. Shortly afterwards the front doors of the building were gummed up with a solidifying agent. A few days later smoke flares were let off in the lifts during the lunch hour; amid the frenzy that there might be a fire, the fire brigade was called. On each occasion the press were alerted and the estate agents informed. A week later the firm acting for the organisers of the Trade Centre announced that they had shelved plans to take a showroom in London.

Anti-apartheid activists concentrated on Barclays Bank which had an extensive South African subsidiary. Barclays maintained the discriminatory staff wages and customer arrangements characteristic of apartheid; it also bankrolled the South African economy, so underpinning apartheid. A 'Boycott Barclays' campaign spread across Britain. Action groups occupied local Barclays branches and disrupted the recruitment drives the bank mounted among new students and which were an important part of extending its customer base. University and student union accounts with Barclays were closed after pressure from campaigners. Labour controlled local authorities and trade unions followed suit. There were vocal pickets outside high street branches. Protesters acquired shares and intervened at the annual general meeting. Like the STST campaign, this one could be successfully focused on direct action at local level. Instead of marching through the centre of London on a weekend afternoon, action could be taken locally and the everyday life of local institutions targeted. Within a few years, the pressure on the bank was so intense that the commercial advantages of its South African operations were outweighed by the disadvantages of losing custom, mainly in Britain. Eventually it took the extraordinary step of pulling out of South Africa entirely, signifying another major success for the anti-apartheid movement.

Barclays had acted as an important channel for overseas investment which so critically underpinned the apartheid economy. Some 60 per cent of all external investment came from Britain and other British clearing banks were also involved in providing foreign finance. They now became a target too. A separate drive, coordinated by the End Loans to South Africa campaign, developed expert tactics, including lobbying and disrupting annual general meetings. Though not as successful as the attack on Barclays which was such a visible target because it alone had branches in South Africa, this added to pressure on the country's economy and therefore its Government. So did the increasingly active campaigns spearheaded by the Anti-Apartheid Movement against British companies which traded with South Africa. The poverty wages paid to their black workers became an embarrassment and also a source of grievance with British trade unions which pointed to the dangers of exploitative labour conditions under apartheid undercutting the standards of British workers.

Meanwhile the consumer boycott continued. In a campaign which applied militant tactics to high street supermarkets, protesters plastered black and white stickers on South African goods with a skull and crossbones marked 'DANGER – PRODUCT OF APARTHEID'. We also filled carriers and trolleys with all the South African produce we could find, had the bill rung up at the till and then suddenly 'discovered' that the contents were all South African and refused to pay, leaving cashiers and managers with angry customers queuing up in frustration as the resulting chaos was sorted out.

In 1974 a major conference in Holland focused on boycotting South African produce. The Dutch anti-apartheid movement had been running a successful boycott of oranges. In Britain the Anti-Apartheid Movement continued to lead the campaign, pushing forward on a number of fronts: arms sales to South Africa, its secret nuclear developments, trade, political prisoners – all these were tackled by the AAM which increasingly became the focus for world-wide coordinated activity.

Also crucial was the International Defence and Aid Fund (IDAF) headed by Canon John Collins. In 1965 its South African group – which had done such important work funding and organising legal defence teams in political trials – had been banned, along with its Chairman David Craighead, a prominent Johannesburg Liberal Party member and friend of my parents. In 1966 the IDAF was declared a prohibited organisation, so it became necessary to operate underground. Over the next 25 years £70 million for legal defence money was channelled into South Africa via a series of trusts with eminent figures as trustees distant from the IDAF. Additionally, £30 million of welfare money was smuggled in. To do this IDAF used 700 individual volunteers from eight countries, who wrote thousands of apparently personal letters to the recipients enclosing gifts of money. Secrecy was vital because within South Africa it was a criminal offence to be associated with IDAF. And, despite their best efforts, the

security services were never able to penetrate the closely
guarded files at IDAF headquarters in London.

Another feature of the struggle was the emergence of the
liberation movements. Having been banned in 1960 the
ANC and the PAC were driven underground. But it quickly
became evident that, such was the extent of repression, resistance could not be carried out exclusively from inside the
country. The 90-day detention without trial law was first
extended to 180-days in 1965 and then in 1967 the Prevention of Terrorism Act allowed indefinite detention without
charge or trial. Like other security legislation it was retro-
spective so individuals could be charged for actions which
were not illegal when committed. Its sweeping nature was
made clear in the legal definition of terrorism as 'any act
with intent to endanger the maintenance of law and order'
and it provided for the detention even of people 'likely to
possess information with regard to terrorism'. The last vestiges of political freedom were extinguished by such catch-all
legislation and ruthless police state repression. The 1967
Defence Amendment Act provided for the call-up each year
of 17,000 white men between the ages of 17 and 25, to form
a citizen force of around 100,000. Suspects continued to be
tortured and ill-treated. More and more black political prisoners died in detention in mysterious circumstances: 'fell down
a flight of stairs', 'slipped in the shower', 'fell out of the
window', 'suicide' – all became regular reasons given for such
deaths.

By the mid-1960s a new front in the struggle had opened
up. Having been suppressed internally, the ANC and its
sister liberation movements in Rhodesia, South West Africa,
Mozambique, Angola and Guine-Bissau, determined upon
armed guerrilla struggle as the only way forward, and
received funds from Sweden and the Soviet bloc. The argument for solidarity within the AAM for the armed struggle
began to gather strength. It welcomed the alliance between
the ANC and the Zimbabwe African Peoples Union (ZAPU)
and hailed their first guerrilla incursion from Zambia into
Rhodesia in August 1967 as a 'historic new phase of armed
resistance'.

Anti-apartheid movements everywhere started to play an
important solidarity role. One of my first activities with the
Young Liberals' Southern Africa Commission had been to set
up a 'Medical Aid for Southern Africa' appeal in 1968 to
assist the ANC and other liberation movements. This was

tactically astute because many people sympathetic to or actually involved in anti-apartheid movements would not associate themselves with the violence of the liberation struggle. I visited the ANC's London office and held discussions with, among others, Thabo Mbeki, then a student at Sussex University and 26 years later the Vice-President of his country. With the help of my mother who was experienced in these things, we typed up and duplicated on a second-hand gestetner machine copies of a pamphlet supporting the medical aid appeal; my father did the artwork for the cover.

At my first national Young Liberal conference in Scarborough in April 1968, I was called to the rostrum to make a brief speech in favour of a resolution supporting the liberation struggle. Despite the radicalism of the YLs then, it was narrowly defeated, with strong appeals by pacifists. I was by instinct and conviction resolutely opposed to violence. For me violence was no academic matter: I had seen too much of it in South Africa and I hated it. We had been brought up to detest the violence of apartheid. But the logic of the predicament of those resisting apartheid convinced me that the ANC and other liberation movements were justified in adopting guerrilla tactics: with all democratic and legal channels blocked, they had no alternative. I started openly advocating the cause of the ANC and its sister groups in Southern Africa when speaking at campaign meetings around Britain. From 1966 the Anti-Apartheid Movement offered an important platform for the ANC and other liberation movements. Fringe meetings were organised at the Labour and Liberal Parties' annual conferences and liberation group representatives spoke at conferences for trade unionists.

However my support for the ANC's *guerrilla* struggle should not be confused with support for *terrorism*. The vital distinction was that the violence of guerrilla movements was directed against the oppressive apartheid state, whereas the violence of terrorists was directed against innocent bystanders. Although the distinction did sometimes become blurred, as when sabotage carried out by the ANC unintentionally caught bystanders, it nevertheless remained a valid and important foundation for political solidarity.

A violent strategy by resistance movements could only be justified when, as was the case with European countries invaded by Hitler during the Second World War or with a contemporary tyranny like apartheid, all other means had been exhausted and there was no viable alternative. To deny people the right to resist such tyrannies violently was to

deny them their humanity and to acquiesce in their oppression. When the crunch came, all the pacifist could do was
bear moral witness, dying bravely as the tanks rolled in.
However, it was still unpopular to support groups like the
ANC. For many years, Nelson Mandela, languishing on Robben Island, was labelled a 'terrorist' in sections of the British
media and by many Conservative MPs; two decades later
these same people greeted him as a saint and jostled oleagi-
nously to be photographed at his side.

Although it was clear to all but a few revolutionary
romantics that the liberation struggle could not on its own
defeat apartheid, it remained a vital and leading part of the
overall struggle. The explicit unity between the guerrilla
struggle in Rhodesia, South West Africa and the Portuguese
colonies of Angola and Mozambique meant that white South
Africa had to fight on a broader front which over-stretched
its resources. And the link to the wider campaign could not
have been made clearer by Moses Garoeb, a leading freedom
fighter in the South West African People's Organisation
(SWAPO). He told me in 1970 that STST had been an
'inspiration' to SWAPO cadres in the African bush as they
heard the news on their radios. I replied that it was the
dedication and sacrifices of people like them which inspired
us to campaign even more vigorously.

5 RESPONSE

The letter bomb suddenly appeared on our breakfast table. My sister Sally, aged 15 at the time, was helping open my pile of mail at home one Saturday morning in June 1972. 'What's this?' she asked and I looked up to see an explosive device recessed into holes in a thick sheet of balsa wood, with metal cylinders and wires protruding. The envelope was postmarked Vienne, in France.

Fortunately it did not explode and I carried it gingerly outside, placing it carefully on the garden path. Shortly afterwards the bomb squad – on red alert at the time for IRA bombings – swarmed all over our house. The device was defused and Special Branch officers later said it was powerful enough to have blown us all up. I noticed that a plastic disc, attached to the inside of the envelope, had been inserted between springloaded contacts. The disc remained behind when the package was removed from its envelope, closing the contacts and completing the circuit. A small electrical fault stood between us and oblivion.

Thereafter I always scrutinised the post with great care, though in practice there was very little that could be done to protect myself against one of the world's most ruthless secret services which had a grim record of eliminating both internal and external opponents. A number of anti-apartheid activists around the world were killed by similar letter bombs sent by BOSS, the South African Bureau for State Security, established in 1969. BOSS's 'Z-squad', set up explicitly to wage terrorist attacks on opponents, took the final letter in the alphabet because it specialised in final solutions: assassination of apartheid's enemies.

One of its first victims was Dr Eduardo Mondlane, the President of the Mozambique liberation movement, FRELIMO, killed in Tanzania in 1969 when a letter bomb exploded as he opened it on his desk. Another victim, Abraham Tiro, a leading figure in the radical black South African Students' Organisation, was killed instantly in exile when he opened a parcel sent to a Roman Catholic Mission near Gaberone, Botswana, in February 1974.

BOSS officially ceased to exist in August 1978, and its functions were transferred to DONS, the Department of National Security. Later this was replaced by the National Intelligence Service, the NIS. But letter bombs continued to be directed all over Africa at organisers of the South African resistance movement. In 1982 one of them killed the writer and ANC activist Ruth First in her study at the Eduardo Mondlane University in Maputo. (Ruth, a leading figure in the Anti-Apartheid Movement, had been one of the most supportive of STST's more militant tactics.) In June 1984 another letter bomb killed ANC member Jeanette Schoon and her six-year-old daughter in Lubango, Angola – it was intended for her husband, Marius.

But letter bombs were just one part of the South African Government's response to growing international resistance. Before the 1969–70 rugby tour started, BOSS printed a leaflet signed 'The Vigilantes' stating that 'counter protest cells' had been established all over the country. It appeared to come from loyalist rugby supporters and warned that any left-wing protesters who interrupted play would be 'carried off and walloped'. The leaflet was distributed to national newspapers and *The Times*, among others, reported it. During the rugby tour, BOSS distributed a press release from a hoax group, the 'Democratic Anti-Demo Organisation', which threatened to spray demonstrators with red paint and cover them with feathers. (At the time I was aware of these initiatives, but did not know BOSS was responsible.) Organisers of the STST campaign identified a number of instances where people involved in some of our special projects appeared to be acting as *agents provocateurs*, deliberately inciting violence. We traced one of these individuals back to the South African Embassy.

In 1981, the former South African agent and journalist, Gordon Winter, described other pro-South Africa interventions in his book *Inside BOSS*. For instance, a Mr Peter Toombs, whom I remember well, launched a mysterious group called the 'Anti-Demonstration Association' from a house in Oxfordshire in 1969. According to Winter, Toombs had previously completed paid assignments for the South Africans. His 'organisation' had no members on the ground, but he seemed well connected and was put up to oppose me in TV interviews. Within hours of the cricket tour being cancelled, Gordon Winter's BOSS handler in London asked him to prepare a detailed report on me and on each one of the activities undertaken by the STST campaign. Winter wrote that it was to be used to 'pin me to the wall'.

Also at this time an English barrister and parliamentary draughtsman, Francis Bennion, publicly announced his intention to bring a private prosecution against me for conspiracy over the direct action demonstrations against the Springboks. To begin with, Bennion's action appeared individually inspired, but this soon changed. The right-wing Society for Individual Freedom (which was closely linked to British Intelligence) backed the prosecution, and Gordon Winter was instructed by BOSS to offer his help and pass over his material on me. This he did, liaising initially with Gerald Howarth, its General Secretary (who entered Parliament in 1983 as a hard-right Conservative close to Margaret Thatcher). In June 1971, the 'Hain Prosecution Fund' was launched to raise £20,000 for Bennion's private prosecution. Howarth was its Treasurer and Ross McWhirter its Chairman. These two, together with Winter, respectively provided links with the hard right, MI5 and BOSS.

Shortly after the launch, Bennion flew to South Africa to raise money and BOSS circulated subscription lists through the South African civil service. The combined effort was described in the South African media as being the 'Pain for Hain' campaign – a title which caught on among right wing circles in Britain where donations were also solicited. In June 1971 I was served with a summons for criminal conspiracy at Heathrow airport as I was about to depart for the campaign against the Springbok rugby tour in Australia and, after a week's hearing at Bow Street Magistrate's Court in October 1971, I was committed for trial at the Old Bailey.

Four counts of conspiracy were levelled against me, covering the sit-down at Bristol tennis court, the interruption of the Wilf Isaacs cricket match, disruption of the rugby tour and the stopping of the cricket tour. I was charged with conspiring with 'others unknown' – even though many were well known, or could at least have been easily identified. Literally hundreds of individual actions (one tally revealed over 900) across the entire United Kingdom (which for these purposes actually included the Republic of Ireland) were laid at my door. They included trespass, breaches of the peace, 'watching and besetting' and intimidation. Some of these individual offences ('particulars', as they were termed) involved activity which did not constitute a criminal offence in its own right but which, when prefixed with 'conspiracy', was transformed into criminal illegality.

I found myself in an Alice in Wonderland world where words were simply reinterpreted to suit the purposes of both the prosecutors and a hostile judge, Bernard Gillis. The law on conspiracy is ancient in origin, dating from 1304, and over the years judges had used their discretion with enthusiasm to enlarge its scope. For example, in 1969–70 when I was running onto sports pitches or helping organise others to do so, 'an agreement to commit a civil trespass' was then 'not indictable', as a leading legal textbook put it. But in 1972 a judge declared in a case of student protesters who occupied the Sierra Leone Embassy that, because this involved a matter of 'substantial public interest', conspiracy to trespass was after all a criminal offence. Despite the fact that this declaration came some two years *after* our protests (though conveniently just before my trial), it was still applied. When the lawyers later disputed this on appeal, Lord Justice Roskill revealingly replied: 'Hain would not have done it had it not been a matter of public interest.' The judges might well have said in my case: 'We don't like what he was up to, interfering with our enjoyment of cricket, tennis and rugby, and we shall find a way of reinterpreting the law to stop him doing it.'

The trial took place in August 1972 during my university vacation and lasted four weeks. Due to the enormous list of activities and offences involved, it took seven minutes for the Clerk of the Court to read out the charges against me. Then the jury was sworn in: nine white men, one white woman, a black Guyanese man and an Asian man. My book about the STST campaign, Don't Play with Apartheid, proved to be the main evidence against me and the trial involved lengthy textual analysis and argument. The prosecution was opened by Owen Stable QC who asserted 'Hain and his friends tried to set themselves above the law.' He then embarked upon a day-and-a-half-long opening speech, referring to my 'fertile, trouble-making propensities' and insisting that the very future of English civilisation was at stake in the trial.

Although in English law one is supposed to be innocent until proved guilty, the reverse applied in my case. This was because, as a judge in an earlier conspiracy trial had determined, 'conspiracy can be effected by a wink or a nod without a word being spoken'. Basically, if it could be shown (as it was pretty easy to do) that I had advocated direct action and played a leading role in the overall movement, then I was guilty of conspiracy – even if I had nothing to do with the individual acts carried out by those 'others unknown'. The only way I could prove I was not responsible was by calling some of those who were. For example, Peter Jordan was a schoolteacher who in Bristol on 31 December 1969 ran on the pitch and sprinkled tin tacks. Although I had nothing to do with it and strongly disapproved, I was charged with conspiracy for this. Calling Jordan as a witness was the only way I could prove we had never met or communicated and that, in his own words, 'it was a spontaneous act'.

The South African connection was all pervasive in court. The 1969–70 Springbok captain Dawie de Villiers was flown over from Johannesburg to give evidence, as was the private cricket tour sponsor Wilf Isaacs. But they were only able to describe the events and could not directly implicate me. Gordon Winter, who later confessed he had all along been working for BOSS while London correspondent for the South African *Sunday Express*, was to be the prosecution's star witness. (Other journalists refused to co-operate.) But, at the last minute, he 'turned'. Nearly ten years later he revealed he was instructed by BOSS to maintain his cover for a more important task – smearing the then Liberal leader, Jeremy Thorpe. We were expecting him to provide the most telling evidence as he was at all the demonstrations, popping up with notebook and camera to hand and we always suspected he might have BOSS links.

But, when called for the prosecution, he switched, under questioning, into a defence witness, alleging that Bennion's team had asked him only for selective photographs showing the demonstrators in a bad light. Giving me a large wink – which I found disconcerting and embarrassing – he ostentatiously pulled out a wad of photos showing police attacking demonstrators. (One officer was convicted in 1974 for planting a knife on a demonstrator.) He also emphasised the defence's reliance upon my role as a *spokesperson* for the campaign, rather than as *organiser* of all the demonstrations which the prosecution wanted to prove in order to find me guilty of conspiracy. His evidence was extremely astute; he argued that I had been 'elected by the press' as STST's Chairman – which was partly true as I had never been formally appointed but simply assumed the role. We were startled at his unexpected helpfulness.

Two weeks into the trial, it was crystal clear that the prosecution were relying almost exclusively on my book as a self-confession of guilt. Their last witness was Wilf Wooller, a colourful cricketing character who had always denounced me in the most personal and extravagant terms. His opening greeting when we met face to face for the first time was: 'I hope to see you behind bars before the tour is out. And I really mean that.' But, in common with all the other witnesses, he was unable to implicate me directly.

However, the oppressive, catch-all nature of the law on conspiracy meant it was almost impossible to prove my innocence. Because of this I was determined not to go into the witness box. I would have convicted myself: although certainly not guilty of over 90 per cent of the particulars with which I was charged, I was nevertheless guilty of coordinating and organising action to disrupt and stop the various sports events and tours. My lawyers thought that the hostile judge, Bernard Gillis, was after an exemplary prison sentence. They were especially concerned that they would be unable to answer a probable question from the judge as to what exactly was my defence 'in law'. It appeared there was no answer to this, in which case my defence would collapse instantly.

On the other hand, I could not be asked that question, as I was not a lawyer. So I decided to defend myself and appeal to the jury on a basis of justice not to convict me. Through making opening and closing speeches for the defence and through examining witnesses we proposed to call, I could talk to and thereby appeal to the jury without going into the witness box. As the *Sunday Times* journalist Derek Humphry reported, the prosecution were 'flabbergasted, as their preparation for the case had been on the certainty that Hain would have to give sworn evidence'. Later, Judge Gillis made clear his unhappiness. As Derek Humphry wrote: 'Lawyers said later that Judge Gillis came close to using improper pressure on Hain by his constant attempts to persuade him not to defend himself and his attempts to alter Hain's decision not to go into the witness box.'

Although taking my own defence was daunting, it made explicit what had previously only been implicit in the rarified atmosphere of the court. Instead of the political issues at stake being submerged in legal niceties, they could now be teased out through my own advocacy. What's more, my destiny was in my own hands. I was fighting for my freedom. I was also fighting for the anti-apartheid cause, as my conviction could have opened the way for other South African-inspired prosecutions.

I 'stood broadly by' what I had written in *Don't Play with Apartheid*, but insisted that it had not been written 'as a confession'. There had been no lawyer vetting every sentence in anticipation that it would be transformed from something written for readability into a legal document in which the interpretation of even the most casual sentence was liable to land me up in prison.

I emphasised my total opposition to violent protest and insisted that I was honest about my role and objectives. I had never hidden my commitment to non-violent direct action – indeed had publicly proclaimed it. This was no sinister, covert conspiracy. STST was disarmingly open and honest. 'The campaign was a loose movement. It was not a rigid organisation. We had no generals. We had no apparatus through which to conspire.' It was quite ludicrous to charge me with nearly 1000 offences committed the length and breadth of the British Isles. It was moreover oppressive to frame the conspiracy charge in such a way that, if I was found guilty of one particular offence, I was guilty of the lot. The jury's verdict would be given only on each of the four counts rather than their contents. This was iniquitous because, even if the jury found I was not guilty of hundreds of offences in each of the four conspiracy counts, there was no way of the judge knowing this when he passed sentence. They might decide I was guilty of only the trivial offences or those which were strictly non-violent. But the judge could not know this and might assume guilt for the most violent offences. It was the *conspiracy* which mattered. And since there clearly *was* an organisation of which I was a leading public figure, this made my defence an uphill battle.

We had lined up a series of activists from across Britain to testify that they had organised local protests – from scattering tin tacks and digging up cricket pitches, to demonstrations outside the grounds – quite independently. But, as they confirmed that they had never met or talked to me, the prosecution objected and Judge Gillis became increasingly testy, until eventually I was stopped from putting questions. The defence witness subject to the most hostile cross-examination was Ethel de Keyser, the Executive Secretary of the Anti-Apartheid Movement, and herself a South African exile. She was asked 218 questions by the prosecution for several hours spread over two days. But, despite being on the receiving end of a QC skilled at tying up witnesses in knots, she never flinched. With almost uncanny precision she skipped deftly between his barbs, her composure never ruffled. So effective was her performance that Stable was unable to make any use of her evidence in his final address to the jury.

But her appearance was notable for another reason. When Stable began asking her about the AAM's annual general meeting in 1969, he seemed remarkably well informed. So much so that it became apparent he was working from a transcript of a tape recording made at the meeting. This must have been done secretly because the AAM itself only recorded minutes of decisions and reports in the normal way. The prosecution must have felt they had a trump card because I, among others, had spoken at the meeting of STST's direct action plans. If Ethel de Keyser had been able to confirm this is in answer to Stable's questions, then the prosecution would have had their first direct evidence which could have supported the conspiracy charges. The transcript could have been admissible as evidence before the jury. But the AGM was three years ago and she was frankly unable to recall points of detail about what had been said in over six hours of reports, discussion and debate, especially since she was engaged in the busy organisation of making sure the day went smoothly. Stable would not reveal in court who had provided the tape recording but we had good reason to believe it was the South African security services who were suspected by the AAM of regularly infiltrating meetings and bugging and breaking into its headquarters.

After Ethel's appearance, which was designed to show that the AAM operated autonomously from STST as a perfectly legal and open organisation, we decided not to call a queue of other witnesses, some of them outside waiting to give evidence. With a hostile judge and the dangers of cross-examination producing ricochet ammunition to the prosecution, we were now in the final stages of the defence case, the conclusion of which was deliberately planned. The former Labour MP Peter Jackson was stopped by the judge while he answered a question confirming his publicly stated intention to run on cricket pitches – again, quite independently of me. Anticipating a similar reaction to the appearance of Colin Winter, Bishop-in-exile of Damaraland, South West Africa, I had prepared my response. His evidence was duly blocked before a battery of objections. I protested that legal etiquette had stopped me from mounting my own defence properly and abruptly announced that in these circumstances, although we had plenty of witnesses ready to be called, I was closing my case. Judge Gillis was disconcerted, as was Stable who, caught by surprise, immediately had to begin his closing statement with the prosecutor's nightmare – a weekend break – intervening. However, he concluded that if I were let off, it would be an incitement to politically inspired law breaking on such a massive scale – by for example homeless families occupying empty properties, Jews protesting at the Russian ballet, Palestinians disrupting performances by Israeli artists – that England's green and pleasant civilisation would be threatened.

My closing speech to the jury took two days and, in another departure from precedent, was interrupted regularly by the judge. I dissected all the evidence to prove it was an open, honest campaign in which I never sought to hide my role or objectives. This was a 'scapegoat prosecution' in a 'politically motivated' trial. I also reminded jurors of the honourable tradition of non-violent direct action – from Chartists and Suffragettes in Britain to Gandhi in India and blacks demanding civil rights in the USA.

After a laborious three-day summing up by the judge, he sent the jury out at 10.35 a.m. on Monday 22 August. Although I had been on bail for the proceedings – able to go out at lunchtimes and home overnight – I was now confined to the cells below the court to await my fate which I knew could be a prison sentence. The hours dragged by. The tension grew. What could be going on in the jury room? At 4.21 p.m., nearly six long hours after the jury had retired, the judge sent for them. The foreman stated that they could not agree on any of the four conspiracy counts. So Judge Gillis informed them solemnly that he would accept a majority verdict 'if ten of you are in agreement'. The tension was now unbearable. At 5.57 p.m. they trooped back in again. Guilty on the third count, the peaceful Davis Cup tennis court sit-down at Bristol – by far the least serious of the counts and the one where I was most culpable as charged. But then the foreman stated that they could not agree on the remaining three counts. It was a dramatic moment. As Derek Humphry reported: 'It was evident that Hain had succeeded in going over the heads of the prosecution and the judge and

influencing the majority of the jury with his political philosophy.' It was confirmed later that the two black jurors held
out even against my conviction over the tennis court disruption. They were joined by others in refusing to convict on
the rugby and cricket tour counts. In the absence of a re-
trial, the judge then directed that 'verdicts of not guilty be
recorded in counts 1, 2 and 4'. He fined me £200.

By this time I was, at 22, more drained than I had ever
been before. The 'Pain for Hain' prosecution failed in its
fundamental objective – to remove me from a leadership role
in the anti-apartheid struggle and the verdict was greeted
with widespread disappointment in the white South African
media. But it certainly succeeded in diverting my time and
energies from the political arena to the courtroom. One way
and another it took several months out of my active political
life – some consolation perhaps to those who wanted revenge
for the defeat inflicted on them in 1970.

The next obvious opposition was a 3000-word broadsheet,
'The Hidden Face of the Liberal Party'. It was almost entirely
about me, using various reports of my activities out of con-
text to smear both me and the Liberals. Hundreds of thousands of copies were distributed in key parliamentary seats
(including Putney) where the Liberals might be expected to
do well in the October 1974 election. Contained in the
broadsheets (one was also produced on the Labour Party,
with a joint print run of about 3 million) were the by now
familiar themes of the hard right: extremism in the Liberal
and Labour parties and allegations of subservience to Moscow. They were published by the hard-right Foreign Affairs
Publishing Company which had strong links with white
South Africa, British Intelligence and the CIA. In view of the
huge production costs it is hard to see how the broadsheets
could have been financed without support from the intelligence services. The broadsheet fitted an emerging pattern of
disinformation, destabilisation and disruption.

During the mid-1970s, South Africa's so-called 'Information Department scandal' was at its height. Under its Secretary, Dr Eschel Rhoodie, the Department moved well beyond
the normal bounds of foreign information and propaganda,
with the active blessing of the Prime Minister, John Vorster.
Rhoodie, in close cooperation with the head of BOSS, General H.J. van den Bergh and Connie Mulder, the Cabinet
Minister in charge and seen as Vorster's successor, mounted
138 secret projects, spending tens of millions of pounds.

They sponsored front organisations, spread disinformation and secretly financed newspapers at home and abroad. Hundreds of people were victims of the activity promoted by BOSS and the disinformation spread by the Information Department. I was just one of their targets.

One of their projects was the Committee for Fairness in Sport (CFS), established in 1973. Funded by wealthy white South African businessmen, and with money laundered through the Information Department, it tried to promote an image of change as a basis for securing sports re-admission. Its Chairman was Gert Wolmarans, former sports editor of the pro-Government newspaper, *Die Vaderland*. The CFS undertook a programme of expensive newspaper advertisements to put South Africa's case. These featured photographs of black and white athletes competing together in 'multinational' events. A well-oiled public relations drive accompanied such initiatives, part of which involved flying over Leslie Sehume to confront anti-apartheid leaders and to call for support for British Lions and New Zealand rugby tours to South Africa.

Sehume had a much publicised half-hour debate with me on BBC television in April 1974. He symbolised a fresh tactic. The sports editor of the black Johannesburg newspaper, *The World*, he was represented as the 'true' voice of the black majority. Putting a black like him up against me (and against my New Zealand counterpart, Trevor Richards, the following year) was designed to put us on the spot. Who did we think we were, foreign whites trying to dictate to black South Africans? However, although he was plausible (even acknowledging that people like me had helped 'accelerate change'), received some favourable coverage in the right-wing press, and was feted by British apologists for apartheid, Sehume was a transparent 'Uncle Tom'. While in London for several weeks, he held forth from a luxurious apartment in London's Waldorf Hotel which was about as far apart from his readers in townships at home as it was possible to get.

In our television debate he told me: 'If you returned to South Africa now, you would be stoned out of the country – by blacks, not whites.' This was powerful stuff. Unfortunately for him it was not true. It was immediately denounced by his own newspaper, *The World*. Although careful not to endorse our boycott strategy (for it was then illegal to advocate sanctions and boycotts), an editorial in the paper took 'the strongest exception to Mr Sehume's remarks' and in an accompanying page-long article reported the views of a range of black sports and civic leaders. Norman Middleton, President of the South African Soccer Federation, spoke for most when he said Sehume was being 'used to exploit his own people' and added: 'Peter Hain would be welcomed to South Africa as a hero because he is a fighter for the blacks.' After a similarly controversial trip in 1975 to New Zealand (where anti-apartheid campaigners had the benefit of briefings on the outraged response to his attacks on me), Sehume was sacked by *The World* and ended up officially on the payroll of the CFS.

Vorster's Information Department devoted considerable resources to improving South Africa's image abroad by attempting to replace the crude introverted image of the country under Verwoerd with a more subtle, outward-looking image under Vorster. The substance of apartheid remained the same but it came in glossier wrapping. For example, under a headline, 'Apartheid becomes "plural democracy" but stays the same', *The Times* reported:

A new term to describe South Africa's segregationist policies was suggested today. It is 'plural democracy' and it is intended to replace 'apartheid', 'separate development' and 'separate freedoms'. The change in terminology was proposed by Dr Connie Mulder, the Minister of Information. He said that both 'apartheid' and 'separate development' had negative connotations abroad. The former was interpreted as 'apart hate', while critics of 'separate development' laid stress on the word 'separate'. 'Plural democracy' on the other hand was an acknowledged international term.

A central feature of this new approach was to avoid unnecessary embarrassment. Thus, visiting black dignitaries were granted 'honorary white' status, international black sports stars such as the tennis player Arthur Ashe were allowed to compete in carefully orchestrated gala events, and some of the more absurd so-called 'petty' apartheid practices were discreetly suspended. But this had an element of farce. Under a headline 'Now blacks can ride donkeys too' the London *Evening Standard* reported:

Black children will be able to ride donkeys at Johannesburg Zoo for the first time ... Mr Monty Sklaar, chairman of the city's health and amenities committee, said four donkeys would be made available for black children ... White chil-

dren can ride donkeys, ponies and elephants at the zoo, but
Mr Sklaar said it had been decided to make only donkeys
available for the black children as they were easiest to train.

However, to court world opinion and achieve even such
cosmetic relaxations without destabilising the basic structure
of white supremacy, internal dissent had to be contained and
clamped down on even more vigorously. The forces of resistance had to be smashed to ensure that even the minimal
changes implemented did not escalate uncontrollably. The
security services, even by the grim 1960s standards, resembled more and more the Gestapo, both in the terror they
induced and the arrogance with which they manipulated
political affairs. BOSS really was boss in South Africa
through the early to late 1970s.

But meanwhile the newly independent African States had
become more influential in world forums such as the United
Nations. They deprived SA Airways of landing rights and
some closed their markets to South African exports. Their
votes had led to South Africa's removal from the Commonwealth and from some United Nations agencies and their
outspoken antagonism to apartheid nourished the spirit of
resistance among black South Africans. In response, Vorster
launched a 'peace offensive', offering technical and financial
aid to black states whose governments were willing to talk.
Malawi had been an early target and when in 1967 South
Africa agreed to pay for the construction of a new capital city
at Lilongwe, President Banda agreed to appoint an ambassador to Pretoria. In 1971 Banda paid a State visit and insisted
on appointing a black ambassador to live in a white suburb
and be allowed to enter whatever hotels or restaurants he
pleased, even when these were reserved for whites.

Such peripheral concessions provoked a battle within the
National Party between the 'Verkramptes' (narrow ones) and
Vorster's 'Verligtes' (enlightened ones). These terms were relative ones, however, since there was no disagreement between
them on the objective of maintaining white supremacy: they
differed only on the tactics. For example Vorster implemented
the keystone of Verwoerd's fundamentalism: the setting up of
the 'homelands' (Bantustans). In 1972 Bophuthatswana (com-
prising 19 fragments some hundreds of miles apart) and Ciskei
were established; in 1973 Gazankulu and Venda; in 1974
Qwaqwa and Kwazulu (made up of 29 major and 41 minor
fragments). This involved moving millions of blacks living in
'white' areas to the homeland in which the government

decided they belonged, and finding compliant black leaders to take these homelands down the constitutional path to 'independence'. The Government retained effective control over the Bantustan legislatures through its appointees who outnumbered the elected members.

The term 'Bantu' designated for them was hated by Africans for the pejorative apartheid terminology it reflected. Official guidelines stated: 'It is accepted government policy that the Bantu are only temporarily resident in the European areas of the Republic for as long as they offer their labour there. As soon as they become, for one reason or another no longer fit to work or superfluous in the labour market, they are expected to return to their country of origin, or the territory of the National unit where they fit ethnically ... No stone is to be left unturned to achieve the settlement in the homelands of non-productive Bantu at present residing in European areas.' The guidelines were Nazi-like in their clarity about the categories of people to be resettled: '(i) The aged, the unfit, widows, women with dependent children and families who do not qualify for accommodation in European urban areas; (ii) Bantu on European farms who become superfluous as a result of age (or) disability ... or Bantu squatters from mission stations and black spots which are being cleared up; (iii) doctors, attorneys, agents, traders, industrialist, etc. (who) are not regarded as essential for the European labour market.' The Government knew that it was sending displaced blacks to bleak land that could not accommodate even another cow or sheep but it continued to insist that all removals were 'voluntary' (some 3.5 million were forcibly moved between 1960 and 1983). The homelands – designated for 70 per cent of the population but occupying just 12 per cent of the land – were designed to be economic and political puppets of the white hinterland. 'Well-disposed little black neighbouring states', said Prime Minister Verwoerd in 1962. 'A chain of labour reservoirs where people are held in a state of compulsory unemployment until the white economy wants them', said the liberal *Rand Daily Mail* in August 1973.

But such separatist policies had an unexpected consequence: excluding blacks from the 'white' universities and sending them to black universities (known as tribal colleges) created the Black Consciousness Movement. The leading protagonist of the movement was Steve Biko, a student at Natal University's non-white medical school, whose home was in King William's Town. With its rejection of the compromises of previous generations, Black Consciousness spread from the tribal colleges to the schools. In January 1975, nine Black

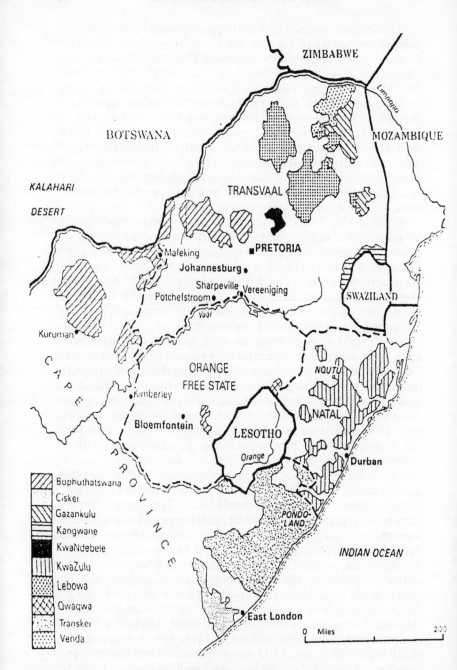

MAP 2 THE BANTUSTANS

Consciousness supporters were tried under the Terrorism Act, not for any act of terror, but merely for publishing the Black Consciousness philosophy – they were found guilty.

Although the League of Nations Mandate under which South Africa administered South West Africa (Namibia) was terminated by the United Nations in 1966, Pretoria remained in illegal control and extended its security laws into the country. This was the beginning of South Africa's strategy of creating a series of client buffer states around its borders at a time when whites had become increasingly perturbed at their isolation and vulnerability to action from the emerging Black Africa to the North.

Until 1975 South Africa had enjoyed the protection of friendly buffer states: on her eastern border, the Portuguese colony of Mozambique, to the north the white settler-ruled Rhodesia (Zimbabwe) and to the north of Namibia (now for all practical purposes an integral part of South Africa) the Portuguese overseas territory of Angola. Then in 1975, following the overthrow of the Portuguese dictatorship, these territories abruptly achieved independence and the ANC was able to establish a presence in both. Angola's independence also provided the Namibian independence movement SWAPO (South West African Peoples Organisation) with the opportunity to make use of a friendly base on Namibia's border. Mozambique's independence did the same for the two Zimbabwe independence movements in their struggle against the racist settler regime – Robert Mugabe's Zimbabwe African National Union and Joshua Nkomo's Zimbabwe African Peoples Union.

South Africa immediately began a destabilisation offensive against these 'frontline' African states. In response to Mozambique's support for the Zimbabwe freedom fighters, the Rhodesian regime created an anti-FRELIMO terrorist organisation, Renamo or MNR (Mozambiquean National Resistance) within Mozambique. When Zimbabwe gained independence in 1980, South Africa adopted Renamo, training and supplying it in order to destabilise the Mozambique Government to terrible effect. With South African support Renamo effectively devastated the transport and infrastructure systems and disrupted the social structure of the country. It terrorised and killed indiscriminately with a force composed largely of kidnapped people. Between 1977 and 1992 an estimated one million died and one third of the total population of 15 million became refugees. Botswana, Lesotho and Swaziland, though black states hostile to apartheid, were powerless to resist South Africa's insistence that they must not allow their countries to be used for ANC guerrilla activities.

Relations were meanwhile fostered with black Africa as part of what was termed a programme of 'detente', culminating in Vorster's historic meeting with the fiercely anti-apartheid President of Zambia, Kenneth Kaunda, in a railway carriage at Victoria Falls in August 1975. Though detente was presented as a reconciliation between white and black in Africa, it was nothing of the kind. Its real purpose was to create a climate of truce in which white South Africa could extend its economic tentacles throughout Africa, so tying African states into a pattern of trading links which would force them to be neutral in the liberation struggle. Detente was pursued assiduously from the early 1970s and looked like being successful until it cracked apart with the invasion of Angola.

In September 1975 a South African force of armoured cars, infantry and artillery crossed from Namibia into Angola and struck 500 miles into the country. The force was acting on a request by the US to support the right wing UNITA in Angola against the leftist MPLA (which enjoyed by far the stronger popular support and had taken over government from the Portuguese). Started on the direct authority of the Minister of Defence P.W. Botha and Magnus Malan, the Defence Force Chief, foreign press reports of the invasion were nevertheless denied. And, although the South Africans had to withdraw, it had been a spectacular performance and had had the same effect upon the minds of Pretoria's Defence Force Chiefs as the Six Day War on Israel. It brought home the fact of South Africa's immense military superiority in the region and how this could be used politically. Botha's Department of Military Intelligence began developing the concept of South Africa asserting itself as a regional superpower, based largely on the example of Israel. Vorster even visited Israel in April 1976 and was warmly greeted by its Prime Minister who seemed indifferent to the irony of a Jew embracing this former Nazi supporter.

However, the compulsory call-up and the pressure to perform active military duties along the country's borders led to growing alienation. An increasing number of young whites, including young Afrikaners, began doubting whether apartheid was worth fighting and, maybe, dying for. A straw in the wind was the public 'defection' in 1976 of Bill Anderson, a young white South African conscript who had fought for the South African army in Namibia. He gave first-hand accounts to the media of torture by South Africa's counter-insurgency forces in Namibia and described atrocities in Angola. Then, in January 1977, he announced that he had joined a white underground group called *Okhela* – the Zulu word for 'spark' – which had been formed in 1972. It aimed to mobilise dissident whites on an undercover basis and, in its commitment to raising 'white consciousness', saw its role in parallel with the growing Black Consciousness movement inside South Africa.

In 1977, I received a covert approach through Basil Manning (then Executive Secretary of the Anti-Apartheid Movement) to meet two members of *Okhela*. At their insistence, we talked in my car in London so as to avoid any surveillance. The two *Okhela* cadres, young Afrikaners, described the group's aims and appealed to me to join them. I said that I would be happy to support them, but that I saw my most effective contribution to the struggle as an anti-apartheid activist in Britain. However, they persisted and, in what I felt was an attempt to make me feel guilty at not being willing to lay myself on the line in the guerrilla struggle, tried to press me to travel to one of the frontline states and be infiltrated into South Africa. I expressed my lack of enthusiasm and was privately unimpressed at what seemed a particularly foolhardy escapade. There was also something about their demeanour which did not ring true. However I said I would think about it, and that they should contact me in a few weeks' time. Although I never heard from them again, after the exposure of the 'masterspy' Craig Williamson as a captain in the South African security services who had operated in London anti-apartheid circles, the two men were also revealed as double agents who had infiltrated *Okhela*.

Meanwhile, sport continued to trailblaze wider social forces. Commenting on the stopping of the cricket tour, a black newspaper, the Johannesburg *Post* (itself constrained by censorship) argued on 24 May 1970 that a sports boycott 'hits South Africa where it hurts most – in the sports breadbasket, and we all know that you don't muck about with South African sports and sportsmen, particularly if South Africa happens to be good at it'. Faced with isolation after 1970, sports-starved whites looked to their Government for an initiative.

It was not long in coming. On 22 April 1971 the Prime Minister, John Vorster, unveiled his new 'multi-national' sports policy. It allowed the different racial groups in South Africa – whites, Africans, Coloureds and Asians – to compete against each other as four separate 'nations' within the country, but only in major international events with foreign participation. The significance of this was that it confirmed the essential case for the boycott: that change would only be forced under the pressure of isolation. However the concession merely expressed the logic of apartheid: that each racial group should develop separately in their own 'nations' – provided of course that whites remained in overall control and kept the spoils for themselves. White teams would continue to represent the country abroad. Crucially, Vorster added: 'I want to make it very clear that in South Africa no mixed sport shall be practised at club, provincial, or national levels.'

Thus, in the 'South African Games', held in Pretoria two years later amid a fanfare of publicity aimed at world opinion, blacks competed against whites for the first time. Photographs of such 'history in the making' were whisked around the world by Government propagandists and their sports allies as if to herald a new dawn. Even in rugby, an image of change was contrived. In mid-1974, when the British Lions toured, almost all their matches were played as usual against white teams (including of course the all-important Tests). But two were played against a 'Bantu XV' (Africans) and a 'Coloured XV'. The reality behind the facade was revealed by official figures from the Minister of Sport. These showed that black participation was minimal. In 1975, a total of 6917 South African sportsmen participated in multi-national events. Of these 6393 (92.4 per cent) were whites, 331 (4.8 per cent) Africans, 135 (2 per cent) Coloureds and 58 (0.8 per cent) Asians. Out of the 39 sports in which multi-nationals were staged inside South Africa, just three (wrestling, golf and tennis) involved people from each of the four racial groups.

In mid-1975, the *South African Swimmer*, newspaper of the non-racial South African Amateur Swimming Federation, expressed black opinion succinctly. 'The purpose of multi-national sports meetings is stark and clear for it is intended to persuade the unsuspecting outside this country into believing that apartheid does not affect sport. How untrue! We would rather deny ourselves the doubtful "distinction" of participating in the multi-nationals and being considered honorary whites for a few days or a week, so long as we suffer, for the rest of the year, the indignity of being contained, confined, controlled and contaminated by the shackles of group areas, separate development, an official state sports policy and the full gambit of racial legislation under which we have suffered since 1652.'

For expressing such views, the SAASF felt the iron fist inside the velvet glove of the new sports policy. Because he refused to collaborate with the policy, Morgan Naidoo, SAASF's President, was served with a five-year banning order which stopped him undertaking a public role such as being a member of any sports body and even prevented him from taking children for swimming lessons. Other non-racial sports officials and sportsmen faced both intimidation by the security services and actual prosecution. Passports were denied to leading black officials, such as Hassan Howa and M.N. Pather, President and Secretary of the South African Council of Sport, preventing them from presenting their case abroad.

Although under apartheid there was no law *specifically* prohibiting mixed sport, a string of apartheid laws and regulations continued to make *multi-racial* (as opposed to *multinational*) sport illegal, just as they restricted any other aspect of life in South Africa. For example, the Urban Areas Act 1945 controlled black sports facilities and restricted their use by permit. The 1950 Group Areas Act segregated the population – sportsmen and women included. In October 1973 the Sports Minister issued Proclamation R228 under the 1950 Act which enabled multi-racial matches to be banned on private grounds as well. The Proclamation was brought in specifically to prevent the Aurora Cricket Club, in Pietermaritzburg, Natal, from playing multi-racial games. The club had been formed early in 1973 by a group of black and white cricketers, breaking new ground in the process. In the event no prosecution was launched using the new regulation, prudence presumably dictating that the government refrain from using its new power – although members of the Security Service at one stage took names of players and spectators and prepared a report for the Attorney-General. Other laws such as the Reservation of Separate Amenities Act 1953 and the 1928 Liquor Act prevented the integration of ground and club facilities for refreshments, seating, toilets and dancing. Black sportsmen and women were also governed by Pass Laws which restricted their movements as citizens and prevented them travelling freely to 'away' matches, or on tours.

Although many of these laws could be and were increasingly circumvented by obtaining permits from the relevant government department, discretionary power over the issue of permits enabled control to be exercised by the authorities. Thus, matches between 'stooge' black groups and whites were automatically cleared for permits, or alternatively granted special 'international licences' on the basis that different 'nations' were competing. Moreover, while the Government was increasingly prepared to turn a blind eye to the flouting of the law by sports groups – especially when foreign teams were involved – a full range of racialist legislation and regulations remained in force and could be applied at any time deemed appropriate. The result was regular incidents such as the one in February 1978 when a multi-racial soccer match in Pretoria was forcibly broken up by police and the participants threatened with prosecution under both the Group Areas Act and municipal by-laws.

In August 1979, the Wanderers Club in Johannesburg was restricted to admitting blacks as 'honorary members' because full membership would have contravened the law in respect of club facilities. In May 1979, Cape Town's international rugby stadium, Newlands, also announced that the law prevented it from integrating facilities, while in March 1980 black spectators and athletes were barred from the opening of a new running track in Oudtshoorn in the Cape Province because it had no provision for separate toilets.

Inside South Africa from the early 1970s sport became the territory in which the ideological battle over apartheid was fought. The ANC encouraged the barriers of sports discrimination to be increasingly challenged. A whole layer of predominantly black sport consolidated under the auspices of the South African Council of Sport (SACOS), formed in 1973. Though still not recognised by the outside world (or rather the Western nations who dominated most world sports federations), it refused to compromise until all vestiges of racialism were removed from the sports system and this was the policy for which the Anti-Apartheid Movement continued to campaign internationally.

By South African standards, the changes introduced *were* significant – in many respects unthinkable prior to 1970. But by world standards they were entirely superficial. The sports system was given a facelift, with racial restrictions being relaxed in certain limited senses and usually during prestige events likely to attract international attention. At club level, however, where fundamental change needed to occur to have any meaning for most sportsmen and women, restrictions were hardly eased at all. The official attitude was that whereas the national level could be controlled and contained, matters could get out of hand in a way that could so easily spill over into the whole of society if integration seriously started to occur locally. As a Government MP said in South Africa's House of Assembly as late as 21 May 1979: 'Integrated clubs and integrated sport constitute far less than 1 per cent of the total sport activities in South Africa.'

International opinion was not fooled and the 'multi-national' policy did not bring the rewards the Government wished. South Africa's remorseless drift into isolation continued, as SAN-ROC lobbied international sports officials tirelessly and anti-apartheid campaigners maintained the pressure from Britain to New Zealand. Hockey, squash, snooker and netball joined the lengthening queue of sports from which South Africa was excluded.

The 1970s proved conclusively that only an uncompromising boycott strategy by opponents of sports apartheid produced results. As was eventually conceded in 1979 by the heart transplant surgeon, Professor Christian Barnard, and by white South Africa's rugby supremo, Danie Craven, isolation *did* work: the protest campaigns more than anything else forced changes. (Both men had previously been fierce critics of such campaigns.) The former England cricket captain, Mike Brearley, put it succinctly when he argued in 1979: 'Any achievements in multi-racial sport over there have been obtained through South Africa being isolated.'

Under continuing pressure on sport, the Government shifted again. This took two main forms. First, attempts were made to move beyond the failing 'multi-national' sports policy to one of what may be called 'co-option'. Second, intriguing overtures were made to leaders of the international campaign against sports apartheid.

Apart from the layer of *non-racial* sports bodies grouped under SACOS, there were also racially constituted black bodies: that is to say, each main sport might typically have an African body, an Asian one and perhaps a Coloured one, in addition to both white and non-racial (but usually exclusively non-white) bodies. Being unable to persuade the non-racial bodies to cooperate, some white sports organisations began working with the separate black groups – which, after all, reflected the grand design of apartheid and its modern sports variant 'multi-nationalism'.

The harassment and intimidation meted out against genuinely non-racial sport contrasted markedly with the rewards given to those few blacks who did allow themselves to be accommodated by the white bodies. Besides being given opportunities to tour abroad always denied to their fellow blacks, these 'collaborators' were often given secure jobs as individuals, and offered financial inducements to improve their club and organisational facilities. Such inducements were naturally attractive, given the abysmal level of facilities available to blacks and given the fact that the Government was spending five times as much money on white sport as it did on black sport – a disparity compounded by the fact that blacks outnumbered whites by four to one.

Even whites who joined the non-racial bodies did not escape attention. Thus, the former white Springbok triallist, 'Cheeky' Watson, who in 1977 resigned from the white South African Rugby Board (SARB) and joined the non-racial SARU, was arrested several times, solely for the 'crime' of entering the black township of New Brighton outside Port Elizabeth in order to play for his new non-racial team in the local Kwaru league. (Whites needed permits to enter black areas and he was refused one.) He was severely reprimanded by white rugby officials such as Danie Craven when he 'defected' and was subjected to harassment by the security services. The family business was targeted and their home mysteriously burnt down. When Cheeky Watson was joined by his fellow rugby-playing brothers, Gavin, Ronnie and Valence, they faced trumped-up charges. He was also jailed for six months during a state of emergency. Their non-racial matches were monitored by the Security Police and even by military intelligence officers. Significantly, the brothers were entirely scornful of the suggestion that multi-racial rugby was on its way in under SARB's direction: the changes were 'just a lot of window dressing', Cheeky Watson said in 1979.

In parallel with the new co-option strategy I was placed in the novel position of being courted by my opponents. Having anticipated that this might happen, I had developed a response to the 'multi-national' and 'co-option' strategies which focused single-mindedly upon sport. We had won the original argument for a boycott on the basis that South African sport was organised on race, not on merit. To middle-opinion it could be presented as an argument about *sport* – which legitimised political intervention in an area which would otherwise have been seen as taboo. If, through relaxation of sports segregation, it could be shown progress was being made, I did not want us to be forced back upon the argument that we would not budge until the whole structure of apartheid was abolished, because that would have placed anti-apartheid forces in the position of having to justify singling out South Africa as against other countries with tyrannical regimes. So, early in 1977 the focus moved on to a series of changes in the law which might 'exempt' sport from apartheid. However fanciful it might be to imagine this actually occurring, it was such demands that would place white South Africans once more on the defensive. I was determined to press on with this strategy, even though it was controversial in some anti-apartheid circles. I also held discussions with the Labour Minister of Sport, Denis Howell, and on 8 February 1977 drafted some notes for his department.

South Africa's 'Mr Rugby', Danie Craven, had been an arch-enemy during the Stop The Seventy Tour campaign. However one spring day in 1977 my phone at home rang. 'Craven, South Africa', the voice said to my surprise, 'I would like to talk. Will you meet me?' Wary that this might be some kind of publicity stunt in which I could be presented as compromising, I pressed him further. What was the purpose? Would it be strictly private? Having partly satisfied myself on these points, I agreed. But not on the basis of his suggestion of a venue near the South African Embassy – only if he came to our flat in Putney where Pat and I had set up home after our marriage in 1975. So it was that, in the evening a few days later, he arrived in a taxi, somewhat apprehensively knocking at our front door.

I began by suggesting that we left politics to one side and talked about sports changes alone. Surely Craven would agree with me that the aim would be to make sport truly non-racial – that is, free of all apartheid restrictions – even if these remained in other spheres of life? It turned the tables neatly on his simmering condemnation of my position as being 'anti-rugby'. He agreed with me and said that he wanted to move faster but the Government was blocking the way.

So I put forward specific reforms confined to *sport alone*. These included: fully integrated club and school sport; a multi-million programme immediately to improve black sports facilities and opportunities; changes in laws – such as the Group Areas Act and suspension of the old Pass Laws for sportsmen – so as to strip apartheid out of sport completely. In return the boycotts could be lifted and Craven could get his beloved Springboks on the world stage again. I also told him he should talk to the ANC and black sports groups inside the country, for their consent and participation was crucial, not mine. Craven took my list away with him. We had got on very well. He warmed to our nine-month-old son, Sam, and even presented me with a Springbok tie which I placed surreptitiously at the bottom of a drawer: the meeting and the gift remained a secret.

Within a couple of months, on 9 August 1977, the former

South African Test cricket captain, Ali Bacher, also beat a path to my door, this time meeting me at my office. Acting as an emissary for the South African Cricket Association, he aggressively sought to persuade me that things were changing for the better and we should call off the boycott. I did not agree, and our exchanges were somewhat acrimonious compared with the down-to-earth honesty and warmth of Dr Craven. It confirmed my view that Afrikaners rather than English-speaking whites would ultimately be the more honest brokers when a settlement with the black majority finally occurred.

Meanwhile, the editor of the liberal *Daily Dispatch*, Donald Woods, had appeared in London acting as a go-between for further discussion. Despite his anti-apartheid inclinations and his growing reputation as an opponent of the system, Donald had been extremely hostile to the STST campaign in 1969–70. I remembered him being used in television interviews (as was another liberal South African, Helen Suzman) to criticise our campaign and especially its direct action strategy; like most white South Africans, he could not stomach attacks on their sport. However he had become progressively radicalised, especially through his friendship with the Black Consciousness activist Steve Biko. He also became involved in non-racial sports bodies, especially the SACOS-affiliated South African Cricket Board of Control and in 1976 helped form a non-racial cricket club called Rainbow which he privately persuaded Dr Piet Koornhof, the Sports Minister, to sanction. In his position as an editor, Donald Woods had extensive contacts with Cabinet Ministers and he had been asked by Koornhof to find out as discreetly as possible whether I, together with the SAN-ROC leaders Chris de Broglio and Dennis Brutus, might be prepared to negotiate an end to the sports boycott in return for the dismantling of apartheid in sport. Koornhof was taking a considerable risk: if news of the initiative leaked, it could be used against him by his more conservative opponents in the National Party who would be horrified at the thought of talking to the likes of me.

We were initially suspicious. Why was Donald carrying messages from the Government we were seeking to destroy? But he assured us there was nothing to lose by testing Koornhof's sincerity and his ability to deliver. In return we insisted that, while we might present a set of proposals, this depended upon Koornhof negotiating internally with SACOS. An agreement could not be made unilaterally by international anti-apartheid leaders and indeed we had no authority from our movements for doing so. At the same time I was clear that we had to keep up the momentum – to push out a boat of proposals and see where it sailed. My whole strategy was to force the Government back to negotiate with the people it was oppressing.

So on 22 June 1977 I drew up a confidential memorandum agreed with Chris and Dennis for a 'Proposed South African Sports summit'. As conditions for our attendance at such a Summit, we insisted that: passport restrictions, bannings and harassment of non-racial sports officials must end; the Government should declare an official moratorium on all sports tours for two years while the sports system was reorganised; a non-racial sports policy must be implemented including the full integration of club and school sport; repealing of all racist legislation in so far as it affected sport; merging separate sports groups into single democratic organisations; and non-racial overseas touring sides. If these conditions were agreed in advance and in full, our statement concluded, 'We would be prepared to accept an invitation from SACOS to attend a formal meeting. If implemented we would be prepared publicly to recommend dropping the boycotts and demonstrations, to take effect at the end of the moratorium period, subject to satisfactory progress having been made in establishing a non-racial sports structure.'

Donald Woods later wrote: 'When I handed Dr Koornhof the letter from Hain and the others he pondered it at length before looking up to say: "We can meet these conditions. We can do a deal. There are certain aspects of it that will be very difficult, but I am sure we can do it."' Arrangements were discussed for me to meet Koornhof for secret negotiations in Switzerland in August 1977. But before flying back to discuss this with me, Woods was phoned by Koornhof and asked to meet the head of BOSS, General H.J. van den Bergh, who warned that Koornhof was going too far too fast, and that *he* would like to meet me in Paris instead. But Woods was by now being drawn increasingly into more radical politics. He was subsequently banned and had to flee the country after the death of his friend Steve Biko. He decided against putting this proposition to me and I only learnt about it some years later.*

However, I was quite content with the outcome. Though

---

* For his account of this episode, see Donald Woods, *Asking for Trouble* (London, Victor Gollanz, 1980). The copy he gave me is inscribed: 'To Peter whom I met on the road to Damascus.'

intrigued by Koornhof's overtures I hadn't expected anything to come of them. On the one hand I was determined to formulate a reasoned response which could be publicly defended and which put whites, desperate to regain world participation, under pressure. On the other hand, I was equally determined not to compromise our position, especially since a major advance had only just been secured at the summit meeting of Commonwealth countries' leaders in Scotland's Gleneagles Hotel. On 15 June 1977 they unanimously adopted the 'Gleneagles Agreement' under which each government pledged to take every practical step to discourage sports links with South Africa. Prior to this, there had been no concerted drive at government level to impose sports isolation; now we had the authority of a Commonwealth agreement and the backing of its member governments to press recalcitrant sports organisations to do so.

In any event, as Chapter 7 shows, political events were moving fast inside South Africa as the black majority emerged from the bleak period of the 1960s and early 1970s in angry resistance. The role of international campaigners changed into supporting that internal fight as the torch of resistance to apartheid passed back to those inside the country. Meanwhile, as the next chapter reveals, the apartheid state maintained, and in some ways increased, its sinister attacks on its international opponents.

6 TRIAL

Enforcing apartheid required not only a range of oppressive methods domestically: intimidation, abandonment of the rule of law, torture, outright terror including assassination – all these were commonplace inside South Africa. But the tentacles of the police state also spread abroad, often assisted by Western intelligence services in ways which infected and compromised the democratic politics of these countries.

From the late 1960s onward, South African agents were responsible for a series of attacks on anti-apartheid organisations across the world. There was harassment and surveillance of activists, and burglaries at the London headquarters of the Anti-Apartheid Movement and the African National Congress. Amongst others, ANC offices in New York, Stockholm, Brussels and Bonn were targeted. One of the worst attacks took place in March 1982 when the ANC's London office was bombed, its officials narrowly escaping injury or death: responsibility for this was eventually admitted in 1995 by Craig Williamson, a Captain in the South African intelligence service.

In one case at least, BOSS was responsible for a murder in London. In January 1970, the British-based South African journalist Keith Wallace was killed at his Kensington flat. He had worked for BOSS for some years, but shortly before his death had threatened to expose BOSS operations in the United Kingdom. There were many other assassinations. In July 1981 Joe Gqabi, the ANC's chief representative to Zimbabwe, was killed outside his Salisbury home. In March 1988, as Dulcie September, the ANC's Paris representative, opened her office near the city's Gare du Nord station, she was shot dead by a professional hitman. Dulcie September was the sixth ANC figure to have been murdered outside South Africa in the first few months of that year. According to *Le Monde* newspaper, the presence of the South African secret agents responsible was known in advance by the French intelligence services. Less than a week later another leading ANC member, Albie Sachs, was fighting for his life after sustaining horrific injuries after a car bomb exploded in his car in Maputo, Mozambique.

In the early 1980s two senior members of the ANC's London mission were coerced and compromised into providing South African military intelligence with information. Official South African involvement was transparent in 1984 when its London Embassy helped four men jump bail and flee to South America. They represented the state arms company, Armscor, and had been charged with acting illegally and breaking the arms embargo. Another conspiracy in Britain, involving plans to kidnap and murder senior ANC officials, was exposed in London in 1987.

When controversy erupted over BOSS's London activities in December 1971, the Labour MP, James Wellbeloved – who was known to have good connections with MI6 – told Parliament: 'There is a spy ring that flows from the South African Embassy in London, who have had British citizens acting as controllers, established a network of informers and infiltrated organisations in this country hostile to the regime in South Africa.'

On Friday 24 October 1975 I had finished drafting a chapter for my doctoral thesis at Sussex University and made a quick trip from our home to the stationers W.H. Smith in Putney to buy new typewriter ribbons.

Later over lunch my wife Pat got up to answer a ring at the door and returned to announce that there were some policemen who wished to see me.

One of the officers asked if that was my car outside, as he pointed to our blue Volkswagen Beetle. I told him it was. Had I been out in my car recently? Yes, I said, to buy typewriter ribbons. Well, they would just like me to go with them down to the police station. I assumed it wouldn't take long and there was no reason for me to be uncooperative.

Pat, who had begun to look rather uneasy, said she would like to go with me, but this seemed unnecessary and the officer confirmed my feelings. It shouldn't take longer than 20 minutes, he told us categorically.

Only when he refused to let me finish eating my lunch, and followed close on my heels as I went to collect my jacket and glasses, had I begun to feel that there was something more serious to all this. Exactly what was it all about? I asked. Couldn't it be discussed here? No, I would only find out when I got to the station.

The atmosphere had grown somewhat tense. The police were crowding into our doorway. Was I being arrested? I asked. If so, what was the charge? I would only go if I was given a proper explanation. In that case he would have to arrest me, he said. My change of manner had obviously put him out. He turned to have a quick discussion with his colleagues – then someone called out from the back to say it was about a 'snatch at Barclays'.

Snatch at Barclays? What on earth could this have to do with me? Pat, at my side, giggled nervously. You must be joking, she told them. My mind had become a jumbled mixture of thoughts: policemen, bank snatch, me. Events had ceased to make sense.

There was obviously a mistake somewhere, but it could not be anything that would take long to sort out. So I followed them down the path and was startled to see that there, parked in the road, were several squad cars and a 'black Maria' together with a further dozen policemen and policewomen.

One of the officers insisted on driving my car down to Wandsworth police station and I was ushered into the back seat of the nearest police vehicle. As we pulled away the officer sitting beside me reached for a microphone and spoke into it: 'The suspect has been arrested. Everything's under control.' In my growing confusion I turned to him. Had I been arrested, then, without knowing it? No, not really, he replied. It was just normal procedure. All would be explained when we got to the station. There was nothing else he could tell me.

Being charged with a crime you have not committed is bad enough for any citizen. Being charged with a bank snatch a few hundred yards from my home in the most bizarre circumstances plunged me into a surreal world that would have done Franz Kafka's *The Trial* proud. Except that it was most certainly for real and did not happen by accident.

Almost exactly as I was getting into my car to drive down to buy the typewriter ribbons, and quite unbeknown to me, a man roughly my age and roughly my appearance snatched a bundle of five pound notes totalling £490 from a cashier in the Upper Richmond Road, Putney, branch of Barclays Bank – a bank which had been a target for anti-apartheid protests. He ran down the High Street, pursued by several staff who were joined by four boys from Putney's Elliott School. He then ran up a side street, turned round, said 'All right, here you are then', tossed the money back, and disappeared.

Minutes later I drove down the very same street toward the High Street and pulled up outside W.H. Smith. As I got out of the car, still totally unaware of what had gone on, two of the schoolboys – who were 12 years old – noticed me and thought I resembled the thief they had just been chasing. They followed me into the shop where they observed me, decided I was their man, took my car registration number and walked to the nearby Putney police station to report it.

After 11 hours in detention – and on the basis only of statements by two of the four boys – I was eventually charged with snatching the money. I protested my innocence when questioned. I didn't even know which branch of Barclays (there were then two in Putney) had been the scene of the crime. The fingerprints on the money did not match mine and there was no other evidence upon which to charge me. Nevertheless, the police proceeded and I found myself hearing and seeing 'HAIN IN BANK THEFT' headlines.

Helpless as the legal process ground its way remorselessly on, I found myself propelled toward another appearance at the Old Bailey.* The bizarre, not to say quite unreal, sequence of events took another twist on the Monday when I was due to appear on an identification parade. There was huge publicity, with my photograph on the front page of the London *Evening Standard* above a caption: 'Peter Hain, due to appear on an identification parade today.' Bank staff later confirmed in court that copies of the newspaper had been in their office and that they had read it before attending the parade. Perhaps this was why the cashier from whom the money had been snatched came down the line and straight back to me, placing her hand on my shoulder. Although none of the other bank witnesses did so, the police now had a 'positive identification' to corroborate that of the two 12-year-olds who had reported my car number.

Later that evening, however, came about the only break I

---

* For a full account see my *A Putney Plot!*

got in six miserable months during which the case consumed my life. Terry MacLaren, the older of the schoolboys who, it turned out, had refused to go along with his friends, was watching the news on television and saw me pictured outside the police station after the parade. 'That's not the man. They've got the wrong one', he told his Dad. Many if not most other fathers would have told their young sons to shut up and mind their own business and few boys would have been as strong willed as 14-year-old Terry. But his father contacted my solicitor the next day.

Quite spontaneously, journalists, political acquaintances and others began discussing whether I had been set up by the South Africans. This was common currency among almost everybody intrigued by the case, especially as it became clear that I was asserting my innocence as a victim of mistaken identity in the strongest possible terms. But although a South African connection seemed all too plausible, direct evidence was absent. For all we knew I was simply a victim of the vagaries of identification evidence (which at the time was being exposed almost monthly for its notorious unreliability) and police malice: during my detention, one of the investigating detectives told me: 'You have caused a lot of trouble with your protests and we are going to make this charge stick on you.'

Then, some two months before the trial was due to start, a South African dimension suddenly emerged. Out of the blue, on 3 February 1976, Mom received a phone call from a Mr Kenneth Wyatt who said he wanted to talk about 'your son's bank theft case'. (My own phone was ex-directory.) I rang him back at a number in St Albans and he said he had some information for me which he did not want to give over the phone. Wary that it might be yet another crank call, I pressed him. He appeared calm and offered to come to my parents' home; an appointment was made for the following day at 10.30 a.m. He arrived on time, a large, bespectacled, shambling figure. Quiet and almost diffident, he seemed concerned that his car might have been followed.

I had never met or heard of Wyatt before and therefore had no basis upon which to judge his honesty. He talked in a disjointed fashion, but his manner was open and reasonable and gave no grounds for supposing either that he was unbalanced or devious. He began by saying that he might not be believed because he had been in the pornography business and had been convicted and served two years for distributing pornographic material. He then said he had been approached by a group headed by a Mr Fred Kamil, formerly a security officer with the South African-based conglomerate, Anglo-American – a corporation which specialised in diamond mining, among other things – and told to contact me. He was instructed to inform me that the Putney bank theft had been carried out by a South African agent specially flown over to Britain for the job.

Wyatt's account, delivered quite flatly, seemed incredible, not to say implausible. When pressed, he was unable to offer any direct evidence. He was simply a courier, he said. However he did explain that information about my case, together with evidence of a plot against the Liberal Party, had come into the hands of the Kamil group. Apparently, Anglo-American's extensive security service worked closely with BOSS. Thus Kamil's own remaining intelligence contacts in the company had access to BOSS. According to Wyatt, one of these contacts inside South Africa had accidentally come across a confidential dossier in BOSS headquarters containing a plan to discredit leaders of the Liberal Party. The plan included the names of five leading figures. My name was among these. So was that of party leader Jeremy Thorpe. A document in the dossier stated that the operation against me had gone successfully and 'action against Thorpe is going according to plan'.*

The rationale for the anti-Liberal activity was that the South Africans wanted to see a permanent Tory Government in Britain: they believed that discrediting the Liberal Party leadership would ensure a Tory victory at the polls. Wyatt said the theory was that the removal of a serious Liberal presence in marginal seats would ensure that they went Conservative (this was accepted by most political commentators at the time). Wyatt further maintained that one of Kamil's female intelligence contacts at BOSS headquarters had come across a picture of an agent who was my 'double'. Further enquiries established that the agent in question had been out of South Africa for several months

---

* Wyatt's visit took place a week after allegations first broke publicly that Thorpe had a homosexual affair with the male model Norman Scott. Four months later Thorpe resigned and in 1979 was tried and acquitted of conspiracy to murder Scott. His three co-defendants did however admit to a conspiracy.

in 1975: he had left for Britain in August and returned at the end of October (the bank theft took place on 24 October). The agent had since gone to ground but not before boasting to colleagues that he had been given a bonus of £50,000 for a 'very successful project'.

Wyatt left saying he was quite willing to try to get additional evidence and would be in touch again if he obtained something more definite. I later arranged for Wyatt to repeat his story to the BBC journalist Roger Courtiour, who was making a documentary on the case. But I had to be particularly careful not to be accused of desperation in resorting to public allegations about a South African plot for which there was no direct evidence.

However, a fortnight later, on 17 February, events took a new turn when it was reported that some people had been charged with conspiracy to extort £1 million from the directors of Anglo-American, and were due to appear shortly in a London magistrates' court. Wyatt was named as one of them. As details emerged, it became clear that everything Wyatt had told me about Kamil and his group was true. It therefore seemed more possible that the alleged plot to discredit the Liberal Party might be true as well.

It emerged in the press that Fred Kamil was born in the Lebanon and later formed a group of mercenaries who successfully apprehended diamond smugglers operating between Sierra Leone and Liberia. During the 1950s he had worked briefly for British Intelligence. After an approach in the early 1960s by the former head of MI5, Sir Percy Sillitoe, who was by then Anglo-American's security chief, Kamil was eventually recruited to work for Anglo's main diamond subsidiary, De Beers. He built up a formidable reputation for trapping illegal diamond operators inside South Africa and was also known for high living on the commission he had obtained. However he lost his job in 1970 after a dispute over £500,000 which he claimed was owed to him from his commissions. In a desperate attempt to get this money, in May 1972 he hijacked a South African Airways Boeing which he believed was carrying a relative of the Anglo-American head, Sir Harry Oppenheimer. But the hijacking was abortive. When the plane landed in Malawi, he was arrested and imprisoned for 11 years. He only served under a third of this sentence, however, and was released in unusual circumstances with the assistance of the South African authorities, which suggests that

Anglo-American may have recognised some justification for his claim; it was reported that the company paid him £50,000. Still maintaining that he was owed the full £500,000, he went to Spain and hired Wyatt and four others to try to extort the money from Anglo-American officials in London.

Events soon took an even more extraordinary turn. Several weeks earlier Norman Scott had publicly broken allegations of Jeremy Thorpe's homosexual relationship with him. Shortly afterwards I had told Thorpe that the *Daily Mirror* was about to publish a story about South African attempts to discredit him. I was informed by the *Mirror* that the South African journalist, Gordon Winter, had been involved in promoting these same allegations two years before. I told Thorpe of the belief in anti-apartheid circles that Winter was a BOSS agent, and he asked to be kept informed of developments.

I now decided to give the Liberal leader a memorandum describing the Wyatt approach and handed it to him personally on 24 February. He read it and, to my surprise, said that the Prime Minister, Harold Wilson, would be interested, picked up the phone, rang 10 Downing Street and despatched the memo there right away.*

Meanwhile I was contacted by a London-based American academic, Dan Hughes, who offered to introduce me to another mysterious figure who had information on my case. She turned out to be a young British doctor, Diane Lefevre. Although vague about substantiating details of the Wyatt allegation, she was anxious to reinforce its general validity. Occasionally she was remarkably well-informed. For example, among my often bizarre mail, I had received anonymously in an envelope postmarked Johannesburg a photograph dated 1964. It pictured Gordon Winter swimming with Mary, the daughter of the Anglo-American chief, Sir Harry Oppenheimer, in the pool at the Oppenheimer home in Johannesburg. We had not mentioned it to any-

---

*   Within ten days Winter, by now back in South Africa, was handed a copy of my memo in Johannesburg by the head of BOSS. This emerged in 1981: see his *Inside BOSS* p. 464. Winter surmised it reached him via British Intelligence, since the memo was still strictly confidential.

one else, but now Dr Lefevre asked me whether I had received it.*

Diane Lefevre also took a keen interest in an anonymous letter sent to Harold Wilson, copies of which had been sent to me, and to leading Labour and Liberal politicians. It purported to come from Johannesburg, though was postmarked London. The letter alleged that Anglo-American had been dealing in arms for the South African Government and that documents revealing a smear campaign against Labour, trade union and Liberal leaders had been taken from the office of the company's security force. Dr Lefevre seemed particularly anxious to boost the credibility of the letter. When Wyatt and his co-conspirators were eventually tried at the Old Bailey in 1977 they were convicted and Wyatt was imprisoned, evidently much to his surprise: he had told journalists beforehand that he would be 'protected'.

Then on 9 March 1976, Harold Wilson astonished the House of Commons when he answered a 'planted' question from Labour MP James Wellbeloved. 'I have no doubt at all, there is strong South African participation in recent activities relating to the leader of the Liberal Party.' He said there had been 'very strong and heavily financed private master-minding of certain political operations' and added that this South African participation was 'based on massive resources of business money and private agents of various kinds and various qualities'. Later he also referred specifically to 'the Hain case'. This set off the media in pursuit of more details. My memo to Thorpe became public knowledge. Wyatt was widely interviewed and new, even stranger, actors soon appeared on the stage.

However, I remained frustrated at the absence of any evidence capable of being introduced in court. We were also conscious that the individuals like Wyatt and Lefevre could be discredited if called as witnesses. We even had to bear in mind the possibility that their appearance might have been designed to achieve precisely that and thereby weaken what

---

* According to Gordon Winter, the photo was sent by the head of BOSS, H.J. van den Bergh, who was anxious to promote rumours that Anglo-American, not BOSS, was behind the plot against the Liberal Party. Winter stated that Diane Lefevre infiltrated the Kamil group for a section of British Intelligence hostile to South Africa (see *Inside BOSS*, pp. 465–7).

was a strong defence. So I had to remain content at fighting for my innocence within the rules of a conventional criminal trial, while wondering whether I was really the victim of a much larger South African plot.

For two full weeks at the end of March and into April 1976 the Queen v. Peter Hain played to a packed house in the Old Bailey's court number 8. Between 20 and 40 reporters sat in: 'The largest number since Christine Keeler', an usher remarked nostalgically. One eyewitness gave evidence that the thief was 'South African' in appearance. And the prosecution tried half-heartedly to suggest that, since I had been active in the campaign to get Barclays Bank to withdraw from South Africa, I might have staged the theft as a political protest. Otherwise South Africa hardly received a mention in the proceedings.

There were no surprises in the prosecution evidence – except that in court it seemed if anything even flimsier. The unreliability – at times incongruity – of identification evidence featured throughout. As the *Sunday Times* reported:

A confusing picture has emerged of the culprit as a sharp-featured, dark-eyed man, sometimes wearing spectacles, sometimes not, aged between 23 and 30 and anything from 5 feet 10 inches to 6 feet 2 inches in height, of medium build, very skinny, quite slim, with a long face, very drawn and white, of normal complexion but needing a shave, a very 'sallow' complexion with a darkish tinge, foreign looking, possibly Spanish, Egyptian or 'Afrikaans', not foreign, with black curly hair worn collar length, not very long fluffy hair reaching just below the ears, shortish wavy brown hair with ginger tints, wearing light-blue jeans and dark trousers as well as a white check shirt, a blue check shirt, a cream shirt with puffed sleeves, a light shirt with dark stripes, a cream waistcoat made of thick velvet wool, white tennis shoes and brown suede 'Hush Puppies'.

The prosecutor, Michael Corkery, opened on the basis that it had been a 'spur of the moment theft'. He called Mrs Lucy Haines, the cashier who had picked me out on the identification parade. But, far from being damning, she was hesitant, saying she had seen the thief only for a 'split second' and at one point seemingly unable to pick me out in court – even though I was sticking out in the dock like a sore thumb. She also confirmed she had seen me periodically on television well before the theft took place.

Apart from the 12-year-old schoolboys – whose evidence was almost embarrassingly inconsistent – and the cashier, no other witness was able to identify me: not even the bank's accountant, Timothy Hayne, who had led the half-mile chase behind the thief. He told the court that he knew my face well from television and the newspapers and I was not the man. None of the police officers called implicated me. The photofit picture was nothing like me. The fingerprint analyst confirmed that my prints had not been on any of the notes – though there was a fresh 'unknown' print on the top note.

But identification evidence remained the central curse of the trial. Once the finger had been pointed at me, I faced a conviction and had virtually to prove my innocence. However, Terry MacLaren's evidence proved decisive. My solicitor John Dundon described him as 'a witness in a million', remarkably composed, fluent – and totally convincing. He said the other boys had been behind him throughout the chase – sometimes up to 30 yards. Terry added that he had got a clear sight of the thief initially some 30 feet across Putney High Street, and later during the chase as he had turned back to glance several times at his pursuers. He described with astonishing accuracy what had happened when I went in to shop at W.H. Smith, including my having greeted a friend there. He also described in detail the differences between me and the thief.

In summing up for the defence, Lewis Hawser pointed out the string of contradictions in the case against me and how the prosecution had been forced to change their opening allegation of a 'spur of the moment theft' by their own witnesses' evidence that the thief had been spotted beforehand acting suspiciously. Hawser then laid out for the jury 'the whole picture as it must be presented by the prosecution' to sustain a guilty verdict:

Peter Hain leaves his house to buy typewriter ribbons. He must park his car behind Oxford Road somewhere. He walks to the bank – over a quarter of a mile – so that would take five to seven minutes. He cases the joint, spends three to five minutes waiting to snatch the money, snatches it and is involved in a tiring chase.

He dodges down Oxford Road, gets in his car and then drives back along the very road down which he has been chased by a man from the bank and some boys. All this within five minutes. He must have passed in his car the four boys who had chased him. He parks right in front of the boys, gets out, goes into Smith's. He doesn't rush to buy the typewriter ribbons as fast as possible – in any case he could have bought them from Surrey Typewriters in Putney Bridge Road without retracing his route – he reads a magazine. He behaves quite normally and looks relaxed within five minutes of a very tiring chase. He then goes home, lunches, doesn't change his clothes. The police come and he volunteers that he had been to Smith's. Members of the jury, the bare bones of the story just don't hang together. This is a classic case of mistaken identity.

However, in an extraordinary summing up, Judge Alan King-Hamilton, a member of the MCC, suggested without any substantiation that my wife Pat, my mother and a friend staying with her, Vanessa Brown, may have been untruthful alibi witnesses. He also introduced a new hypothesis which he then had to withdraw under joint challenge from defence and prosecution. His open hostility to the defence shocked even the most experienced lawyers and was the talk of the Bar for some time. He must at best have confused the jury and at worst have raised serious doubts in their minds as to my innocence – which is perhaps why they took nearly five long and tense hours eventually to acquit me.

Shortly afterwards, the apartheid connection reappeared in a series of exotic new twists. On 16 March 1976, a fortnight before I first went into the dock, Harold Wilson had unexpectedly announced his intention to resign as Prime Minister. There was much private and semi-public speculation that his previous cryptic references to nefarious activities by South African agents had in some way affected his decision.

A month later, on 15 April, a 20-year-old male prostitute, Andre Thorne, approached the *Guardian* newspaper, a consistent critic of apartheid. He claimed to know of a 'blue' movie in which a well-known Liberal MP dressed as a scout-master had engaged in sexual acts with young boys. When a *Guardian* journalist investigated, the trail led back to the South African Embassy, one of whose attaches offered to buy the film from Thorne. However, the attache turned the tables on the newspaper by taping a conversation between himself, the journalist and Andre Thorne. A carefully edited version of this tape was then used to claim publicly that the

Guardian had plotted with Thorne to smear the Embassy. However the attache had clearly exceeded his role as a diplomat and was ordered to leave the country after an angry statement from the new Prime Minister, James Callaghan. Shortly afterwards Thorne gave an interview to the *Sunday People* in which he retracted his story and claimed to have lied about the blue movie. Coming after the earlier, inconclusive interviews with Wyatt, this seriously discredited efforts to expose any South African plot.

A rather similar sequence of events occurred a few weeks afterwards. On 17 May Frederick Cheeseman rang the office of the Liberal Chief Whip, David Steel, claiming to be an ex-intelligence officer with some information about a smear campaign against the party. When interviewed by Steel's aides he claimed he had been visiting BOSS headquarters in Pretoria in September 1974 when he was shown a series of dossiers profiling leading Liberal and Labour figures which were to be used as the basis for a smear campaign. After extensive reading of the documentation he provided, and checks on his identity with security services across the world by the BBC television journalists Barrie Penrose and Roger Courtiour, the Nine o'clock News ran the story as a lead exclusive, and other media followed it.

However, a day later, Cheeseman did a complete *volte face*. In an exclusive interview with the *Daily Express*, he claimed to be a hoaxer: a Walter Mitty character on the dole. This effectively killed investigations into the possible role of BOSS and other intelligence operatives in my case, that of Jeremy Thorpe and possibly other Liberal and Labour politicians. The same pattern of allegation and retraction had featured in the role of Andre Thorne and the press showed little further interest. A few years later it emerged that Thorne had indeed been 'put up to it' by South African Embassy officials and that Cheeseman, far from being bogus, was in reality an intelligence agent on active service – and remained so.* A former British Intelligence officer, Colin Wallace, told me in 1987: 'The Colonel Cheeseman saga is known in intelligence circles as the "double bubble" because it contains a second dimension in deception and not only deflects attention from the main target, but also "bursts", leaving the investigator doubting everything he has

---

*   This is confirmed by, among others, Winter in *Inside BOSS* and Barrie Penrose and Roger Courtiour in *The Pencourt File.*

uncovered so far. I have no doubt that Pencourt [Penrose and Courtiour] did get quite close – possibly too close – to the truth and various deceptions were put into action to discredit their investigations.'

While these events were unfolding – and quite out of the blue – Harold Wilson had contacted the two BBC journalists, Penrose and Courtiour. In an unusual step, he had volunteered a great deal of information on tape on the role of the security services and offered to advise them further if they would agree to investigate leads he provided. Interestingly, Wilson warned Penrose and Courtiour that Cheeseman would probably turn out to be what he intriguingly called a 'non-admitted person' (in other words, an agent who could not be directly linked to the intelligence services). Cheeseman's sudden switch from extremely well-informed contact to hoaxer bore witness to this.

Wilson's key claim was startling. Despite being head of the nation's security services, he told the reporters: 'I am not certain that for the last eight months when I was Prime Minister I knew what was happening, fully, in Security.' During this period – spanning summer 1975 to his resignation in the spring of 1976 – he had become more convinced of an earlier suspicion that there was 'a very right-wing faction' in MI5 and to a lesser extent MI6. This faction had sought to smear himself and others in his administration. It had indulged in various 'dirty tricks', including burglaries at his home and his offices. Both MI5 and MI6 officers had assisted with newspaper smear stories against him. MI5 was actively promoting stories that there was a communist cell at Number 10 Downing Street, and was assisting in a 'well orchestrated campaign' against the Labour Government. In August 1975 Wilson had complained to MI5's Director General, Sir Michael Hanley, and the MI6 head, Sir Maurice Oldfield.

He also believed the British Intelligence agents involved worked closely with their South African counterparts and some individuals in the CIA too. It was clear that he felt he could not trust anyone in Intelligence. He wanted a Royal Commission to investigate. These revelations were extraordinary to say the least, particularly since they were made through the medium of two BBC journalists he had never met before. Wilson continually stressed the South African connection as he later expanded on his account in a tape-recorded interview. But at the time his central claims were not taken as seriously as they should have been because he would not elaborate. He did not persist with his demands for

a Royal Commission after being strongly warned off by
James Callaghan's Cabinet Office with advice that to do so
would breach national security and the Official Secrets Act.
That there was indeed a plot involving elements in the British and South African security services to disrupt the Liberal
and Labour Parties was, however, substantiated ten years
later by the retired MI5 agent Peter Wright and by the
former British Intelligence officer Colin Wallace.

My bank theft coincided with a concerted drive to establish a
new right wing dominance in Britain during 1974–6. This contained a number of different threads which, even if not part of
a conspiracy, certainly converged into a common purpose.*

By the mid-1970s key sections in the British establishment had become increasingly alarmed at what they believed
was a leftward political drift in Britain, and had taken steps
to reverse this. The escalating crisis in Northern Ireland, the
growth of the left in both the unions and the Labour Party,
successful extra-parliamentary protest and direct action such
as STST, trade union and student militancy – all were seen
to pose a major threat.

Many on the right believed they really were faced with
'the end of civilisation' in Britain as they had known and
controlled it. In 1972 striking miners using flying pickets
had beaten the Heath Government. At Saltley coke depot in
Birmingham, then the nation's main supply of coke for gas
and power stations, 15,000 pickets proved too much for the
police who were forced to close the gates. The miners' success horrified many on the right who viewed it as a seditious
victory for trade union power over the state. Brendon Sewill,
a senior adviser to the Tory Chancellor of the Exchequer,
spoke for many when he later wrote of Saltley:

> At the time many of those in positions of influence
> looked into the abyss and saw only a few days away the
> possibility of the country being plunged into a state of
> chaos not so very far removed from that which might
> prevail after a minor nuclear attack. If that sounds melo-
> dramatic ... it was the analogy that was being used at the
> time. This is the power that exists to hold the country to

---

*   For a fuller account see Robin Ramsay and Stephen Dorril,
Smear!

ransom: it was fear of that abyss which had an important effect on subsequent policy.*

The Conservatives were to suffer a series of further defeats at the hands of the trade unions, most notably following another miners' strike in the winter of 1973–4. After imposing a three-day working week to limit energy demand, Edward Heath called an election on the theme 'who governs the country' – and lost. Labour formed a minority government in February 1974.

The right moved onto the offensive. They were able to do so with the active or tacit support of leading figures in the British state. There was a move within the Tory Party against Edward Heath who was felt to be too liberal. He was eventually replaced in 1975 by Margaret Thatcher after another election defeat in October 1974. There was an intellectual resurgence from new right thinkers like Milton Friedman who had previously been treated with some derision, and who provided much of the ideological foundations for the Thatcherites who began strengthening their hold over the Conservative Party. They also relied upon various research organisations and pressure groups which were found to have clear links with British Intelligence. Among these were the Institute for the Study of Conflict, the Society for Individual Freedom (which had helped sponsor my 1972 prosecution) and the National Association for Freedom (which BOSS helped fund).

At another level activity was less open. Back in 1971, with terrorism and conflict escalating in Northern Ireland, Edward Heath sent MI6 into the province. At the same time the British Army established an 'Information Policy Unit' which it officially denied existed but which became an instrument of 'disinformation' and 'black propaganda'. Its leading operative was a local army information official, Colin Wallace, who became Senior Information Officer at the Army HQ in Lisburn. His main task was 'Psychological Operations' – or 'psy ops' as they are known in the trade. Wallace worked in Northern Ireland for the Ministry of Defence between May 1968 and February 1975; he left the service in 1976 and has since provided detailed evidence on the psy ops he and his

---

* See my *Political Strikes* for further background.

colleagues carried out, including establishing front organisations and organising paramilitary projects within the North.

It is now clear that the distinction became increasingly blurred between 'legitimate' targets such as the IRA or the Protestant paramilitaries, and 'illegitimate' targets in Britain. Wallace confirms that, over the years, his psy ops work was steadily widened to cover figures and groups on the left in British politics – and here 'left' was defined in very broad terms indeed to cover anybody not identifiably on the hard right, including members of the Labour and Liberal Parties, and even 'liberal' Tories such as Edward Heath.* By 1973 Wallace and his colleagues were working very closely with the British security services on 'British' rather than 'Irish' intelligence work. The 'Irish crisis' had come to be merged with what they perceived to be a 'British crisis'.

Among the many people Wallace recalls being asked to monitor and sift intelligence upon was me. Although I had paid a brief visit there in February 1972 as Chair of the Young Liberals, I had done very little political work on Ireland. But this was not the point, as Wallace told me in an interview early in 1987: 'We saw you as an important target in the long term. You were clearly on your way up in politics. Through your anti-apartheid activities and your involvement in radical campaigns, you had offended many people on the right and it was important to neutralise you.' The information on 'indigenous' British figures like myself on Wallace's psy ops target list was provided by MI5. The list included individuals such as Lord Avebury who was a target simply because he had headed the 'Peter Hain Defence Fund' for my 1972 conspiracy charge. The psy ops activity across the Irish Sea was also linked closely to American intelligence services.

A former MI5 intelligence officer, Cathy Massiter, confirmed in a TV documentary in March 1985 that a fundamental shift of emphasis occurred between 1970 and 1984 when she was in the service. From being a counter-espionage organisation aimed at hostile foreign powers, MI5 switched towards a domestic surveillance organisation. She found herself being directed to monitor individuals in CND and leading trade unionists. The F Branch in MI5 expanded enormously to cover these domestic targets. Apart from tapping phones and maintaining surveillance, MI5 infiltrated individuals into various

---

*   For a fuller account see Ramsay and Dorril, *Smear!*

groups and organised illegal burglaries of target houses and offices. (Amongst many others, my own phone was tapped and there was evidence of infiltrators in the various anti-apartheid, anti-racist and political campaigns in which I had been active.)

Colin Wallace stated that intelligence information fed from MI5 to his office in Northern Ireland was then 'recycled' with the assistance of the CIA to news agencies in America including Forum Features,* Transworld News and the North Atlantic News Agency. When it appeared either in US papers or in international dispatches from these agencies, Wallace and his colleagues would then pick it up in Belfast as 'hard' information and supply it both to MI5 and to his political masters (first Tory, then Labour ministers).

Thus MI5 could use its own recycled information, 'disinformation' or 'black propaganda' – Wallace says all three types were involved – contained in apparently independent sources to give credibility to its activities against its political opponents or provide corroboration for its suspicions. Amongst the people who were targets in this process were Edward Heath, Harold Wilson and Jeremy Thorpe who between them headed all three major democratic parties in Britain at the time. Wallace confirmed that Heath was a target because he was too weak, Wilson because he was the main alternative to rule by the right, and Thorpe because the Liberals might become influential enough to block the return of a new, rightist Conservative government. (Much the same story with which Wyatt had approached me; and in 1977 the Liberals did actually conclude a formal pact to sustain Labour in power.)

Psychological operations against these politicians and others had begun before the defeat of Heath's 1970–4 Government and the return of Labour. Prior to this, MI6 (the security service which operates mainly outside the UK) had been more active in liaising with psy ops in Northern Ireland. But when Labour came back to power, events took an even more serious turn. MI5 (which has responsibility for domestic security) became dominant in Northern Ireland. At this point the attention of Wallace and his colleagues became

---

* Forum World Features was a CIA front news agency which was used as a conduit for the distribution of information furthering CIA objectives from 1966 until 1975.

even more directed at domestic British politics – a switch which later led him to become alienated from his work and depart from the service in 1976.

At the time Wallace recorded that MI5 was particularly anxious because it believed Labour would: phase out internment without trial in Northern Ireland; withdraw from the EEC; succumb to growing trade union power and left-wing influence; establish greater control over the intelligence services; and introduce a Freedom of Information Act. Significantly, MI5 was also concerned Labour would take tougher action against South Africa and the illegal Smith regime in Rhodesia – thus 'encouraging Marxist influence in Southern Africa'.

Wallace added: 'Most of my work during this period was being used by others for totally unconstitutional ends.' He explained that this created an atmosphere in which he and his colleagues found it steadily more difficult to distinguish between, for example, a suspected IRA bomber and a British anti-apartheid activist. Information on both was being fed across his desk. Both appeared on target lists and in his security files. Both represented a common threat and both therefore were legitimate targets.

The way in which intelligence information could be abused is evident in Wallace's contemporaneous files which he showed me in 1987. For example there is a cutting from the *Irish Press* dated 7 February 1972 which describes Russian reaction to the events on 'Bloody Sunday' the previous week when the army killed unarmed civilians in Derry. Russian journalists working for TASS and *Pravda* were quoted in the article. Wallace had underlined their names and noted alongside the cutting: 'KGB – link to Labour activists. See also Bloody Sunday Commemorative vigil Peter Hain. Hain's family deported SA 1966 for Communist activity.' (As a leaflet in Wallace's file confirmed, I had sponsored a vigil to commemorate Bloody Sunday on its anniversary in 1973.) Another article clipped from the *Irish News* of 16 November 1972 reported the meeting of an international tribunal in Belfast to investigate army harassment of civilians in the North. It was chaired by Kadar Asmal, then a South African exile lecturing in international law at Trinity College, Dublin (and from 1994 a Minister in the Mandela government). Wallace had recorded alongside the cutting in a red pen: 'Asmal is a SA lawyer. Hain's family deported from SA for Communist activity.'

His note made an additional reference to the KGB and the Irish Anti-Apartheid Movement which Asmal also chaired.

Fifteen years later Wallace described to me this technique as 'guilt by tenuous association'. I was just one of many to whom it was applied. A false entry on MI5 records about my parents' 'Communist activity' provided a pretext for my name to be associated first with the KGB and then back full circle to Irish terrorism. As Wallace also confirmed, it is not hard to envisage how, on this basis, action to discredit me could be rationalised by the security services. Wallace states that, not only did he work closely with MI5 and the CIA but that both these agencies worked with BOSS. What began as part of a counter-terrorism war project in Ireland, widened significantly to cover intelligence work on, and psy ops against, all manner of activity which had nothing strictly to do with Irish affairs.

Unusual activity was meanwhile mounted on another front. The experience gained by the armed forces in Northern Ireland had accustomed them both to the task of controlling civilian populations and to a more overtly political role. And there was some discussion in senior military circles as to whether the armed forces should intervene in British politics, possibly by organising a coup. Field Marshall Lord Carver, Chief of Defence Staff in 1974, later acknowledged that such discussion had occurred amongst 'fairly senior officers', but said he personally 'took action to make certain that nobody was so stupid as to go around saying those things'.

In 1974–5 there were reports of private 'citizens armies' being prepared by retired military figures. They included General Sir Walter Walker (until 1972 Commander-in-Chief of NATO's Northern Command in Europe) and Colonel David Stirling (known for his wartime exploits in the Special Air Service). The purpose, as Stirling expressed it,* was to 'provide on a volunteer basis the minimum manpower necessary to cope with the immediate crisis following a general strike or a near general strike in the knowledge that the government of the day must welcome our initiative'. The 'government of the day' happened to be a Labour one, at that stage still pursuing a relatively left-wing programme. Although these private armies were ridiculed by some commentators, their purpose was really to pressure the government. David Stirling explained later that he thought a general strike was likely and that he was forming

---

* See Carol Ackroyd's *The Technology of Political Control.*

a group of trained cadres because Labour was unwilling to make the necessary preparations for an appropriate military response. It was not known at the time, however, that Stirling's group, GB75, and Walker's group, Civil Assistance, were covertly assisted by British Intelligence. So was another group which had been launched in 1973 called 'Unison'.

According to Colin Wallace, GB75, Civil Assistance and Unison were in part psychological operations. There are other connections. One of Civil Assistance's Kent area co-ordinators was Lieutenant Colonel Frederick Cheeseman, who had surfaced publicly in May 1976 as the source of the South African plot allegation. The link to more overtly right-wing activity was apparent through Unison's founder members Ross McWhirter and George Young. Both had close links with British Intelligence and both were key figures in the Society for Individual Freedom.

In August 1977 Harold Wilson told the *Observer*: 'My impression is that what has been going on over a period of years has come from or been fed by, a small mafia group of MI5 who have contacts outside in one or two sections of the Press, and a few self-appointed private enterprise security agents.' There is other corroborative evidence from two important sources. In 1978 the author Chapman Pincher, a right winger with extremely good Intelligence sources, wrote in his book *Inside Story*: 'the undermining activities which Wilson complained of were not only genuine but far more menacing than he revealed. Certain officers, inside MI5, assisted by others who had retired from the service, were actually trying to bring down the Labour Government.' Colin Wallace added: 'Information supplied by the CIA to MI5 was used to justify a number of in-depth investigations into Harold Wilson's activities and those of other Labour MPs/supporters to find out if sufficient "hard evidence" could be gathered to wreck the Labour Party's chances of gaining power ... When the investigations failed to uncover anything of value, elements within the Security Service, supported by others in Whitehall including former members of the Intelligence and Security Services, embarked upon a disinformation campaign to achieve the same objective.'

There is a great deal of other evidence of action aimed at disrupting and destabilising the Wilson Government contained in accounts by Pincher, Colin Wallace, Dorril and Ramsay and Penrose and Courtiour. In *The Wilson Plot*, the investigative journalist David Leigh also confirmed how elements in MI5 and the CIA sought to discredit Wilson and bring down the Labour Government in the mid-1970s.

The important point is that this activity was orchestrated by a distinct group within MI5. Wilson referred to it as a right wing 'mafia' or 'faction' (there is good reason to suppose he had been briefed by sympathetic officers within MI6). Wallace states that it numbered at least 40 agents. Perhaps the most significant supporting evidence comes from Peter Wright. He was a leading, if not the leading, member of this MI5 group in the mid-1970s who were in the F4 and F6 branches of the Service at the time. In his 1987 book *Spycatcher* he confirmed the validity of the earlier and quite separate accounts given by Wallace and Pencourt.

To summarise: throughout the 1970s there was what may be described as a 'hard right' project to roll back the post-war social democratic political consensus supported by all the major parties – a project which eventually succeeded with the advent of Thatcherism in 1979. This contained perfectly legitimate elements, such as the espousal of new right ideology and the open promotion of Mrs Thatcher for the Tory leadership and subsequently the premiership. But it also contained less legitimate elements. At one end of the spectrum these included rightist pressure groups and shadowy military networks. At the other was Peter Wright's MI5 faction deliberately promoting right-wing political forces such as the Thatcherites in the Conservative Party, and engaging in psy ops to undermine the Labour Government and discredit people who were regarded as a threat to the 'hard right' project.

The interests of this British hard right and the South Africans coincided. Leading figures in pressure groups such as the Society for Individual Freedom and the National Association for Freedom made no secret of their support for South Africa and were in turn supported by it. Peter Wright testifies that the MI5 faction was openly sympathetic to white South Africa because it was seen as an ally in a mutual war against 'international communism'. Colin Wallace corroborates this, adding that information was regularly 'traded' between MI5 and BOSS. Even joint operations were carried out where the agencies shared common objectives, as the former BOSS agent Gordon Winter also confirms.

With hindsight, it now seems likely that BOSS was involved in the bizarre events surrounding the Putney bank theft and the subsequent court case, possibly with the help of sections within MI5 who were disposed to support the apartheid regime in South Africa and prepared to discredit its critics by the use of a variety of black propaganda and psy ops tactics.

According to Gordon Winter, BOSS had indeed been directly involved in the set-up. At the time of the theft a BOSS agent with a walkie-talkie radio had been watching my home from a parked car. When I left to go shopping, the agent alerted the real thief – a man with a criminal record who, after my arrest, was flown to Paris and then to South Africa to start a new life. In Winter's account, the only minor slip-up was that the thief's hair had been styled to resemble mine – but by coincidence, I had changed my hairstyle only shortly before the event.

Immediately after the theft, BOSS arranged for Scotland yard to be notified that I was linked to the crime. The caller apparently told the Yard to check in Special Branch files where they would find that I had campaigned actively against Barclay's involvement in South Africa, and had once taken part in a picket outside the very same branch of the bank (which was true).

How far do Winter's claims of BOSS involvement square with the facts? First, the intervention of the schoolboys would need to be unplanned: they were clearly no part of any BOSS plot. But then their role was confined purely to implicating me through reporting my car number. Similarly, the local police force need not have been a party to the plot: they came into the picture only from the time my name was reported as a suspect, whether by BOSS or not. Second, one interpretation of the thief's behaviour (as reported by nearly a dozen eyewitnesses) is fully compatible with the role of a BOSS operative. About 20 minutes before I left the house, one of the cashiers had spotted the thief behaving suspiciously; she later surmised in court that he must have been 'casing the joint'. He had peered through the window and come into the bank. Other witnesses reported seeing what they assumed was the same man in the area even before this. Nearly an hour before, one witness, Elizabeth Forshaw, spotted a man while she was shopping in Putney High Street: 'I saw a familiar face, and immediately I thought it was Peter Hain ... Suddenly, when he was within a few feet I did not think it was Peter Hain. Before I was absolutely convinced, but when he came within two or three feet I knew it wasn't him.' (She explained that she was particularly interested in people she had seen on television and knew what I looked like.) After the theft, the thief turned round while running from his pursuers and threw the money back – not the behaviour of someone desperate for the money but maybe that of someone keen to allow witnesses to see his face since everybody accepted that he resembled me.

Third – and perhaps most significant – is the evidence of the phone call to the Yard. Neither Winter nor BOSS could have been aware of one fact which was never made known outside the few most closely involved in my defence team. This was an unexplained incident which both confused and intrigued my solicitor, John Dundon; so much so that he later made a separate statement about it in front of a solicitor colleague. At one point during my detention, while Dundon was in the police station waiting to see me, the officer in charge of the investigation referred obliquely to telephone conversations with senior officers in Scotland Yard, and to important evidence they had. The Wandsworth detective hinted that this evidence was being weighed in the decision on whether or not I should be charged. But he would not elaborate. Neither Dundon nor I could make any sense of it at the time. He was convinced that something more was involved than simple consultations with Metropolitan police chiefs over a potential political embarrassment if a mistake was made charging a public figure. But he had no proof and so had no basis for pursuing it.

If BOSS (or perhaps a British Intelligence source) did phone the Yard as Winter described then this could be the elusive factor in those key hours when the decision was finally made to proceed against me. It would make sense of Dundon's conversation with the detective, of the lengthy delay while consultations took place, and of the relative importance which the detective attached to those consultations. With knowledge of police procedures it is not hard to see how, to the investigating officers, 'evidence' via Scotland Yard could seem important as corroboration for local evidence gathered quite independently – especially since that local evidence (the sum total of which at this stage came from two of the schoolboys alone) was extremely thin.

In February 1987 Colin Wallace told me he had established through a then serving British Intelligence officer the contents of a record held by the security services in London. According to him, it stated that the Metropolitan police were tipped off by MI5 almost immediately after the bank theft that I was responsible. This tip-off occurred well before the schoolboys implicated me by reporting my car number. Wallace said the security service record confirmed BOSS' involvement. The record also showed there had been an earlier attempt to set me up some weeks before, but that this had failed to implicate me sufficiently. (I was completely unaware of this at the time. However, just before my trial my solici-

tor was shown statements from a witness who saw me on
TV and had reported to police that I looked like the thief in
a bank snatch across the river from my home at Fulham one
month before the Putney theft.)

Once my arrest had been accomplished, however, it seems
that a section of MI5 or, more likely, MI6, wanted the South
African plot to be known through a source which could not
be traced back. As Colin Wallace recalls, by 1975 the battle
for power in Northern Ireland between MI5 and MI6 meant
that 'they were much more at war with each other than with
the IRA', and this affected domestic British operations as
well. The two intelligence services were also known to have
quite different political attitudes towards South Africa. MI6
tended to be more anti-apartheid, reflecting Foreign Office
policy. By contrast, MI5 – particularly Peter Wright's faction
– were actively pro-South Africa, reflecting their anti-commu-
nist obsession which virtually 'equated anybody not blue
with being red', in Wallace's words.

According to the *Pencourt File* authors, Kenneth Wyatt
himself may have had British Intelligence links and, if his
allegations were encouraged or even inspired by MI6, this
might also explain the appearance on the scene of the del-
phic and extraordinarily well informed Dr Diane Lefevre. Her
approach to me could have been timed deliberately to corroborate the Wyatt account. She actively promoted the South
African connection at the same time as the Prime Minister,
Harold Wilson, was doing so. Coming shortly after my
memorandum on Wyatt's approach had been forwarded to
Downing Street by Jeremy Thorpe, Wilson's intervention
specifically referred to the involvement of private agents and
business resources in the South African disruption of British
politics. In his later statements to the *Pencourt File* authors,
Wilson also drew upon intelligence briefings to back up his
own suspicions.

Another common thread between Kamil and British Intelligence is the political scenario sketched by Wyatt. He
could have said that motivation for the action against me
and the smear attempts on other Liberal and Labour politicians was limited to the fact that we were known to be
strongly anti-apartheid. Given BOSS's history of dirty tricks
in Britain, that would have been believable; indeed many
people speculated at the time that this was the explanation. But Wyatt did not say that. Instead he gave an account which at the time seemed surreal. He linked the

plot to the power balance within British politics. The
objective, he claimed, was to discredit the Liberals and prevent the formation of a pact with Labour that might block
the prospect of a Tory Government. Of course, undermining Labour and securing the election of the Tories would
benefit white South Africa indirectly. But, as we now
know, exactly the same political objectives were being
actively pursued by the rightist MI5 group at the time.
The political arguments used by Wyatt to substantiate his
main allegation were virtually identical to the analysis
within the hard right, including MI5, which was revealed
ten years later, notably in *Spycatcher*. It is too much of a
coincidence to suppose they were unconnected. Nobody else
was discussing this scenario publicly at the time – which
is why, until Peter Wright and Colin Wallace provided
credible confirmation, it was hard to take it seriously.

Finally, BOSS had a history of disrupting anti-apartheid
activity in Britain. Framing me on a bank theft does not look
unusual when it could be seen as part of a general pattern. It
would also have been what is known as a 'deniable operation' – which is precisely why it remained so difficult to
prove. As with many South African intelligence activities
across the world, the *real* crime remained conveniently un-
solved.

7 RESISTANCE

In the two years to mid-1976 white South Africa enjoyed a good press: whites-only signs were reported being removed from some park benches; black athletes were pictured competing against whites; and Prime Minister Vorster was courted as peacemaker in the Rhodesian deadlock. Apartheid's propaganda machine had reason to be pleased with itself.

Suddenly that illusion was shattered by a six-letter word: Soweto. On the morning of 16 June white policemen fired on schoolchildren protesting peacefully against being taught in Afrikaans, and the township exploded. Shock waves tore through the country as black communities took to the streets in a display of defiance at the hated white oppression greater even than that which followed the Sharpeville massacre 16 years before. They met with the predictable response of a police state: shot down mercilessly, in the back, the head, the chest. By the end of the year at least 600 were dead and over 6000 had been arrested. From behind its public relations façade, apartheid had once again reared its ugly head before the world.

Although the eruption may have been a surprise, its roots were clear. In 1975 the Minister of Bantu Education had issued an instruction that arithmetic and social studies in all black secondary schools must be taught in Afrikaans. Parents, pupils and teachers protested – they regarded Afrikaans as the language of their oppressors. Their protests were rejected. Desmond Tutu, the Anglican Bishop of Johannesburg, wrote to Vorster in May 1976 warning him that unless something was done very soon 'bloodshed and violence are going to happen in South Africa'. The warning was ignored.

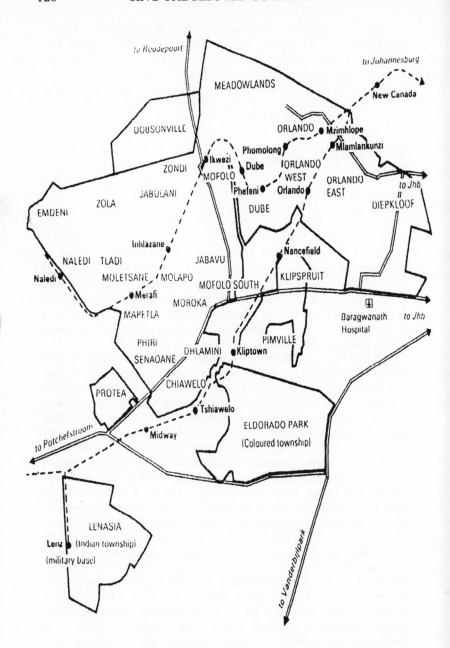

MAP 3   SOWETO

Soweto (South Western Townships), a complex of 28 townships covering 23 square miles situated 10 miles from the
centre of Johannesburg, had started life in the 1930s as bar-
racks for migrant blacks, mostly mine workers, called Orlando.
It had no electricity, no shops, no modern amenities. The
1950s and 1960s saw rapid expansion: roads were constructed,
acres of box-like concrete houses were built and water supplies
and drainage installed. The lack of electricity meant that coal
stoves were used for cooking, causing a smoky pall over the
township. The absence of shops and the fact that most
Sowetans were employed in 'white' Johannesburg, required
residents to commute to Johannesburg daily by train, bus or
shared taxis. Most had passes, some had education and jobs
and so they were among the elite of black South Africa. By
1976 the houses were officially supposed to accommodate
600,000 people, but most experts believed the population to be
well over a million.

Opposition to the Bantu Education Policy had been growing in the Soweto schools and representatives from the
schools had elected an Action Committee to organise a
demonstration, which took place on the morning of 16 June
1976. The demonstration was to be peaceful, but the
students knew the police would try to stop them, so secrecy
was essential. Over a dozen assembly points had been chosen
at various schools and each had a set time of departure, ten
minutes apart, so that each time the police received a report
that a group of students was marching, another group would
begin before they could react, leaving the police too stretched
to respond. The groups were to converge on Orlando West
Junior Secondary School, then march together to Orlando
Stadium for a mass rally, some 15,000 strong. The columns
marched through Soweto chanting slogans, singing freedom
songs and carrying placards protesting about the imposition
of Afrikaans. The slogans were 'Down with Afrikaans',
'Blacks are not Dustbins', 'Afrikaans Stinks', 'Afrikaans is
Tribal Language', 'Bantu Education – To Hell with it'.

Police vehicles raced to the scene and tried to seize placards and stop the march, firing tear gas at the students. No
order for the marchers to disperse was heard and a senior
police officer admitted that no warning shots were fired
before the police opened fire, killing several children. The
first child killed was 13-year-old Hector Petersen in Orlando
West. His photograph was flashed around the world as he
died being carried by his crying brother.

Then Soweto erupted – police vehicles were stoned and set

on fire, police dogs that were unleashed upon students were knifed. Vehicles belonging to the West Rand Bantu Affairs Administration Board which administered Soweto on behalf of the Bantu Affairs Department (BAD), were burnt and most of its offices in Soweto destroyed. Commercial vehicles of white-owned businesses were also set on fire. Beerhalls and liquor stores were burned and looted and a bank and several post offices were also set alight. Two white officials of the West Rand Board were killed. The Government closed schools and sent its anti-riot squad into Soweto in armoured cars (called 'Hippos' in the townships). The army was placed on alert and troops were mustered. In just over 24 hours the violence and shooting had spread throughout the township. Within a few days 143 vehicles (including 53 police vehicles) and 139 buildings (including 33 BAD buildings) had been damaged by fire or burnt out.

But the violence was not confined to Soweto. Within a week, other townships in the Johannesburg area, and Atteridgeville and Mamelodi in Pretoria, also erupted and there were outbreaks as far afield as the Eastern Transvaal, the South-Western Transvaal, the Orange Free State, the Northern Cape, Langa and Nyanga in Cape Town, and at the Universities of the North and Zululand. During July the unrest spread to other parts of the Transvaal, to the Vaal triangle and to Natal, Kwazulu and the Eastern Cape. In August the Bophuthatswana (the Tswana Bantustan) legislative assembly building in Mafeking was burned down. Disturbances in Port Elizabeth claimed 33 lives and there were outbreaks in East London. Two months after 16 June, some 80 black communities all over the country had expressed their fury and within four months this had risen to 160. All the provinces and all the Bantustans had experienced unrest and there was also a disturbance in Namibia.

A storm of resistance had been unleashed with Soweto at the centre. Although the violence subsided within a few days, calm did not return to the townships until the beginning of 1978. During the second part of 1976 and throughout 1977 there were repeated skirmishes between students and police and more students were killed. Despite this they continued to organise protests and demonstrations and their campaign against Bantu Education grew. During this period Soweto was virtually under martial law as an occupied territory.

The Afrikaans decree was withdrawn and about six weeks after the initial eruption Soweto schools reopened and attendance began to increase slowly. But many school

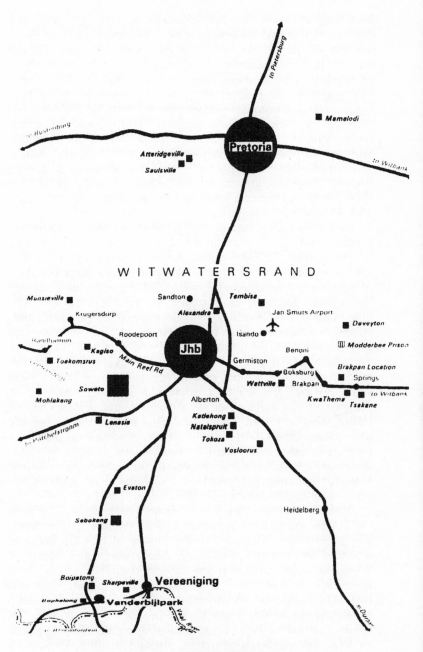

MAP 4 TOWNSHIPS IN
PRETORIA—JOHANNESBURG—VEREENIGING

buildings were set on fire, possibly by militants who did not want a return to school. On 4 August 20,000 students set off to march to police headquarters at John Vorster Square in Johannesburg, to demand the release of those arrested in the troubles, but were stopped by the police. On four days in August the students organised work boycotts – stay-at-homes – by Soweto workers which seriously crippled business in Johannesburg. During one of these, some migrant workers living in a hostel in Orlando stormed through the neighbourhood, attacking and killing other residents. The police were later accused of having incited them to attack schoolchildren. During September there were further incidents and 6 children were shot dead and 35 injured.

In October 16 teachers and 62 students were detained in a police raid on a high school and the police opened fire on a funeral killing 7. This signalled the beginning of raids and arrests in Soweto and in the following weeks large numbers of pupils were detained and many fled the complex to escape the police, some seeking refuge in neighbouring countries and joining the liberation struggle being organised from outside. There was an almost complete boycott of the secondary school exams at the beginning of November and these were eventually taken only in March 1977. A month later the students marched against rent increases imposed by the West Rand Board. This led to a successful campaign which also resulted in the collapse of the Soweto Urban Bantu Council (UBC), the only civic body recognised by the WRB, and the formation of the Committee of Ten, a Soweto local authority interim committee, chaired by local doctor Nthato Motlana, which was widely representative and had the support of the Soweto Students Representative Council and Black Consciousness organisations.

The first anniversary of the Soweto uprising on 16 June 1977 was marked by commemoration services in the township's churches. The one in the Regina Mundi Church was attended by between 5000 and 7000 people and broke up when the police fired tear gas into the building. On 23 June there was a second march to John Vorster Square, but this time the students outwitted the police by travelling into Johannesburg in small groups and wearing workers' overalls, before converging on a central rallying point. They marched to John Vorster Square carrying placards reading 'Vorster release our leaders' and 'Bantu Education is for the Education of Slavery'. About 150 were arrested.

But the repression only fanned the flames of resistance. In the second half of July 1977 Soweto schools were again burned and arsonists were warned that they could get the death sentence. Another boycott of classes began and gathered strength so that by the end of November it was supported by almost all Soweto secondary schools and by many primary school pupils. By then some 500 secondary school teachers had resigned and so, 18 months after the 16 June march, the pupils of Soweto had brought about the collapse of secondary school education in the complex. But the boycott was not confined to Soweto. By the end of November it had spread to the Pretoria townships, to the Venda and Ciskei Bantustans, the Orange Free State and Port Elizabeth.

Then, on the 12 September 1977, there was further outrage when the Black Consciousness Movement leader, Steve Biko, died in police custody in Pretoria after having suffered brain damage in a police cell beating in Port Elizabeth and then being transported naked on the floor of a police van for some 600 miles. Biko had become a symbol of internal black resistance and had been banned in 1974 and detained under the Terrorism Act in August 1977. For his courageous determination to ensure that the truth about Biko's brutal murder came out Donald Woods – who, just a month before had been acting as a government intermediary in promoting sports dialogue with me and others – was first banned and then forced to flee, dramatically escaping disguised as a priest across the Lesotho border. Biko was the forty-sixth political prisoner to die in police custody and his death provoked international outrage, especially since the police tried to cover it up.

Official figures put the casualties from the beginning of the uprising in Soweto as 575 killed and 2389 wounded but these are almost certainly underestimates. In Britain the Anti-Apartheid Movement stepped up its campaigns, giving expression to international outrage. The uprisings also boosted the struggle by politicising young blacks, and many activists slipped into exile to join the ANC, now well enough established in the frontline states to be able to give them a thorough guerrilla training.

After the government crackdown in 1960 there had been no liberation group for those leaving South Africa to join. But that year the ANC Deputy President, Oliver Tambo, left the country and set up an ANC post in Dar-es-Salaam, Tanzania, and another one in London. ANC representatives soon called for economic sanctions at the United Nations in New York. At the 1961 Commonwealth Conference the ANC lobbying contributed to South Africa leaving the organisation. In 1962 Mandela (on his overseas visit while underground) addressed the Pan-African Freedom Movement Conference in Ethiopia and obtained pledges of assistance. Former members of the SA Communist Party in exile successfully lobbied the Soviet Union and its allies for aid for the ANC, which had to rely heavily on the assistance of Communist countries because of the reluctance of Western states to help it. Also in 1962 the first batch of volunteers left for military training in Tanzania and Ethiopia (where Mandela was able to meet some of them). However, many volunteers were intercepted by the security forces on the escape routes.

The ANC's military wing Mkhonto (MK) began its sabotage campaign in December 1962 with bomb attacks on power stations and government offices and also attacked police informers, state witnesses and collaborators. But this first sabotage phase of resistance was over: the ANC was decimated by arrests and riddled with police infiltrators and by the end of 1964 seemed close to internal collapse. Mandela had been joined on Robben Island by other ANC leaders after the Rivonia trial. Under Tambo's leadership it was decided that a commitment to armed guerrilla struggle was the only way forward.

During the next 12 years the ANC regrouped and reorganised. The underground was largely purged of counter-espionage agents. An external command was set up. Bases were established in friendly countries and infiltration routes were organised. Consequently, after the 1976 uprisings, the radicalised students had the ANC ready and waiting in the newly independent frontline black states (by then only Namibia and Rhodesia of the the six frontline states were still governed by anti-ANC elites). Military camps, administrative offices and educational institutions had been established in the outer 'sanctuary' states of Angola, Zambia and Tanzania. Clandestine infiltration routes had been organised in the inner 'transit' states of Botswana, Zimbabwe, Mozambique, Swaziland and Lesotho, and the National Executive Committee (NEC) had moved its headquarters from London to Lusaka in Zambia. There were two bases in Mozambique until 1984. And after Zimbabwe's independence in 1980 an office was opened in Harare. The ANC had originally established camps in Tanzania. But from 1977 camps were set up in now independent Angola to provide guerrilla training for their recruits; after receiving training, groups were infiltrated back into South Africa. With Angola sharing a border with Zambia, communications and visits between ANC headquarters and the camps were easy and frequent.

The first 'in exile' ANC Consultative Conference in 1969 in Tanzania had formed a new multi-racial Revolutionary Council to command Mkhonto and taken the decision to begin moving the ANC back into the region. The second, held in 1985 in Zambia, confirmed Tambo as the effective leader and Alfred Nzo as Secretary-General. Joe Slovo became the first white elected to the NEC, which also included Mac Maharaj representing Indians, Reg September representing Coloureds, Thabo Mbeki (Govan Mbeki's son) as Director of Information and Joe Modise, the Commander of Mkhonto. Prior to 1975 the total estimated number of ANC personnel outside South Africa was 1000. By 1980 it had risen to 9000 and by 1986 to 13,000 (8000 under arms with Mkhonto and 5000 in civil service departments or enrolled in educational programmes).

The response from whites to the Soweto uprising had been characteristically intransigent: in the general election in late September 1976 the Nationalists were returned with an increased majority. Prime Minister John Vorster made it plain that the fundamentals of apartheid would continue. But whatever his public stance, Vorster knew that a policy of no-change was unsustainable. The uprisings had provoked all the financial problems which followed the Sharpeville shootings in 1960, except these became even more severe. Capital left the country, businesses collapsed and the housing market went into sharp decline. Instead of the usual annual influx of whites, 1977 and 1978 saw more than 3000 nett departures. The whites were in a despondent state and could see no way ahead.

For three months after Soweto Vorster had made no comment. Then, gradually, the reformers regained the ascendancy and Verwoerd's strict recipe for apartheid continued to be jettisoned. But the Government did not embark on reforms because it was shaken by the post-Soweto disturbances or by the international criticism of Biko's death: although these certainly concentrated minds, they reformed because of economic and social changes.

For the first two decades of apartheid there had been sufficient white workers to fill most skilled jobs and hundreds of thousands of blacks had been removed from towns.

But then the growth in manufacturing overtook the capacity of the white population to produce skilled workers, especially as the Government's vigorous 'Afrikaner-first' policies had moved many Afrikaners out of blue-collar jobs. Compared with 1948 when the Nationalists came to power and Afrikaners controlled 9.6 per cent of private business (excluding farms) 1 per cent of the mines and 16 per cent of all posts in professions, by 1975 these figures had jumped to 20.8 per cent, 18 per cent and 38 per cent respectively. Sanlam, the Afrikaner insurance group, had become one of the most powerful companies in the country and had bought the General Mining Company from the English-dominated Anglo-American mining corporation, so securing Afrikaner control of a major company in the country's main foreign exchange earner, gold. The civil service, before 1948 dominated in the upper echelons by English speakers, was by the end of the 1970s almost 90 per cent Afrikaans.

As a consequence, factory managers could not find the white workers that the apartheid laws said they must employ, so they evaded the law by promoting whites who had previously done the job and calling them 'supervisors', then recruiting black workers at lower wages to do the work. Job titles were altered to conceal the fact that black men were doing white men's work. But when white trade unions complained of this the police charged the offending black workers, who were fined, imprisoned or sent away to a homeland. The law blamed the black worker, not the employer who had offered him the job. Informal deals to resolve these problems became increasingly common. Once satisfied that there were no whites to fill the jobs, some white trade unions accepted the situation. Black workers and their employers bribed the police. And the shrewder managers managed to persuade Bantu Affairs Department officials to re-classify black recruits to the workforce as having Section 10 rights, i.e. the right to remain in an urban area for more than 72 hours. Even before we had left in 1966, one of my uncles, Hugh Stocks, who owned the large construction company Stocks & Stocks, managed to obtain permission to recruit black crane drivers. He did so, not for liberal motives, but for the very practical reason that crane driving was a much more desirable occupation for blacks than for whites and so attracted a higher standard of applicant.

In 1971 the running of African townships had been transferred from local authorities to centrally-appointed Bantu administration boards which took their cue from Pretoria.

Instead of reacting primarily to local needs and pressures the boards followed the official line which called for the reduction of the flow of blacks to towns. So at a time when the needs of industry were drawing blacks in their thousands into towns, black house-building was reduced and the newcomers settled in shanty towns or caused overcrowding in township houses – illegal acts punished by eviction to the homelands which again depleted the industrial workforce.

The economic basis of apartheid was gradually being challenged by its own contradictions. On the one hand the system of race domination and discrimination had created a vast opportunity for exploitation which boosted profits and sustained white privilege. On the other hand, its very racial rigidity was by this time an obstacle to further economic expansion and prosperity. Thus, economic imperatives were nibbling away at the edges of apartheid. Although the erosion of racial job reservation provided immediate relief for the system and thereby shored it up in the short term, in the long term it forced further reforms.

In 1977 Vorster appointed two commissions: the first, the Riekert Commission, examined influx control and recommended that blacks with skilled jobs and proper housing be accepted as permanent residents in towns, with influx controls enforced against all others; the second, the Wiehahn Commission, which included one black member, looked at industrial relations and advised that job reservation be abolished and black trade unions be recognised and have equal status with white unions. This would bring them into South Africa's statutory industrial relations system, with its conciliation procedures and right to strike after an official 30-day notification period. Thus skilled black workers would become a 'permanent part of the economy'.

Granting blacks trade union rights was not so much a concession as a legitimation of what was in any case becoming the status quo. Although black trade unions were not recognised and black strikes were illegal, many industrial managers chose to avoid trouble caused by unofficial or wildcat action by dealing with the unions. Many black unions had successfully called illegal strikes. A major series of strikes in Durban in 1973 and the country-wide strikes following the Soweto riots showed black trade unionism to be a growing force. And the market was driving up black wages faster than white ones: between 1970 and 1976, real white earnings rose by 3.8 per cent and black by 51.3 per cent. In the mines, where black wages had been abysmally low even by South African standards, between 1970 and 1978 (a period of heavy capital investment and the build-up of a skilled labour force to man it) white earnings rose by 79 per cent and black by 390 per cent.

At the same time trade unionism also experienced the familiar characteristic of apartheid rule during this period: on the one hand, reforms conceded as of necessity, on the other vicious repression. For example, late in 1976, the officials of two organisations set up to train trade unionists – the Urban Training Project in Johannesburg and the Industrial Educational Institute in Durban – were banned. Even more sinister were the deaths while in police detention of at least two blacks arrested for promoting trade unionism. On 2 September 1976, Luke Mazwembe of the Western Province Workers Advice Bureau was found dead in his cell within two hours of being picked up by police. On 9 January 1977, Lawrence Ndzanga, the former National Secretary of the South African Railway and Harbour Workers Union also died in detention. In 1976 there were 13 known deaths of detainees, compared with 22 in the previous 14 years since detention without trial was first introduced.

After the Soweto riots anti-apartheid groups in Britain and America put pressure on international companies not to operate in South Africa and some companies resisted this by claiming to pay black workers the same rates as whites. In reality, though a few atypical companies may have done so and though there had been some convergence in wage rates for skilled industrial workers, there were still huge differences between the earnings of most whites and most blacks. As a result, a new front was opened up for the international anti-apartheid movement to show solidarity with the black majority. Promoting and supporting black trade unionism became an important objective of British trade unions and others across the world. There were high-profile campaigns around British companies with South African subsidiaries and the AAM worked hard to build support for economic sanctions.

After the two commission reports the Government decided in 1978 that it must accept the inevitable and turn the skilled black workforce into collaborators in maintaining the system. So apartheid was to be largely dismantled within the white economy. Blacks essential to the economy would be conceded a share of the nation's wealth and granted residence rights. The aim was for them to become a stable labour force which would act as a buffer between white society and the mass of less skilled blacks who would remain outside the new system. But there would be no concessions towards political power and if they were involved in an illegal strike or a riot or were dismissed from work they would forfeit their residence rights.

Training schemes to prepare blacks for skilled industrial work were to be financed by the Government and by industry helped by 100 per cent tax rebates. Years of apartheid legislation had virtually removed all houses in black townships from the protection of property laws, so that blacks could neither own them freehold nor on long lease. They were to be made legally purchasable on 99-year leases. However, before these proposals could be implemented, Vorster was forced to resign.

Concerned about South Africa's poor image, Vorster had been preparing the Information Department for the task of 'selling' apartheid South Africa and had pumped money from the Prime Minister's discretionary fund into it. When he needed more, he turned to the Defence Department's budget, the safest source of secret funding. Between 1974 and 1978 Vorster put about £30 million into special projects, including an undercover attempt to buy the *Washington Star* (he had to settle anonymously for a less important American paper, the *Sacramento Union*). There was also an undercover attempt to buy the British publishing company Morgan Grampian. Vast sums were spent on persuading Western journalists and broadcasters of the justice of his reforming policies.

Eventually this misuse of funds by the Department of Information was exposed by two Johannesburg papers, the *Rand Daily Mail* and *Sunday Express* in the second half of 1978, bringing about the fall of Vorster and his heir apparent Connie Mulder, the Minister of Information and leader of the Transvaal National Party, in what became known as the 'Muldergate' affair. The chief of police, General H.J. van den Bergh, was out and his Bureau of State Security (BOSS) was dismantled. P.W. Botha, head of the National Party in the Cape, became Prime Minister, Magnus Malan Defence Minister and Constand Viljoen Chief of the Defence Force.

With Vorster's security empire discredited, the country's new leaders relied much more on the military and presided over the militarisation of South Africa from Government downwards. Security superseded ideology as the dominant theme and the centre of decision making shifted from the party and the intelligence services to the military-security establishment. The Defence Force budget rocketed and its fighting strength soared. The State Security Council, headed by Botha and including an inner core of Cabinet Ministers plus the military intelligence and police chiefs, met fortnightly to take the major security-related decisions, which were then ratified by the full Cabinet the next day. In foreign policy the militarists on the Council completely superseded the Foreign Ministry in devising a more aggressive regional strategy, basically offering economic cooperation to neighbouring states that cooperated and destabilising those that did not. The latter included armed strikes into neighbouring countries by both land and air, killing local civilians, and arming and supporting insurgent bands such as Renamo in Mozambique and UNITA in Angola. Also included was the use of economic force.

This strategy eventually reduced Mozambique to economic ruin and forced it to sign the Nkomati Accord, in which it agreed to exclude ANC bases in return for the South Africans withdrawing all support from Renamo (which they did not). But in Angola the policy failed and the South Africans overreached themselves, provoking Cuba into a massive build-up of its military assistance to the MPLA. In 1988, for the first time, the Cubans were sent south to engage in force a South African column which was trying to take the MPLA's main southern stronghold of Cuito Cuanavale. The column encountered heavy resistance and was surrounded. As South Africa tried to supply and relieve its force from the air it found that it had lost its accustomed air superiority and the beleagured column began to suffer heavy casualties. This was a major blow: never before had the powerful white state been defeated militarily. South Africa then agreed to accept withdrawal from Angola and independence for Namibia in exchange for Cuban withdrawal and the removal of ANC bases from Angola.

Botha's new strategy had required the maximisation of South Africa's economic and military power, which necessitated forging an alliance between the Afrikaner Nationalist Government and the English-speaking business sector, relations with which had deteriorated during the Verwoerd years. A tacit working arrangement did exist, for example in Armscor, the national weapons industry formed after the UN arms embargo in 1977, which involved both private and public sectors.

So in 1980, as a symbolic gesture, Botha convened two large national conferences with business leaders. The businessmen convinced Botha that the economy could not expand with apartheid's ideological brakes in place: job reservation had to go to meet the industrial sector's need for skilled manpower and blacks had to be trained for skilled jobs, which meant upgrading their education and admitting them to white-only technical institutions and universities. Businessmen also convinced him that a skilled workforce must be allowed to unionise in order to regularise labour relations, so black trade unions were granted increased recognition. The businessmen pointed out that there was no sense investing in training staff if they had no security of tenure. So this was introduced together with measures to make life in the townships more bearable, such as home ownership and some commercial development. Mortgages were made available for some high quality housing in black townships. In Soweto a new suburb called Selection Park was developed with elite houses beside a golf course, many with swimming pools. Black entrepreneurs and professionals bought them and they became a potent weapon in the Government's propaganda armoury as foreign journalists were brought in to see them.

Co-opting certain blacks and controlling those who dissented became part of a total strategy by whites who recognised that the old approach of brazen apartheid was not viable socially. It was also restrictive economically because an economy which was industrialising and growing as fast as South Africa's required a large pool of skilled labour, which in turn required racial barriers in the labour market to be reduced. And so, whites sought deliberately to cultivate a black urban middle class, offering the prospect of jobs to more skilled black workers and relaxing aspects of so-called 'petty apartheid' such as segregated park benches. Blacks in the Defence Force were given the same status as whites of equal rank, for the first time requiring whites to take orders from or salute senior blacks. Even initiatives to legitimise certain black trade unions could be seen as a method of co-opting and thereby bringing within an orderly official bargaining framework previously unruly unofficial and militant action by black workers.

These changes from the top down coincided with the changing needs and desires of a large section of the Afrikaners themselves. There was by now an Afrikaner entrepreneurial and technocratic class that made common cause with its English-speaking counterparts against some of apartheid's sacred cows. The aim of sending all blacks back to Bantustans was inimical to the interests of Afrikaner businessmen who, with the lack of skilled white workers, were also

desperate to train and employ skilled blacks. A better edu-
cated, more urbane and travelled generation of Afrikaners
had emerged at many levels, aware of the impracticability of
apartheid; of the manner in which it was thwarting
economic advance; and embarrassed by its crudity.

But by identifying with this new Afrikaner middle class,
Botha alienated the original constituency of the National Party
– the farmers and white workers. By then nearly half of all
economically active Afrikaners worked for the Government in
one capacity or another, including all those who administered
apartheid day to day. They were a vulnerable group who realised that, if apartheid went, they would go with it. Thus it was
that, although in the 1981 general election the National Party
was re-elected with a comfortable majority, the 'Verkrampte'
HNP – the hardliners who had quit the NP in 1969 – took
nearly 30 per cent of the Afrikaner vote, and Botha therefore
decided to slow down the pace of change.

The Government did decide to dump what it described as
'outdated' and 'unnecessary' apartheid laws, such as the prohibition of mixed-race marriages and sex across the colour
line, in an attempt to present itself to the world as reformist.
But there was never any intention of dismantling apartheid
by changing any of the fundamentals which entrenched political separation and ensured white domination and control.
A black middle class was to be allowed to develop which,
with the Coloureds and Indians, was to be co-opted into a
new alliance of insiders, to be rewarded with a greater share
of the economic cake and limited political rights over their
own race groups. These proposals were bitterly opposed by
Hertzhog's HNP. There was also deep discontent among
'Verkramptes' still within the National Party and 14 MPs
quit to form the Conservative Party in 1982 under the leadership of Andries Treurnicht, the powerful head of the
Transvaal NP. His breakaway Conservative Party was the
beneficiary of the discontent Botha's changes engendered
among Afrikaner traditionalists. This was extremely significant because it solidified the fracture in Afrikanerdom which
had first appeared in the battle inside the National Party
between 'Verligtes' and 'Verkramptes' a decade earlier.

But the Government was now locked into a programme
to cement a new order involving some concessions and the
co-option of key groups while retaining white dominance and
privilege. In April 1982 there was a concession to the ANC
when Mandela, Sisulu and three other Rivonia prisoners were
moved from Robben Island to the less bleak confines of

Pollsmoor Prison on the outskirts of Cape Town. In 1983 the Government put forward new constitutional proposals similar to those that Botha, as Chairman of a constitutional commission set up by Vorster, had proposed in 1977 but which were shelved. These envisaged a tricameral Parliament with separate houses for whites, Coloureds and Indians in which the white chamber was able to outvote the other two at all times. Black 'political rights' were to be limited to allowing them to elect local authorities in the townships. A whites-only referendum approved the proposals.

The Indian Congress called upon all Indians to boycott the elections of the Indian House and in January 1983 invited the Rev Allen Boesak, a Coloured and President of the World Alliance of Reform Churches, to address a meeting in Johannesburg at which he called for 'churches, civic organisations, trade unions, student organisations and sports bodies ... to unite on this issue, pool our resources, inform the people of the fraud that is about to be perpetrated in their name, and expose those plans for what they are'.

In August 1983, when the inaugural rally of the campaigning body Boesak had called for took place in the civic centre at Mitchell's Plain, the Coloured township near Cape Town, over 400 organisations sent delegates. About 10,000 people of all races attended and launched the United Democratic Front (UDF). The UDF proved a powerful force because it was so difficult for the Government to act against. Its member organisations had committees and many had premises: but the UDF had neither – nor did it have property or formal leaders for the police to seize. When Boesak and other UDF patrons were detained the UDF continued in limbo until its member groups next decided to activate it. The only policy it adopted was a watered-down version of the ANC's Freedom Charter, so bland that not even the Government could object to it. And the UDF declared that it did not 'purport to be a substitute movement to accredited people's liberation movements', which meant that it did not seek to replace the ANC or oppose it. Effectively it was acting as a surrogate ANC, as many of its members privately acknowledged. Meanwhile in May 1983 the ANC's military wing, Umkhonto, exploded a car bomb outside the Air Force HQ in Pretoria, killing 19 and injuring 200, both black and white. Later that year in a daring mission that shook the white community, Umkhonto also blew up a section of the Koeberg nuclear power station near Cape Town, delaying its commissioning by 18 months.

In a whites-only referendum in November 1983, the Conservative Party opposed Botha's new constitution on the grounds that it opened the gates to the black flood. The UDF and the Progressive Freedom Party (PFP) opposed it for failing to bring in blacks and the PFP further pointed out that by dividing the legislature itself on racial lines the new constitution actually strengthened apartheid. But predictably, the white electorate voted for it with a two-thirds majority.

For a year the UDF ran a strong campaign against the new constitution. Addressing mass rallies and recruiting supporters, it organised the most sustained and vigorous political campaign that black South Africa had ever been able to run. Partly because of this, the elections in August 1984 saw a derisory turnout of Coloureds and Indians as less than 20 per cent of those who were registered voted – one parliamentarian took his seat on the strength of a paltry 154 votes. Nevertheless the new three-chamber legislature met in September 1984 and for the first time Coloured and Indian representatives joined whites in the Parliament House in Cape Town. The UDF campaign for a boycott of the council elections in black townships in October 1983 was even more successful. An almost total boycott was secured. In many seats no candidates could be found to stand, and only 2 to 3 per cent of those registered bothered, or dared, to vote. Many of the councillors elected were middle-class blacks who were attracted by political office and the economic opportunities they expected it to deliver.

But the black anger which had fuelled the UDF's massive support was not extinguished and on 3 September 1984 violence erupted once again in the townships. It started in Sharpeville and five neighbouring Vaal Triangle townships after a build-up of grievances. These began with the council elections (in which less than 10 per cent of those eligible voted). There was ongoing dissatisfaction with rent rises and corruption by the new councillors who had privatised the state monopoly of township liquor stores, divided the stores equally among themselves, granted themselves 100 per cent loans repayable over 20 years and agreed that no new liquor licences would be issued until the loans had been repaid. Then some built themselves two-storey mansions with two-car garages, which stood out provocatively among everyone else's little matchbox houses and mud-daub shanties.

The violence had been triggered when the police shot dead a local hero, the captain of the Bophalong township

soccer team, on the night of 2 September. Early next morning an enraged mob of youths descended on the ornate
homes of the councillors, the first to die being the Deputy
Mayor, who was hacked to death in Sharpeville and whose
car and house were set on fire. Two more councillors were
killed that morning, one in Sebokeng and another, with a
guard, in Evaton. From there the youths went on the rampage and by mid-morning Sharpeville, Sebokeng and Evaton
were all ablaze. A peaceful protest march to the council
offices the same morning was fired on by the police and
from then on chaos reigned for two days as angry youths
stoned the police, burnt cars and set alight every commercial
building and police opened fire on anybody moving in the
townships. Thirty people were shot dead.

The rioting spread across the country – from the Vaal
Triangle to the East Rand to the squatter camps of Cape
Town and the townships of the Eastern Cape, to Durban's
Inanda and Umlazi and then back to Soweto. The unrest
spread wider and deeper than any previous disturbances,
from city to countryside and into South African *dorps* (small
towns). Outlying *dorps* of the Orange Free State and Northern Cape, where blacks had always been docile, suddenly
erupted. The Bantustans of Ciskei, KwaNdebele, Bophuthatswana and KwaZulu all saw outbreaks.

A wider range of groups was involved than had been in
Soweto in 1976, which had seen a youth revolution. This time
the UDF spanned generations and interest groups – trade unionists, educators, students, politicians, exiled ANC leaders
and former Black Consciousness leaders were all members.
White liberals and radicals were also involved, including the
National Union of South African Students (NUSAS). A variety
of strategies were employed: consumer and rent boycotts,
school boycotts, strikes and stay-aways, rallies, protest demonstrations and a mix of street confrontation with public and
private negotiation.

The 1984 troubles were more intense and lasted longer
than previous ones, raging for three years and resulting in
over 3000 deaths, 30,000 detentions and untold damage to
property and the national economy. The army was mobilised
and a state of emergency declared on two occasions to control it. But this was only partially achieved. The central aim
of the unrest was to make the townships ungovernable.
However this was not a plan decided upon by ANC strate-
gists in exile or its underground activists. Although the ANC
remained influential, there was a spontaneous reaction from

the grassroots in the townships. Thus, when black councillors fled or resigned, street or area committees were set up
which formed a rudimentary alternative administration that
effectively took over control of the townships. Residents
stopped paying rents to the government agencies and instead
the street or area committees collected fees. They also con-
scripted their supporters and decided when to call strikes or
boycotts. Black police were driven out of some townships and
the committees organised their own crime prevention forces.
People's courts were set up – Pretoria's Atteridgeville township had 12 of these, with an appeals court known as the
Advice Office, which heard cases ranging from political col-
laboration to assault, theft and even civil cases.

In the Port Elizabeth townships the UDF attained such
control that it was issuing hawkers' licences. White businessmen negotiated safe passage for their vehicles with the UDF.
Its leader in the area, Mkhuseli Jack, was in such demand
that he carried a bleeper so that he could be contacted easily.
The UDF called a consumer boycott in Port Elizabeth to
pressure businessmen into supporting demands for the release of political prisoners and an .end to the state of emergency. When the police detained Jack and his colleagues the
businessmen pleaded with the police to release them so that
they could negotiate an end to the boycott – and the police
complied. In a small harbinger of things to come, business
came before politics.

But although the movement effectively controlled the
townships – and the police and the white authorities were
forced to negotiate with it on township matters – its offers to
talk at national level met with little response. Instead, in
January 1985, Botha announced that Mandela would be released in return for a promise not to take action that would
lead to his rearrest. Mandela disdainfully rejected the offer in
a reply read to a UDF rally in February by his daughter
Zindzi.*

Frustration increased, and the violence intensified.
Umkhonto freedom fighters infiltrated townships and trained
groups of 'comrades' (as the young activists were known). In
February 1985 the police were confronted with organised

---

* See Mandela's autobiography, *Long Walk to Freedom*, for an
account of these initial contacts which eventually led to proper
negotiations.

street fighters as bursts of AK-47 automatic rifle fire scattered them. In KwaNdebele the unrest swelled to civil war as the 'comrades' fought pro-Government vigilantes and by the end of 1986 several administrators had quit and the request for independence was withdrawn. Though the leaders tried to impose restraint there was inevitably much savagery by the 'comrades', especially against those considered to be collaborators, and the gruesome practice of 'necklacing' began – placing a tyre filled with petrol around the neck of the victim and setting it alight.

Then in March 1985 police fired on a peaceful demonstration in Langa township, outside Uitenhage in the Cape, killing 20 people and wounding 27 – the worst massacre since Sharpeville. The Government met the rising black anger with increasingly repressive violence on the ground. But at the upper echelons there was a desire to avoid appearing ruthless in order not to jeopardise the Government's projection of itself as reformist. Botha's year of reformism had coincided with the advent of friendly conservative governments in Britain (Thatcher), the United States (Reagan) and West Germany (Kohl) – South Africa's most important trade and spiritual links with the outside world. All asserted that Botha should be given a chance and resisted moves for sanctions against South Africa, and Botha had no wish to disturb these promising relationships by using strong-arm methods. He was thus caught between a rock and a hard place. Relative Government restraint continued through much of 1985. But in mid-July a state of emergency was declared in 36 of the 300 magisterial districts. Hundreds of activists were detained briefly but the UDF was not banned.

Partly because of his friendship with Steve Biko and partly because he was a newspaper editor, Donald Woods' escape with his family in January 1978 had been given world-wide media publicity. Unusually, he was invited to address the UN Security Council, where he called for mandatory international economic sanctions. He also met President Carter, briefing him and arguing for economic sanctions, the cancellation of export–import bank credits and the withholding of visas for security force personnel (General van den Bergh, the head of BOSS, was refused entry soon afterwards). Having the advantage of being considered a moderate and conservative in European terms, Woods was invited to give personal briefings on South Africa to the heads of government in most of the democratic countries of Europe as well as

Australia, New Zealand, Canada, Japan, India and several African countries.

Woods' major effort was concentrated on the USA, where the American lecture circuit became a significant part of his life. Between 1978 and 1990 he lectured at 462 universities and addressed 18 state legislatures and over 50 major city governments – all of which held important investment portfolios related to South Africa. But the critical factor that made the USA the first major Western state to initiate effective economic sanctions against South Africa was its black vote which no voting district was able to ignore totally. Black Americans started insisting that the price of their vote was economic sanctions against South Africa. Another factor that added momentum to the sanctions campaign, particularly in countries not noted for strong anti-apartheid movements, was the production of major motion pictures against apartheid, including Richard Attenborough's *Cry Freedom* (based on Donald Woods' link to Steve Biko and seen world-wide by more than 600 million people). In these ways media pressures were mobilised world-wide in support of the rising level of internal struggle.

At the beginning of August 1985 it was said that Botha was about to make a speech signifying a giant step away from apartheid – the 'Rubicon speech' as it came to be known. But Botha became furious at extravagant speculation in the international press and believed he was the victim of a plot to push him well beyond where he intended to go. So when he came to speak at the Natal Congress of the National Party on 15 August it was a huge anti-climax, delivered with finger-wagging belligerence. He warned the world that he would not be pushed around by outside pressures or internal unrest.

For some time South Africa had experienced difficulty raising foreign loans and had been forced to take out high-interest short-term loans to raise much needed foreign capital, then getting the banks to roll these over each year. By August 1985 some 67 per cent of South Africa's $16.5 billion foreign debt was in loans that could be called up at any time. Botha's speech caused them to be. The first to move were the American banks, led by Chase Manhattan, followed by Britain, Germany and Switzerland. By the end of August there were demands for the repayment of $13 billion within four months and the Rand fell by 35 per cent in 13 days, reaching an all-time low.

Introduced at long last, these loan sanctions started to

create precisely the impact which had led anti-apartheid forces the world over to advocate them for decades. South Africa was unable to meet the repayments, froze debt and imposed foreign exchange controls, including the introduction of a two-tier exchange for the Rand: a 'commercial Rand' rate internally and a lower 'financial Rand' externally. The effect was to create a siege economy. Foreign exchange and development capital was denied and white living standards plunged. This was a decisive factor in the accelerating downfall of apartheid.

The apartheid Government's options were running out. And when Nelson Mandela was taken from Pollsmoor in November 1985 for surgery on an enlarged prostate gland to a hospital in Cape Town, the Minister of Justice, Kobie Coetsee, had a secret meeting with him there. After he was returned to Pollsmoor he was put in a cell in the prison hospital, away from his colleagues. Mandela asked to see them and explained that it was probable that the move might be to enable the Government to begin talks with him, and it was agreed not to protest at the change. Thereafter Coetsee had several more secret .meetings with him in a guest house in the prison grounds. Later that year Mandela was able to communicate the substance of these meetings to Oliver Tambo, who was then in Zambia, through his senior legal adviser George Bizos. Bizos flew to Lusaka and met Tambo, then made a second trip in February 1986, by which time Tambo had been able to consult with other exiled ANC leaders. He told Bizos that they had confidence in Mandela's ability to handle the situation and that he should carry on with their full support. After informing Mandela, Bizos met Coetsee to advise him of the position.

Botha made a more reformist speech when opening Parliament in February 1986, announcing that a national Congress of the National Party would be held in August to endorse a new constitution. In March he lifted the state of emergency. But the township unrest intensified and open rifts in the Government between political reformers and the 'securocrats' began to surface.

The visit to South Africa of the Commonwealth Eminent Persons Group (EPG) in May 1986 brought the rifts to a head. Headed by Malcolm Fraser, the Australian Prime Minister, and General Obasanjo of Nigeria, the EPG helped to initiate the first indirect dialogue between the ANC and the Government. General Obasanjo visited Mandela in February 1986, then the whole EPG met him in March and May in the Pollsmoor guest house. Following the May meeting the EPG drew up a 'possible negotiating concept', which they put to both the ANC and the Government. This included the release of Nelson Mandela and other political prisoners, unbanning the ANC and PAC, withdrawing the army from the townships and allowing free assembly and political activity, with the ANC agreeing to suspend its guerrilla activities and to enter into negotiations. The ANC indicated it might respond positively, but awaited the Government's reaction before finally deciding. From Pollsmoor Prison Mandela indicated his personal approval. But the securocrats won at a Cabinet meeting on 13 May, the EPG initiative was rejected and the Government dispatched military raids against 'ANC bases' in Zimbabwe, Botswana and Zambia. That such raids were often indiscriminate was shown by the fact that the 'base' in Zambia bombed by SA planes was in fact a United Nations camp full of Angolan and Namibian refugees.

In June another state of emergency was declared, more comprehensive and stringent than the last, placing the country under martial law. With the securocrats firmly in the saddle the reform programme was dropped and the Government launched the crackdown that the hawks had been demanding for so long. At the big National Party congress in August 1986 Botha made another defiant, belligerent speech to the world.

Then the total onslaught began. Organisations were banned, open-air gatherings prohibited and the police and military moved into the townships to detain 30,000, including 8000 children and 3000 women – more than in the entire 25 years since Sharpeville. The Government recruited special constables from the ranks of the unemployed and gave them six weeks' training in political repression. Vigilante bands were formed from township residents with cause to resent the 'comrades'' excesses, armed and turned loose on the more radical townships. Activists' homes were burnt and the offices of anti-apartheid organisations bombed. Political rivalries within the black community were exploited. As repression intensified and black leaders were detained, discipline slackened and groups vented their frustrations on each other. Bloody confrontations occurred between the UDF and the fundamentalist Black Consciousness organisation Azapo in Soweto and the Eastern Cape, and between the UDF and Buthelezi's Zulu force, Inkatha, in Natal.

As members of the street and area committees were detained or fled, the Government reinstated its own administrations and these regained control of the ungovernable townships. Roads were paved, sewerage installed and a massive housing programme commenced in 200 townships to eliminate the 'underlying social and economic factors which have caused unhappiness in the population'. Thirty four troublespots were targeted where troops cordoned off the township and conducted door-to-door searches, detaining anyone who seemed suspect. In the Port Elizabeth township of New Brighton, Mkhuseli Jack was again detained (and held until May 1989). Between 17 May and 12 June 1986 in the Crossroads squatter camp outside Cape Town, vigilantes (called 'witdoeke' because of the white scarves they wore) conducted two well-organised and massive raids which razed to the ground four satellite camps, driving some 75,000 people from their homes and killing hundreds. The security forces looked on, content that their clandestine strategy of arming and organising these vigilantes was proving fruitful.*

Abroad, anti-apartheid activists joined demonstrations organised by the AAM in solidarity with the resistance. There were also regular pickets outside South Africa House in London in support of political prisoners and those UDF leaders, trade union officers and others prosecuted in political trials. However, observing and offering support was often an anguished experience. In December 1986 we heard that our friends, Fabian and Florence Ribeiro, had been shot dead in their home in Mamelodi. (Fabian had been detained during the emergency and earlier that year their house had been petrol-bombed – he maintained by Government agents.) The Government reported that the assailants were black and gave the impression that the killing was the result of violence between black factions. But neighbours reported seeing two masked white men at the scene of the shooting who, when they tried to follow, fired upon them. And the registration number of a car seen outside the house was later traced to the security forces. Fabian had been compiling a dossier of injuries and torture to children he had examined after their release from detention and was interviewed on British television. My parents tried to send flowers, but were told that a public funeral had been banned, and they had to settle for a message sent through a relative in Pretoria.

---

* Despite denials at the time, it was confirmed in the 1990s that this strategy was authorised at the highest level of the Government.

By late 1987 the rebellion was virtually over and 97 townships were under military occupation. But the repression did
not totally crush the resistance nor win support for the Government's reform programme. Though disrupted organisa-
tionally, the resistance continued to retain the support of the
black community. UDF calls for stay-at-homes drew mass
responses and municipal elections in 1988 were heavily boycotted. And no black 'moderates' appeared to cooperate with
the Government in negotiating a new constitution that
would fall short of majority rule. The uprisings ended once
more with an outflow from the country of young black activists to continue the struggle with the ANC forces in exile.

However, Mandela's meetings with Botha and other senior
Government figures were paralleled by secret meetings between prominent Nationalists and the ANC from 1986 to
1990. These helped to break down the stereotypes that each
harboured about the other. In exile the ANC had established
an increasingly influential international network and the role
of anti-apartheid activists was increasingly directed at supporting it. In 1986 the ANC Director of Information Thabo
Mbeki, attending a Ford Foundation Conference in New
York, met the Chairman of the Broederbond ('Brotherhood'),
the Afrikaner secret society which had devised the apartheid
ideology and was the think-tank for Government strategy
after 1948. The meeting had a profound effect upon the
Afrikaner who, on his return home, resigned his job in order
to devote himself to promoting inter-racial understanding.

Other Broederbond members and Government advisers,
including F.W. de Klerk's brother Wimpie, became involved
in a series of 12 clandestine meetings in London between
November 1987 and May 1990. In another sign of business'
increasing pressure for change, these meetings were set up at
the request of the ANC by Consolidated Goldfields, a major
British mining house. A Stellenbosch academic, Willie Ester-
huyse, reported back to Botha via Niel Barnard of the
National Intelligence Service and Wimpie de Klerk did the
same for his brother. Mbeki and Jacob Zuma, the key ANC
figures, knew of the report-back arrangements from the
beginning. The meetings enabled the Government informally
to sound out the ANC's position on various matters and the
ANC to do the same on the Government's attitudes. For the
Afrikaners the meetings demolished the demonised image of
the ANC built up by years of propaganda, while the ANC
became sensitive to white anxieties, particularly to Afrikaner
fears of survival under black majority rule.

International business was anxious to promote some sort of rapprochement and there was now a tentative basis for further dialogue. At a meeting between a group of Afrikaner dissidents and the ANC in Dakar in 1987, both sides were surprised to find they had much in common and that there was a great deal of flexibility and negotiability. Meanwhile there was a realignment of white opposition forces to the left of the NP in 1988 when the PFP, the National Democratic Movement and the Independent Party combined to form the Democratic Party. Although peripheral to the main motors of change, this symbolised the more focused drive for reform which existed among a section of whites, mostly English speaking, who did not support the ANC and would in previous years have looked either to the old United Party or to Helen Suzman's Progressive Party.

Meanwhile sport had continued to be an important catalyst for change and an arena where the dynamics of apartheid's fracturing politics were contested. As we saw in chapter 5, during the mid-1970s there was a strategy of co-opting certain compliant black sports groups, with cricket and rugby leading the way. The white South African Cricket Association was able to incorporate some of the smaller non-white groups, but the dominant non-racial South African Cricket Board of Control refused to go along with this and its leading officials had their passports withdrawn and experienced police harassment. Co-option became an increasingly transparent attempt to preserve the racist power structure of white sport behind an image of integration, though it did present anti-apartheid campaigners with some of the dilemmas I had anticipated in 1977.

In 1979 a South African 'Barbarians' rugby side had toured Britain. It was organised by Danie Craven's South African Rugby Board (SARB) and had a mixed squad of eight whites, eight Africans and eight Coloureds. This was a new departure and illustrated how rugby had moved on, first from the all-white rigidity of 1969–70, and then from the 1974 concession when the touring British Lions were for the first time permitted to play two matches against separate African and Coloured teams. In this Barbarians team the Africans were drawn from the Africans-only South African Rugby Association (SARA) and the Coloureds from the Coloured-only South African Rugby Federation (SARF). SARA and SARF were affiliated to the white SARB, but only on a subservient basis, for SARB also had 22 white provincial units which could outvote the two black 'national' bodies. SARA and

SARF between them represented under 10,000 black rugby players, concentrated in the Cape. Most black players – over 50,000 – belonged to the non-racial South African Rugby Union. SARU was affiliated to the determinedly non-racial South African Council of Sport (SACOS) and rejected all overtures from SARB, did not cooperate over the Barbarians tour and condemned the blacks in the touring party as 'collaborators with apartheid'.

As a section of the AAM, the Stop All Racist Tours campaign coordinated demonstrations against the Barbarians tour. But it was clear that there was neither the appetite nor the political mood to repeat the direct action tactics of ten years earlier. It was also announced that the British Sports Council would be sending out a fact-finding commission to establish whether there was a case for relaxing the ban established under the 1977 Commonwealth Gleneagles Agreement. The Sports Council's Chairman Dickie Jeeps, a former rugby international, was known to have close contacts with the South Africans, and I had discussions with him.

Partly because of this, and concerned lest we lose the initiative in public argument over South Africans tours, I decided to firm up the proposals first developed in 1977 for reforms to banish apartheid from sport, and secured support for these from the annual meeting of the Anti-Apartheid Movement. In a memorandum submitted to the British Sports Council on behalf of the Stop All Racist Tours Committee in January 1980, I put forward a series of conditions to be fully satisfied for South Africa to be considered for readmission to world sport. These included an Act of Parliament specifically exempting all aspects of sport from the apartheid laws and regulations which restricted it: the Group Areas Act, Separate Amenities Act, Urban Areas Act, Liquor Act, Pass Laws and permits regulations. Part of the Act would forbid racially exclusive rules or conditions of membership in the constitution of any sports club or federation. All players, spectators and trainers would have the same rights of access to all sporting clubs and ground facilities throughout the territory of South Africa. The organisation of each and every sport would be entirely integrated on a non-racial basis. School sport would be fully integrated and a sports development programme was needed to raise black sport as a whole to the level of all sport in South Africa, with each citizen enjoying an equal proportion of state funds devoted to sport. All restrictions (banning orders, the confiscation of passports, refusal of exit visas) regarding the representatives of non-racial sport would be lifted, and police harassment of the non-

racial officials and players ended. If these conditions were ful-
filled, an international sports commission would go to South
Africa to establish whether a basis existed for their readmission
to world competition.

In fact the Sports Council delegation did not recommend
South Africa's readmission. But rugby – true to its reactionary ideology – continued with occasional breaches of the boycott, in open defiance of the Gleneagles Agreement. In 1980
a British Lions team toured, though it inadvertently exposed
the reality of sports apartheid. Despite playing against the
odd handpicked black player or co-opted side, one of the
Lions, Tony Ward, refused in 1981 to return with the Irish
rugby team, saying: 'At the end of the day you and I play a
game and then we go to the bar for a pint. If you are a black
in South Africa that is not possible. I go to the bar and you
go to your township or wherever ... That's neither rugby,
sporting nor moral.'

At the same time – although there had been no official
response to my proposals – further reforms were indeed hesi-
tantly implemented. First an elaborate system of special
licences was introduced to enable certain approved sports occasions to get around the apartheid laws restricting sport. When
this proved insufficient, some minor changes were made to
some of the key laws (for instance lifting liquor restrictions)
which had first been identified in my 1977 memorandum,
passed to the Sports Minister Piet Koornhof.

But virtually all sports activities still remained segregated
under the law and black sports facilities remained abysmal.
Where young white cricketers enjoyed green fields and well-
manicured pitches (such as I learnt to play on in the early
1960s as a schoolboy in Pretoria), the typical 'pitch' for a bud-
ding black cricketer was a dusty, rutted strip in a township.
While there were changes for the better in cricket, as in other
sports, they had not gone anything like far enough to warrant
South Africa's readmission. The problem all along was that
changes were made, not with the honest objective of establishing truly non-racial sport, but on the basis of seeing what the
Government or white sports leaders felt was the minimum
they could get away with. The irony is that, by their pathetic
catalogue of delay and prevarication, whites dug themselves
deeper and deeper into sports isolation. The price was remorselessly raised until reforms in sport were no longer sufficient.
Ultimately, fundamental political changes were necessary to
eradicate apartheid before South Africa could win a ticket back
into international sport.

By the early 1980s the non-racial sports organisations under the umbrella of SACOS were becoming more assertive
and confident that the bulk of world opinion was starting to
look to *them* rather than to white-dominated bodies decorated with 'Uncle Toms'. When the townships exploded,
arguments over the niceties of sports changes looked almost
obscene when viewed against police state brutality all over
the world's television screens in 1985–6. SACOS's slogan,
'No normal sport in an abnormal society', increasingly struck
a chord. Its insistence that sports isolation could not be
broken until apartheid itself had been broken appeared more
convincing, and anti-apartheid campaigners like myself were
more than content to stand back, support SACOS and let
events take their course. There was no need to put forward
the 'constructive' initiatives I felt had been necessary before.
Although international cricketers and other sportsmen were
enticed over with lucrative financial inducements for 'rebel'
tours, these were merely irritants to anti-apartheid movements. So was the case of the long-distance white South
African runner, Zola Budd. Although never criticising sports
apartheid, she was granted British .citizenship in record time
in 1984 in a transparent manoeuvre, sponsored by the *Daily
Mail*, to get her into the British Olympics team. But after
four miserably controversial years facing demonstrations in
Britain, and breaching athletic regulations by living in South
Africa for too long during the year, she fled back home.

During this period in the 1980s I also received periodic
invitations from white cricket leaders, other sports figures
and a national newspaper to go out to South Africa and 'see
for myself'. I always accepted these invitations in principle,
subject only to being able to go anywhere, talk to anyone
and – crucially – that the invitees persuade the Government
voluntarily to withdraw its 1969 ban on my entering the
country. This last condition was deliberately framed. Despite
private criticism within anti-apartheid circles, I was determined not to spurn the invitations. To have done so would
have played right into the hands of apartheid apologists who
would have been able to portray me as being unwilling for
dogmatic reasons to go and to acknowledge the 'changes'.
This would have undermined my credibility in the media
and with the middle-ground opinion which we had always
managed to secure for the sports boycotts. However, I was
equally only too aware that any such visit could be used by
the South Africans for propaganda purposes. So I refused to
apply for the entry ban to be lifted. The Government had

imposed it, and they must withdraw it. I was not going down on my knees to request it and to agree to any restrictive conditions that would doubtless have been imposed. The result on each of the four occasions over about nine years that these invitations were issued, was always the same: first there would be huge interest in the South African media at my acceptance of the invitation. Then there would be speculation and a certain amount of to-ing and fro-ing between the Government and the relevant sports officials (or national newspaper as the case may be). And finally a Government minister would refuse voluntarily to lift the ban. The impasse remained.

Then came an extraordinary meeting in October 1988 at Harare in Zimbabwe between Danie Craven and a top ANC delegation led by Thabo Mbeki. Also present were colleagues of Craven, leading ANC members such as Steve Tshwete and Ebrahim Patel of the non-racial South African Rugby Union (SARU), a SACOS affiliate. After two days of talks, they reached agreement that the ANC would press for the ban on the Springboks to be lifted if rugby was reorganised on a fully non-racial basis. Thabo Mbeki indicated a softening in the ANC's position on the sports and cultural boycott, stating that while the boycott should be maintained against racist institutions in South Africa, non-racial organisations had to be treated differently. This was a concession on the position that apartheid had to be abolished before sports links could be resumed.

It also followed a more interventionist role by the ANC in the sports issue which it had previously left to others, notably SAN-ROC and anti-apartheid groups externally, and SACOS internally. Five months earlier, in May 1988, SARU together with leaders of the UDF had set up a new group, the National Sports Congress (NSC). With the legal UDF acting in a tacit alliance with the illegal ANC, the NSC was effectively the sports arm of the ANC and publicly welcomed the Harare initiative. SACOS was more circumspect in public and extremely angry in private. Its more fundamentalist stance had served the anti-apartheid cause very effectively in 15 years of struggle and in the most difficult circumstances it had built up a well-run grassroots organisation in 24 sports. But its ideological rigidity was unsuited to the emerging era in which the ANC was increasingly able to assume centre stage as the open and legitimate voice of the black majority – and was more or less tacitly encouraged to do so by international political and business forces, as well as pragmatic elements within the South African Government. In this climate, although SACOS continued to play an important role, the NSC gradually started assuming the leading position which it was to display in organising grassroots demonstrations against the rebel Mike Gatting cricket tour early in 1990 (see next chapter).

The Harare meeting had been set up by one of South Africa's leading Afrikaner businessmen, Louis Luyt, also Chairman of the Transvaal Rugby Union. Over ten years before, he had been a leading sponsor of the apartheid front organisation, the Committee for Fairness in Sport, which had spent millions trying to get the boycott lifted. But with the ANC illegal, the meeting was highly controversial. President P.W. Botha was reported to have exploded with rage when informed. Craven's fervent desire for a tour to celebrate the following year's centenary of the white Rugby Board had led him to do the previously unthinkable and treat with the ANC – still regarded by most whites as the 'terrorist' arch-enemy. His action was an important sign of whites' growing desperation. The fact that Craven was encouraged by the business elements represented by the powerful Louis Luyt reflected the increasing impatience of the business world with the apartheid regime. It was also the final vindication of the anti-apartheid movement's sports boycott strategy. Within 18 years of stating at the time of the STST campaign that he would never have a black in his side, Craven, as the leading sports figure in South Africa, had moved from first talking to me in 1977 to finally talking to the hated ANC in 1988.

In the event Harare proved almost the last throw of the dice from the old sports era. If Craven had been allowed to implement his agreement with the ANC, it would have been a historic step forward. But he was blocked, both within his own rugby board and by the Government; ironically in view of his later reforming role, the Sports Minister, F.W. de Klerk, condemned Craven and Luyt for 'plunging politics knee-deep into rugby' and spelt out to them 'the negative consequences of this kind of action for South Africa in its fight against terrorism'. After an initial period of silence, President P.W. Botha's public condemnation was itself revealing of how powerful the ANC had become. He insisted that the ANC was wrapping itself in a cloak of piousness 'in order to stab you in the back with a dagger'. Sport, Botha added, was part of the ANC's terrain of 'subtle subversion' and 'there are still politically blind moles in this country who fail to see this'.

The result of the failed initiative was that the international forces remained solid in enforcing the boycott. Although many anti-apartheid activists were privately deeply unhappy with the ANC's tactics, I personally was always supportive. As it was later to show in political negotiations, the ANC was extremely sophisticated – sometimes too much so for international activists schooled in the harsh and necessary arts of no compromise. In reality our position had actually been strengthened by the ANC's demonstration of flexibility at Harare, for it revealed to the world that all the blockages were from white South Africa. From then onwards, sport – instead of being a means of confronting whites with the realisation that they had no alternative but to change – became a means of offering them a glimpse of a new post-apartheid South Africa in which their beloved sports tours could resume.

In the run-up to Nelson Mandela's seventieth birthday in July 1988, the cry went up around the world to 'Free Mandela'. The campaign had been carefully planned by the AAM and other anti-apartheid groups throughout the world. Mandela's international stature was by now immense and the signals that the Government had been courting him only reinforced his influence. He had become a symbol both of the oppression of apartheid and of the alternative to it. The climax of the campaign was a spectacular 'Free Mandela' concert at Wembley Stadium in London organised by the AAM and attended by 100,000 who saw some of the world's leading pop groups perform. International television rights had been negotiated by the AAM and the event was beamed by satellite to hundreds of millions across the globe. The success of the AAM's operation underlined its key new role as an agency for pressing the South Africans into making more concessions to the ANC and enhanced Mandela's stature as a household name across the world.

Against this background, and after a successful operation for tuberculosis later that year, Mandela was transferred from Pollsmoor prison and installed in a warder's house in the Victor Verster prison outside Paarl, about 35 miles to the east of Cape Town. Here he increasingly held court, sensing that his moment of destiny was coming, his lifestyle a bizarre mixture of prisoner and statesman. He responded to queries from the Government on the ANC's attitude on various issues, had family visits and received visitors (including leaders of the UDF and trade unions). He was even taken on drives into Cape Town and the countryside at weekends to familiarise himself with the country he had not seen for a quarter of a century.

His wife, Winnie Mandela, had become another symbol of the struggle for freedom, widely admired internationally for her courage and determination in raising a young family while her husband remained in prison. In 1977 she had been banished to the hostile and barren Brandfort in the Orange Free State. But in 1986 when her house was petrol bombed and burned down she defied her ban and returned to her home in Soweto. The Government did not move against her and, tragically for those like my parents who had known her when she was young, and to her many anti-apartheid admirers, she increasingly became a law unto herself. She refused to work in a collective way with the UDF and instead surrounded herself with a group of young men called the Mandela United Football Club, who accompanied her as bodyguards. Within months they were terrorising the neighbourhood and late in 1988 kidnapped four young men from a church refuge, interrogating and assaulting them. A week later the body of one of them – Stompie Moeketsi Seipei, a popular teenage activist – was found in a field, and the 'trainer' of the 'football team' was found guilty of his murder. From exile the ANC criticised Winnie's 'judgement' and in February 1989 the leaders of the UDF and COSATU declared that Mrs Mandela had abused 'the trust and confidence of the community'.

Meanwhile the ANC in exile had decided to set up a leadership group to enter South Africa and link up with activists, to give direction to their activities. This initiative, called Operation Vula (a shortening of the Zulu Vulindlela – 'open the road'), was to be led by Mac Maharaj, an Indian member of the ANC's national executive committee, an ex-Robben Island prisoner and an exile since 1976. In 1988 Maharaj and Siphiwe Nyanda entered South Africa through Swaziland and established the main base in Durban, where they set up an expanding underground network. In the next year Maharaj worked out a very effective communications link with Lusaka. Using a small laptop computer with a modem, he transmitted coded messages from public telephone booths to contacts in London and Amsterdam, who re-transmitted them to Lusaka. For the first time the ANC headquarters in Lusaka were in direct and regular contact with an underground agent inside South Africa. Later, Maharaj established a method of communicating with Mandela in prison and so acted as a conduit for messages between

Tambo and Mandela. He became Tambo's eyes and ears
inside the country. Ronnie Kasrils, a former Mkhonto Chief
of Intelligence, joined Maharaj in 1990.

In January 1989 a planned meeting between Mandela and
Botha was postponed when the President had a stroke. In
March Mandela sent Botha a ten-page memorandum in
which he said: 'The deepening political crisis in our country
has been a matter of grave concern to me for quite some
time, and I now consider it necessary in the national interest
for the African National Congress and the Government to
meet urgently to negotiate an effective political settlement.'
On 5 July Mandela was taken to meet Botha in the President's official residence in Cape Town. But, though the
meeting was warm, Botha was not forthcoming on the question of negotiation.

Botha meanwhile furiously resisted calls that he resign
because of ill health. But Cabinet Ministers led by F.W. de
Klerk, now installed as National Party leader, insisted. Botha
was deposed and, after the general election in September
1989, F.W. de Klerk became President. Despite having shown
no visible reformist signs he promised a 'new South Africa, a
totally changed South Africa'. And shortly afterwards, when
20,000 marchers led by Archbishop Desmond Tutu were
allowed to demonstrate in Cape Town against police killings,
things began to look hopeful.

De Klerk only became aware of the secret negotiations
with Mandela in 1988, four years after they had begun. But
he says that when he found out he supported them. He had
been regarded as a conservative and said that his change to
reformer was not a question of morality, but of practical
politics – part of a gradual realisation within the National
Party that apartheid was unworkable. He always refused to
apologise for apartheid, maintaining that it was merely a
policy that 'didn't work' and that his predecessors had been
dedicated, sincere people. Nor did he give any hint in the
September 1989 election campaign of any intention to negotiate with the ANC or to unban it, but instead denounced
the Democratic Party because some of its leaders had met
with the ANC. Yet within weeks of taking power he had
begun making dramatic changes.

De Klerk's real emancipation from apartheid ideology had
begun with his election as National Party leader in February
1989, after Botha's stroke. As party leader he made several
trips abroad – most unusual for a National Party leader –

where the heads of state that he met all emphasised the need for South Africa to change. Also crucial was the new international climate of an end to the Cold War following Mikhail Gorbachev's dramatic reforms, his internal *glasnost* and his foreign policy of active rapprochement with the West. This meant that neither Washington nor Moscow any longer had a strategic interest in perpetuating a regional conflict in Southern Africa which was instead becoming more of a headache. For Washington, white South Africa's role as a 'bulwark against Communism' had become obsolete. For Moscow, there were more pressing domestic demands for funds that had gone to support liberation groups like the ANC. The US was increasingly under pressure to take a more proactive anti-apartheid stance from a more assertive constituency of 40 million black Americans led by Jesse Jackson, a high profile candidate for the Presidency in 1988. For his part Gorbachev wanted to focus on the task of *perestroika* at home to revitalise an ailing Soviet economy, not to be bogged down any more in long drawn-out liberation wars. This meant that Pretoria's deeply-held perception of the black struggle against apartheid as a conspiracy orchestrated from Moscow was now redundant.

And of course, the biggest pressure on de Klerk to change was economic. Contrary to what apartheid apologists from Margaret Thatcher and Ronald Reagan downwards had maintained, the imposition of financial and other sanctions had bitten deeply. The chorus of white complaints about falling living standards was becoming more insistent, even hysterical. A final decisive factor was resistance to white rule. Anti-apartheid activists abroad were operating in a more favourable climate than ever. Boycotts were proving effective, from sports to arms. Within South Africa the ANC was increasingly powerful, operating through what were effectively surrogate organisations. There was growing internal resistance orchestrated by the UDF and the new Mass Democratic Movement formed in 1989 out of an alliance between the UDF and the black trade union movement, COSATU. The ANC's military wing Umkhonto had the ability to strike and wound. The trade unions were also a major threat, the 1987 miners' strike showing how the economy could be paralysed if subject to a general strike, which could be sparked off almost at any time.

A fortnight after de Klerk's election in September 1989 events began to accelerate at a breathless pace. First he ordered the release of one of the leading ANC figures, Govan Mbeki, from Robben Island. Shortly afterwards Walter Sisulu and seven other top ANC political prisoners were released and 80,000 people gathered in a football stadium in Johannesburg to welcome them. During December Mandela had three meetings with de Klerk. Speculation about his own release was rife. At long last it seemed as though events were beginning to take a more positive course – though those of us involved in the bitter decades of struggle could hardly believe that the end was beckoning.

8 TRANSITION

Spotting the white police van tailing us took me back with a jolt over 25 years to my childhood when surveillance by Pretoria's Security Police was the norm. This time the police were on our tail in the black township of New Brighton outside Port Elizabeth. It was December 1989 and I was with a camera crew on a secret visit to make a film for Granada Television's *World in Action*. Our guide was the local UDF leader, Mkhuseli Jack.

The idea for the visit had come from Linda MacDougall. One of Britain's most original and incisive TV producers, she had suggested to me a year before that I might go back to make a film. At first I had dismissed the very idea. I was banned from returning. It could be very dangerous. Old scores could well be settled. New evidence that officially sponsored 'death squads' were responsible for the murder of over 50 anti-apartheid activists would make it especially hazardous. In any case, how could such a visit be accomplished? If I were granted permission (itself improbable), the State would know exactly what I was doing and I could be a target, if not from an official agent, then certainly from an unofficial one. On the other hand, even though Linda had herself filmed there secretly on two occasions, surreptitiously entering the country on a train from Zimbabwe or Botswana, I was so well known that doing something similar was fraught with danger.

Still, Linda persisted. We met on and off for about a year. The prospect of being able to expose in a television film the still deeply entrenched racism in the sports system was an attractive one. But the logistics of a visit seemed impossible, and furthermore I was doubtful about its political impact. Then two things changed. First it was announced that the former England cricket captain Mike Gatting was taking out a 'rebel' England Eleven cricket tour in early January 1990. This could have been the start of a serious breach of the boycott. Second, Linda came up with an ingenious solution. I was to change my name by deed poll and *World in Action* would negotiate a new passport.

I was still in two minds about the idea. My wife Pat and my parents were implacably opposed because of the obvious dangers, but I decided to go ahead under conditions of strict secrecy. Only Linda, the programme's senior editors and my immediate family were in the know. (Pat was concerned that our sons, Sam aged 13 and Jake aged 11, should know in case something happened to me and so I told them the night before I left with a warning that I might be captured if they breathed a word: they didn't.) I took a week off work, assembled a new identity as a telecommunications businessman (an easy task since I was Head of Research for the Communication Workers' Union) and boarded a British Airways flight from Heathrow to Cape Town. My new passport bore the name 'Peter Western-Hain': Pat's maiden name being Western, this provided a half plausible reason for the Passport Office and my old solicitor friend Larry Grant who privately made the deed poll arrangements without being aware of the purpose. We assumed that the computer check on arrival would not spot the hyphenated Hain in my new name.

The overnight flight out was surreal. I was booked in Club Class among business travellers, reading a *Financial Times* and various telecommunications journals, and hoping there would not be a chance encounter with someone who would recognise me. We judged that the risk of recognition was slight because nobody would have imagined me going back and I wore glasses which I only used occasionally for long distance. My mood was one of both excitement and apprehension. What would it feel like being back again? Would I get through immigration security? If I was caught, what would happen to me, my family, my job, my hopes of being selected to stand for Parliament?

The plane stopped over at Johannesburg on the flight to Cape Town and, suddenly, there was the familiar old chatter of Africans as black cleaners appeared in the cabin to tidy up before we took off again. Ahead was the first major hurdle: getting through security at D.F. Malan airport. Linda

MacDougall had travelled out, also in secret, two weeks before to set up interviews and research locations, and we had kept in touch clandestinely by phone. As the plane circled down past Table Mountain I knew she would be waiting for me in the crowd greeting arrivals. Blinking in the Cape brightness and feeling hot in my suit, I walked across the tarmac and tried to appear relaxed as the official in the entry kiosk examined my passport. He looked up disinterestedly and muttered 'purpose of visit?' I replied 'business' and he waved me through into the unknown.

But my mood of relief soon altered. For then came one of those farcical coincidences which could have undone all our careful preparation. My luggage was missing. It wasn't on the carousel at baggage reclaim for our flight, and eventually I went to enquiries. If I left it, a stray bag turning up might provoke unwelcome interest; on the other hand I was attracting attention to myself by enquiring. I started filling in a form as directed, almost certain that the Coloured clerk was looking quizzically at me with what seemed like a half smile. Then, thankfully, there was a shout. The case had appeared at the other end of the baggage area. I picked it up in relief and walked through to find Linda outside, frantic with worry. Hardly speaking, we jumped into her hired BMW and started driving, checking we weren't being followed. (I was conscious of the way the anti-apartheid exiled poet Breyten Breytenbach had been allowed to enter in 1975 while the Security Police followed and then picked up all his contacts; he was arrested and imprisoned.)

During the following nine days in which we travelled illicitly around the country, I felt I was always on borrowed time. There were mixed emotions: it was eerie, it was dangerous – but exciting too. It was extraordinary to see the ANC's distinctive green, gold and black colours worn so openly and with pride. ANC graffiti decorated townships to an extent unimaginable when I was last there in 1966.

While I was interviewing activists who produced a monthly newspaper, *Saamstaan* (Solidarity), in Oudtshoorn, a backwater in the Karoo desert, Security Police patrolled busily in cars outside. One of their colleagues was bugging the office and phoned up, issuing threats over the 'shit' being told to 'these foreign journalists'. (Since my name had not been mentioned they were unaware of my presence inside.) Only four months previously, I was assured, the police would have burst in and rounded us up. Over the past two years they had harassed the paper's sellers, wounded one of the journalists with gunshot, burnt down its offices and restricted its editor, Reggie Oliphant. Yet here was Reggie telling me he had 'unrestricted himself' by talking to us and, though confined to his home between six at night and six in the morning, showing he would not be intimidated by threats to his family and on his own life. The old certainties of the iron-fist regime were crumbling.

Reggie, who had lost his job as a teacher in 1981 because of his campaigns for non-racial sport, was a fierce opponent of the Gatting rebel tour. Whatever impression of reform was being projected abroad by white cricket officials, he greeted with incredulity the very idea of mixed sport in a town like Oudtshoorn. Sports facilities for blacks and Coloureds in the town were almost non-existent by comparison with lavish provision for whites. Oudtshoorn's black pupils, deprived not just of sport but of school places, were prevented by the Government from filling an empty white high school, a training college and a technical college – all unused because of over-provision for whites and which together could have offered nearly 1000 places to desperate black children.

Carefully staged coaching sessions for blacks in a handful of well-known townships like Soweto could not conceal the reality that sports apartheid was alive and well in his town with its 80,000-strong population still rigidly segregated. Across the country, it was officially estimated at the time that well over 90 per cent of sport was still segregated. In Guguletu, one of the squalid townships on the Cape Flats to the south-east of the city, teachers spoke to me about the absence of sports facilities in their Government-controlled schools. As we talked on the township's only football field, covered by an uneven stretch of fine grey gravel littered with glass, they could not give their names for fear of dismissal. The very idea of *any* sports facilities seemed macabre in nearby Brown's Farm: a squatter settlement where 15,000 people lived in flimsy, hastily erected shacks and where women spent a good part of their day in an exhausting mile-long walk to collect water. On each journey they had to struggle across a motorway, several having been badly injured over the previous year by busy traffic. Yet the Government had refused to supply piped water. The kids there were so dirty and diseased, I couldn't help myself flinching as they gathered round for a friendly hug.

The Cape Flats, a mosaic of townships and squatter settlements, stretched over miles of flat sand down to the sea and was divided by buffer strips from white suburbs with swimming pools and blooming Jacaranda trees. Unemployment was estimated at 60 to 70 per cent. But still the population rose relentlessly beyond a million. Khayelitsha – 'our new home' – was the Government's name for one of the 'controlled squatting' areas. When people were first forcibly resettled there in 1981, most got a tiny block containing a toilet and cold water, standing on 90 square metres of sand. As there were no street names, each block was helpfully numbered. On these small sites, people had to put up their own homes – mostly made from old corrugated iron or timber. A lucky few were able to construct brick dwellings. For others home was under black plastic sheets stretched across rickety frames, with cardboard inside to keep out the wind. In the winter, it was wet and cold. In the summer, particularly when the South-Easter blew, it was like a dust bath. The sand got in your eyes, in your hair and (so it felt) under your skin too. After a few minutes I was desperate for a warm shower, wondering how on earth the local women could keep motivating themselves to hang out washing scrubbed pristine clean in cold-water tubs.

In Port Elizabeth, Ronnie Pillay and Khaya Majola, top black cricketers with the non-racial South African Cricket Board, told me despairingly how cricket was dying among their people because of abysmal facilities. They explained that they could not afford the plane fares to travel hundreds of miles to away matches in towns like Johannesburg, with the result that a three-day match turned into a five-day excursion by road – and their players could not get the time off work as white cricketers did. Official statistics showed that for every 1000 Rands the Government spent on sport, just *one* Rand went to blacks. Of every 100 cricket fields only 15 were available for blacks to play on – and most of these of very poor quality. More than this, the deliberate squashing of non-racial sports bodies outside the white-dominated racial structures continued. Non-racial sports officials still had restriction orders imposed on them. When I interviewed him, the President of the Western Cape National Sports Congress, Ngconde Balfour, had only recently emerged from nine months detention, mostly spent in solitary confinement.

Meanwhile white companies refused to offer sponsorship except to Government-approved bodies like Ali Bacher's South African Cricket Union which had invited the Gatting rebel tourists. The idea that cricket could be separated from politics remained incredible, especially since the Government was bankrolling the rebel tour by granting 90 per cent tax rebates to companies providing the several millions of pounds needed in sponsorship. Significantly, however, the sponsors, once keen to proclaim their support, were now keeping very quiet for fear of a black consumer boycott and trade union reprisals – another indication of the changing balance of power.

When I spotted that we were being followed by the Port Elizabeth Security Police in New Brighton township, we hastily dumped all the camera equipment in a dry cleaners' considered secure by Mkhuseli Jack. Linda MacDougall then confronted the tailing driver in her best 'English lady' style asserting loudly that this was her first time in a township and demanding to know why she couldn't travel about freely. I remained seated anonymously in the car whilst the officers backed off in embarrassment under her torrent.

Apart from that scary episode the trip proved highly successful. We were not detected. None of the interviewees knew I was coming, only that a 'British journalist' wanted to talk to them. Nonetheless, the moment I stepped off the plane at Oudtshoorn, Reggie Oliphant, waiting alongside the runway, claimed he recognised me. (We had never met before.) Most people couldn't believe I was there. Some stared as if seeing a ghost and Khaya Majola had tears in his eyes as we were introduced. In an audacious move, we even interviewed Danie Craven at his beautiful rugby headquarters in Stellenbosh. It was risky, but Linda was concerned that there should be some balance in the programme. He reacted in amazement as I walked in on camera: 'Aren't you scared?' he asked. We had counted on his old-fashioned sense of honour in upholding a promise he had made to Linda beforehand not to mention the interview until we had returned safely. To his credit he kept his word, despite not having been forewarned that I would be the interviewer, and the meeting produced a somewhat dramatic moment in the film.

The final hurdle was getting safely out through Jan Smuts airport, then notorious for its steely security. Again we had no trouble – though the tension obviously got to me because, unusually for me, and despite a very smooth flight, I was sick on the plane. There were a few curious questions on my return about having a tan in the middle of a British winter, but we managed to keep the venture secret over Christmas until two weeks later when the film had been edited and was ready for transmission. News was simultaneously broken in the *Guardian* and the South African morning papers.

We also alerted those who had helped us film that they could now talk about it. Val Rose-Christie, a white civil rights worker, had shown us round the Cape Flats which she knew so well. She was looking forward to telling friends, when she was startled on the drive into work to see banner headlines on posters alongside the road stating 'HAIN WAS HERE'. There were angry questions in the South African Parliament about how I had got in. When they eventually discovered the 'Western-Hain' connection, expensive modifications to the computer system at points of entry were put in place.

As an exercise in raising the protest profile around the Gatting rebel tour, it could hardly have been more successful. There was widespread media attention in Britain and the film got good ratings. More important, my predictions that the tour would be disrupted by angry demonstrators helped create a frenzy of interest within South Africa as there were stories in all the papers, making the link between the STST protests and the opposition likely to be faced by the rebel cricketers. (I had had private talks with some of the organisers about the tactical lessons which could be applied from STST.) With momentous political change in the air a sports tour had suddenly propelled itself into prominence, threatening to undo a lot of the goodwill that had been carefully built up between the Government and the ANC. The anti-apartheid sports campaign had come full circle. Where direct action had set the seal on tours abroad, now it was about to inflict fatal damage at home over a serious breach of the boycott. Such a prospect had been inconceivable seven years before when there had been another rebel cricket tour.

The departure of the Gatting team was delayed for several hours at London airport after an anti-apartheid activist had telephoned a hoax bomb warning. At Johannesburg, dogs, tear gas and batons were used to attack peaceful demonstrators awaiting their arrival and exposed to the world's media the brutality still at the heart of apartheid. The police action also showed how worried the authorities were about the growing movement which threatened to disrupt and maybe even curtail the rebel tour. Whites, both in Britain and inside South Africa, had seriously underestimated the strength of feeling and bitterness the tour had provoked among the black majority. Not only was there understandable resistance to a move which sought to smuggle white South Africa back into international competition, there was also a burning resentment that the rebel tourists were getting millions of pounds in fees which could have gone towards upgrading the pathetic level of black sports facilities.

The demonstrators – focused around the National Sports Congress which was aligned to the Mass Democratic Movement inside and the ANC outside – had a victory almost right away. The first three matches were rescheduled away from urban strongholds of political militancy to isolated towns. Carefully staged photo-calls for Gatting & Co to coach black youngsters in a handful of well-known townships like Soweto had to be abandoned. The furore following the ugly scenes at Johannesburg airport simply compounded the grotesque miscalculation made in staging the tour in the first place. Such was the pressure that, over drinks after one of the clandestine meetings in London between the ANC and the Government, there was discussion on the Gatting tour, after which it was suggested that an agreement be negotiated to stop the demonstrations in exchange for abandoning the second stage of the tour. One of the Afrikaners telephoned the white South African Cricket Union while the ANC called the NSC and the non-racial South African Cricket Board. The deal was made: the demonstrations ceased and the second stage was cancelled. Its organisers humiliated, the cricket rebels came home prematurely, their disappointment tempered by pay-offs averaging over £100,000.

I remained convinced that the sports boycott was as necessary as it had ever been. Rebel tours were simply postponing the day when South Africa could be readmitted. Even the Gatting tour organiser Ali Bacher appeared to concede that it had been a mistake. Following the deal to cut it short, he began to negotiate with the National Sports Congress, to agree upon a democratic, non-racial structure for cricket from school and club level up to national sides. From this followed the establishment of the United South African Cricket Board – the first unified sports group in the country's history.

Although some mixed sport existed in 1989–90, it was overwhelmingly in the larger cities like Johannesburg and Cape Town. In small towns in the middle of the country, such as Oudtshoorn, for example, there was no mixed sport at all. A survey of sports facilities in the Natal town of Pietermaritzburg found that whereas 11,567 white school pupils shared 32 cricket fields and 65 cricket nets, 13,608 Coloured and Indian pupils shared just 1 field and 5 nets, and there were *no* sports facilities in black schools. In the black townships of Umlazi and Lamontville outside Durban, 330,000 Africans shared 6 soccer fields and 2 swimming pools. In Durban itself, 212,000 whites had 146 soccer fields and 15 public swimming pools. For the country as a whole, despite being under one-fifth of the total population, whites possessed 73 per cent of all athletic tracks, 93 per cent of all golf courses, 83 per cent of all hockey fields, 85 per cent of all cricket fields, 93 per cent of all squash courts, 80 per cent of all badminton courts, 98 per cent of all bowling greens, 84 per cent of all swimming pools and 83 per cent of rugby fields.

I deployed these facts in campaigning with the Anti-Apartheid Movement after making the *World in Action* film. Building upon proposals first put forward 13 years before, I also proposed a charter for change which if implemented could permit South Africa's readmission to world sport:

1. White South African sports bodies should begin immediate negotiations with the NSC (National Sports Congress) and SACOS (South African Council on Sport) to establish unitary, non-racial, democratic sports organisations covering every sport and under the jurisdiction of a new, national, supervisory South African Sports Council.

2. These negotiations should run in parallel with political negotiations between the de Klerk Government on the one hand and the ANC and Mass Democratic Movement on the other. It is not possible to conceive of the readmission of South Africa to international sports competition on the basis of a sports settlement in isolation from a political/constitutional settlement. However, timing may differ.

3. The Government must pass laws specifically prohibiting the organisation or playing of sport on a racist basis. Legislation must prohibit racially exclusive clubs and racially exclusive school sport. All sports leagues and competitions – whether at school, club, provincial or national level – must by law be non-racial.

4. Legislation must open up all sports and leisure facilities – including swimming pools, parks, sports centres – to all races, with the right of appeal to a Race Relations Court to grant access should it be denied (the same right would exist for club and school sport etc).

5. Government and business must together ensure that the per capita expenditure on sport is equalised across all races. There should be a multi-million Rand crash pro-gramme to upgrade black sports facilities.

Having been there and seen for myself, I was in a strong position to puncture the arguments of apologists for South Africa. Back in STST days, my recent South African back-ground had always put me in a strong position in public debate: I had been there, I *knew*. The secret visit gave me a new authority over those apologists who had been back and forth at the invitation (and expense) of the Government or white sports bodies. The visit had also provided a unique opportunity to make sense of the tumultuous changes about to be unleashed in the country.

Among African National Congress activists (from Govan Mbeki downwards) operating through the UDF and the Mass Democratic Movement, there was a mood of confidence I had not expected. At all levels of the movement people who had just emerged from long years of detention spoke with deter-mined optimism about their plans for the future and their belief in the inevitability of white rule ending in a negotiated solution.

For its part, white authority seemed rather punch-drunk, unsure about the new ground rules. Thus, the press were banned from carrying Nelson Mandela's picture, but the ANC's colours were worn or displayed openly. Some protests were being permitted, provided they received prior police per-mission and conformed to tight restrictions. Others were still repressed – as when the Gatting rebel cricketers arrived at Johannesburg airport and when 4000 people marching for better education were dispersed with water-cannon in Cape Town. Despite having been agreed in advance, protests around the rebel tour quickly degenerated into violent clashes with police. At the same time morale among white police had collapsed due to Government legitimisation of protest and defiance. The exposure of officially sponsored 'death squads' also destabilised the security forces. So did President de Klerk's moves to dismantle the apparatus of his military-dominated predecessor around the National Security Council to reinforce his own power base.

The striking thing about going back was the extent to which the Government was being forced to change, not out of desire, but of necessity. The pressure from an increas-ingly defiant black majority was growing, their trade unions

powerful and their consumer power threatening white business. Even the very limited sanctions over loans and
investment had an impact: the economy was in bad shape
and whites complained constantly about depressed living
standards and economic expectations.

I was shown a confidential report of a top consortium of
white businesses, *Policies for a new Urban Future in South
Africa*, which came from the Private Sector Council on
Urbanisation. It charted the explosive growth in the black
population and described the urban crisis facing South Africa.
Already there were over seven million 'shack dwellers',
mostly squatting around large cities. About 70 per cent of
urban blacks did not have electricity or running water. Up to
40 per cent of economically active blacks were unemployed.
The consortium argued that this urban crisis was a major
threat to the development of a modern economy. It called for
the rapid eradication of all apartheid legislation and the
proper planning of urban development. With this sort of
pressure on the de Klerk Government, the respected South
African journalist, Phillip van Niekerk (who had helped
research the film and accompanied us) maintained we had
seen the 'last whites-only election'. The very thought was
difficult to comprehend, such had been the stranglehold of
apartheid.

Time did seem to be running out for whites-only rule.
There seemed a realisation that they no longer had sufficient
bullets. But I also sensed that whites were losing their *political will* to govern in the old way, ruthlessly maintaining
their privileges by force and, where appropriate, outright terror. Perhaps it was a little premature to seek parallels with
the still fresh tumult in Eastern Europe following Gorbachev's reforms and the collapse of the Soviet bloc. But
there was a sniff of the same demise of an old order which
in East Berlin had allowed people to pour buoyantly into
Security Police buildings which they had passed by in terror
only days before. The armed might of South Africa's police
state was still intact and the white political power still immense. But there comes a psychological moment when that
doesn't count any more, as in Romania at the same time as
my visit. South Africa appeared not too far from that point.

A minority of (mainly working class) whites were still
opposed to negotiations. They had lost out through economic
recession. White unemployment stood at 9 per cent – very
high by postwar standards. Privatisation to boost Government revenues had shaken out the jobs of Afrikaner loyalists

traditionally employed in the huge state sector. But – contrary to the much trumpeted apartheid folklore – Afrikaners were not going to retreat into their *laager* and 'fight until the blood rises to the horses' stirrups'. President de Klerk's reforms seemed to have the backing of a majority of whites. He at least appeared to realise that the game was up and that the Government needed to take advantage of the opportunity for a negotiated settlement now held out by Nelson Mandela, the ANC outside the country and the Mass Democratic Movement inside.

Events were moving very quickly. Nelson Mandela was gradually being transformed among many white media commentators from feared ogre to national saviour. Mandela's role was crucial: hugely popular at grassroots level in the townships and tactically sophisticated. But this was probably the last opportunity for a peaceful transition. If it failed, the balance of power within the resistance movement would shift downwards to younger, more militant elements sceptical about the prospects for successful negotiations. Also, if it failed, the world would turn its back as the country toppled into the abyss.

On 2 February 1990 de Klerk opened the first session of the new Parliament and made good his promise of a 'new South Africa'. The President surprised everyone by announcing the unbanning of the ANC, PAC and other outlawed organisations. He gave notice of the impending release of Mandela and hundreds of other political prisoners. And he declared his readiness to enter into negotiations with all of them to work out a new constitution in which everyone would enjoy equal rights. The impact of the speech was breathtaking. Listening to it broadcast live in London, I found that the implications took some time to sink in. Relatives, friends and colleagues phoned each other or chatted excitedly as they gathered in front of televisions or radios. We could hardly believe what we were hearing. But there was no going back – either for whites or for anti-apartheid forces: an entirely new political agenda had opened up.

The release of Nelson Mandela himself followed on 11 February. It had been announced in advance, indeed carefully orchestrated: Tim Bell, one of Margaret Thatcher's media gurus had been hired by the South African Government to advise and had carefully released the first photograph of Mandela for decades, meeting de Klerk in the President's rooms. It revealed, not the burly bearded freedom fighter in

the prime of his life which image for years had appeared the
world over, but a slim, dignified old African statesman with
a smile of destiny that hovered somewhere between the be-
nign and the all-knowing.

However, all the careful choreography nearly came un-
stuck, as Mandela revealed four years later in his autobiography. Without any notice he was told by de Klerk at a
meeting in the President's residence that he would be released the following day. He objected, explaining that his
family and the ANC would have no time to prepare. He
wanted a week's notice. He also insisted upon walking out of
Victor Verster prison, rather than being flown to Johannesburg as the Government had planned. After some to-ing and
fro-ing, they finally settled on a compromise: he would walk
out of Victor Verster, but, because the world's press had
already been informed, it would have to be the next day. 'It
was a tense moment and, at the time, neither of us saw any
irony in a prisoner asking not to be released and his jailer
attempting to release him', Mandela wrote.

I was in the South Wales Valleys, on what became the
first step in my eventual selection as the Neath constituency's Member of Parliament. Having slept the night in the
former coalmining village of Seven Sisters, I left at dawn to
hurry up by train for media interviews. Few who watched on
television will ever forget the image of the world's most
famous political prisoner, kept out of sight for over 25 years,
stepping to freedom through the gates in the prison fence: it
was one of those defining moments in history which many
ordinary onlookers will remember forever, recalling exactly
where they were and what they were doing. Millions of view-
ers in his country and across the world wept openly. With
his wife Winnie by his side Mandela walked towards the
massed ranks of TV cameras and spectators. Except for his
obvious humility and humanity, he looked almost regal, a
giant among his people. He then climbed into a car in an
ANC cavalcade for the 35-mile drive to Cape Town along a
road lined with smiling, waving crowds of all races.

Later, on the balcony of the City Hall, with the eager
upturned faces of the crowd filling the Grand Parade below,
raising his fist in the ANC salute he cried out,'Amandla!
Amandla! Mayibuye iAfrica!' ('Power! Power! Let Africa
return'). With Cyril Ramaphosa, the UDF and COSATU
leader, holding the microphone he said: 'Friends, comrades
and fellow South Africans, I greet you all in the name of
peace, democracy and freedom for all. I stand here before you

not as a prophet but as a humble servant of you, the people.'
The next day the Mandelas flew to Johannesburg and drove
to his small house in Orlando West, then on to Soweto's
football stadium where he spoke to a crowd of 85,000 in the
stands and about 120,000 outside. The exhilarating mood
surrounding his every appearance captivated not just black
South Africa but a world watching almost continuous live
broadcasts.

So the most turbulent era in South Africa's turbulent history had come to an optimistic end: Mandela and other leaders freed, the ANC and other outlawed organisations
unbanned and with an Afrikaner leader at last prepared to
negotiate with the 75 per cent of South Africans who had
never enjoyed democratic rights in their own country. But
although the new South Africa beckoned, its birth pangs
were still fraught with anguish.

Negotiations between the South African Government and the
ANC, previously *ad hoc* and exploratory now began in
earnest. The initial meetings had taken place in secret in
Switzerland, the only European country apart from Britain
that did not require entry visas for South Africans. The first
two had been at Lucerne on 12 September 1989 and 6 February 1990 – the third in Berne a fortnight later and the
final one two weeks after that in Zurich. The ANC representatives were led by Thabo Mkebi, the Government's by
Mike Louw, deputy head of the National Intelligence Service,
who had been present at the early meetings with Mandela.
They had discussed and agreed critical issues such as the
release of Mandela and the unbanning of the liberation
movements (the conclusions of which were reported back to
de Klerk). The later meetings made preliminary arrangements
for the return of the overseas ANC leaders to South Africa to
commence discussions with the Government.

There was much to settle before constitutional negotiations
could commence and this was done at a series of preliminary
meetings within South Africa for which representatives of the
ANC's external leadership returned. The first took place on 2
May 1990 at Groote Schuur, the official residence of the Prime
Minister in Cape Town, and lasted for three days. Temporary
indemnities against prosecution for having violated the security
laws were issued to all the ANC members who were to attend
and they were flown to Cape Town. The second meeting was
held on 7 August, after which Mandela announced the unilateral suspension of the ANC's armed struggle. Although there

was private criticism within the ANC and among anti-apartheid activists of this suspension, Mandela's supreme authority in the movement and his skill easily carried the day. He knew that for a peaceful transition to succeed there had to be give and take, and he and his fellow ANC negotiators progressively squeezed further concessions out of the de Klerk Government.

After these preliminary agreements the black parties set about the problems of returning exiles, released prisoners and local activists reacclimatising themselves and integrating themselves into cohesive political movements. For the ANC in particular the major challenge was to change from the culture and habits of an underground revolutionary movement to those of a political party about to engage in conventional politics.

With preliminary negotiations underway the ANC decided to keep the sanctions, Operation Vula and the guerrillas in place until it became clear that the negotiation process was irreversible. So Operation Vula remained operative. In July 1990 Mac Maharaj and Siphiwe Nyanda were arrested and in October, with seven others, were charged with 'attempting to overthrow the Government by force'. In March 1991 charges were dropped and they were all freed. (Maharaj later became Transport Minister and Nyanda General Secretary of the National Union of Mineworkers.)

Meanwhile international solidarity movements were changing their role too. Although maintaining a vigilant guard against premature breaches of sanctions and boycotts, the priority for groups like the Anti-Apartheid Movement was to strengthen the ANC's hand in its negotiations with de Klerk. This was tackled principally by building up Mandela's international profile with a punishing series of tours abroad. The AAM organised a 100,000 strong rock concert at Wembley Stadium to welcome him as a free leader. He appeared on stage between acts to deliver a powerful appeal for support and received a rapturous reception. I was also in New York's Yankee sports stadium during an American visit in June 1990 to hear him speak to another bumper crowd. He had earlier received the kind of ticker-tape welcome in the city normally reserved for only a select few. He took America by storm, dominating the media and being feted by its top politicians; significantly, his visit preceded that of de Klerk whose appearance went almost unnoticed. There was no doubt that the world, like black South Africa, was receiving Mandela as the country's leader-in-waiting, and awaited his imprimatur before sanctions could be lifted and normal relations established.

This was very significant, because, although de Klerk acted with courage and vision during this period, he was not about to hand over control. When he spoke of a 'New South Africa' he was not envisaging majority rule. Rather, he wanted 'power sharing' between what he called 'a nation of minorities' – the ten black tribes, the two white tribes and the Indians (for him the Afrikaans-speaking Coloured people would be regarded as Afrikaners). His strategy was to build an anti-ANC alliance with Chief Buthelezi's Inkatha movement and with other Bantustan leaders, and also with the Coloured and Indian minorities, which he assumed would share the whites' fear of majority rule. He wanted to allow time for Mandela to go from being the messianic figure he was at the time of his release, to just another fallible politician, pressured by the constraints of the situation into losing credibility with his mass of followers. And de Klerk wanted Western sympathy to shift from the ANC to his Government, as the world responded to his boldness, lifted sanctions and shrank from the ANC's commitment to socialism.

He produced a complicated constitutional plan, the effect of which would be that, while a black majority in the House of Representatives could pass legislation, a white minority in the Senate and the Executive would have the power to veto it. It was essentially a plan to retain white control, and black leaders attacked it as a fraud that would give the appearance of majority rule without the reality and would freeze apartheid's inequalities. And this was where the momentum for change de Klerk had unleashed began to take a life of its own, remorselessly undermining his strategy. Having once freed black leaders and legalised black politics, de Klerk had to make compromises; the white Government increasingly realised that it could no longer decide the future by itself.

The critical decision of how the new constitution was to be agreed became the main stumbling block. De Klerk wanted it done by a convention of all the existing political organisations. The ANC wanted it written by authentic representatives of the people, who could be determined only through an election. The procedure adopted would effectively decide the outcome of the constitutional negotiations before they began: whether the constitution would deliver a power-sharing or a majority rule system. Again, a combination of internal mass action and external solidarity from anti-apartheid movements was brought to bear on the Government in support of the ANC, and the pressure for a much more thorough democratisation than de Klerk had envisaged gathered force.

The ensuing deadlock was broken in January 1991 by Mandela, who called for an 'all-party congress' to negotiate the route to an elected Constituent Assembly. This offered the basis for compromise: first would come the multi-party convention the National Party wanted, which would negotiate an interim constitution under which one person, one vote elections would be held for a Constituent Assembly as the ANC wanted; and this Assembly would negotiate the final constitution for a new South Africa. But the multi-party convention would have the power to lay down certain binding principles restraining the Constituent Assembly – such as the requirement of special majorities on certain issues – so that the latter would not have an entirely free hand in drafting the final constitution.

The ANC endorsed the compromise in October 1991 and a preparatory meeting of all the participating parties took place. But the PAC insisted that the convention should be held outside South Africa, under a neutral chairman and rejected the two judges who had been appointed to chair it. When the ANC and NP overrode their objection, the PAC withdrew from both the preparatory meeting and the convention that followed. This process – that once the two major participants agreed, the proceedings went ahead – now became a pattern for the negotiations.

While all this was going on most of the apartheid laws were repealed. Nelson Mandela also continued his international visits and, in May 1991, came to the House of Commons in London to meet the Labour leader, Neil Kinnock. I was invited along with my mother – she to reunite with him for the first time since his Pretoria trial in 1962, I to meet him for the first time ever. As everyone else who was privileged to be introduced to Mandela confirmed, he had a gentle sense of authority that was unique. Around him raged the tensions of the negotiations and the bitter birth pangs of the new emerging politics. On international visits he would be pushed from pillar to post, with thousands of people – all important in some way – anxious to meet him. Yet he was relaxed, dignified, courteous to a fault and somehow above the ordinary mortals who pressed his flesh. He had the stillness of a man at the eye of a political storm. Of course he remembered her, he assured my mother. And he said to me how the direct action sports protests had provided such a fillip on Robben Island. I even taught him to say goodbye in Welsh: *'da bo chi'*, he repeated with a smile, his pronunciation perfect.

The first phase of the negotiations took place within a forum called the Convention for a Democratic South Africa (CODESA). The two main parties had promised that negotiations would begin before the end of 1991, so the first session was hastily convened to take place on 21 and 22 December, the weekend before Christmas. There were 228 delegates representing 19 political parties – the most representative cross-section of the country's leaders ever to meet. Mangosuthu Buthelezi was a conspicuous absentee: he had complained that one delegation for his Inkatha Freedom Party (IFP) was not enough and that there should be another for his Kwa-Zulu Bantustan administration and another for the king of the Zulus; when the CODESA organisers refused he stayed away, leaving the IFP delegation to be led by its chairman. He was the only political leader never to attend any session of the negotiating conventions and his behaviour became more erratic and egocentric.

The first plenary session of CODESA was a ritualistic event, with speaker after speaker reading prepared speeches. But it erupted after de Klerk, the last speaker, attacked the ANC for failing to disband its guerrilla force (despite a secret agreement between the Government and the ANC that Umkhonto need not be disbanded until the transition to democratic government was completed). Mandela responded angrily, accusing de Klerk of being 'less than frank' and describing him as 'the head of an illegitimate, discredited, minority regime'. De Klerk was visibly rattled, the exchange a portent of things to come.

CODESA had been divided into five working groups to cover different issues and the groups were supposed to submit their reports for endorsement to the second session, which had been scheduled for 15 May 1992. Working Group 2 was dealing with the central issues on which the settlement depended and whilst the other groups moved ahead fairly smoothly, Group 2 became bogged down. The ANC's negotiators in this group included Cyril Ramaphosa and Joe Slovo, the Government's included Gerrit Viljoen, the Constitutional Affairs Minister. The critical issues causing the delay were when and where the decisions would be made between power sharing and majority rule. The Government had accepted that the final constitution would be drafted by an elected Constituent Assembly, but the ANC had conceded that CODESA should agree on some binding basic principles. The Government's aim was to get as many issues as possible accepted under this procedure and thereby entrench its power-sharing model as a binding principle. The ANC, understandably, would not agree.

In March 1992 de Klerk called a whites-only referendum to seek approval for the negotiations. Mandela urged supporters not to disrupt the referendum and called on white ANC supporters to vote in favour. Once more, sport played a key political role. The ANC had encouraged the newly formed United Cricket Board to re-establish South Africa's international links. For the first time in a quarter of a century South Africa participated in a cricket venture abroad – except that it was agreed the team could not be called 'Springboks', its symbol instead being the national flower, a protea. The Cricket World Cup was staged in Australia and media coverage back in South Africa was intense. Live television and saturation press coverage enthralled the white population. And the Government, in a programme of carefully orchestrated political advertisements and TV broadcasts, used pictures from the World Cup to urge a YES vote as the only means of keeping such international sports participation. Where sport had been used as a stick to force change, now it was a carrot. De Klerk won with a two-thirds majority on an 85 per cent turnout. However he used this mandate, not simply to press ahead with the changes, but to toughen the National Party's negotiating stance at CODESA.

The second session, CODESA 2, began in May 1992 with the ANC trying to hurry things along and the NP trying to draw them out. The participants had decided on a decision-making formula they called 'sufficient consensus', which allowed the chair to judge whether there was sufficient agreement among the parties to allow negotiations to proceed. In practice this meant that if the ANC and NP agreed, the issue was considered settled and if not, there was deadlock. This enabled the NP to slow things down. The Working Group 2 confrontation arose when it transpired that the Group was still deadlocked over percentages – the ANC wanted ordinary clauses in the new constitution to require a two-thirds majority and the Government insisted upon 75 per cent which would effectively have given whites and a few allies a veto. The plenary session of CODESA 2 was delayed while Group 2 attempted to resolve these differences. Finally Cyril Ramaphosa announced the withdrawal of the ANC from Working Group 2. CODESA 2 collapsed and the plenary session met solely to receive a report of the failure and then to adjourn. It did not meet again.

Tensions had been rising outside CODESA while the

negotiating process was under way. The expectant masses in the townships grew restive at the Government's intransigence and delaying tactics, at a time when they were being subjected to increased political violence by Inkatha vigilantes from the migrant workers' hostels. These vigilantes were supported (and in many cases orchestrated) by the police. There was also growing evidence of the malevolent consequences of what became known as a 'third force', including security service resourced and inspired killings of black commuters to Johannesburg in trains and taxis. The balance within the ANC shifted towards its militant wing in mid-1992 and pressure intensified for a more activist campaign. Although Mandela and other ANC leaders continued to express optimism, the process of transition was in crisis.

In July 1990 Buthelezi had turned Inkatha, a self-styled Zulu 'cultural and liberation movement', into the Inkatha Freedom Party (IFP), a political party which he said would seek to establish a nationwide support base. Soon afterwards violence broke out in Sebokeng, a township 35 miles south of Johannesburg, between supporters of the IFP and the ANC. More than 30 people were killed and residents reported having seen busloads of rural Zulus brought into their township to take control of the hostels. A rash of similar attacks followed, using the hostels as bases to launch assaults upon residents, provoking reprisals against the hostels and starting a cycle of violence in the Witwatersrand townships.

In September 1990 attacks in commuter trains began, with armed men shooting and stabbing passengers, followed by attacks on the minibuses used as taxis. No arrests followed these savage outbursts, and there were allegations of the police either joining in the township attacks or standing by watching them. As the death toll mounted the ANC began accusing the Government of conducting a systematic destabilisation campaign and this soured relations between Mandela and de Klerk. In December 1992 independent investigations by the Goldstone Commission revealed that a group in Military Intelligence was behind the anti-ANC operations 'to sabotage reform', and de Klerk was obliged to fire or suspend 23 officers.

It was only in March 1994 that the Goldstone report revealed a terror campaign systematically organised by a 'third force' which reached right to the top of the security services, the police, the defence forces and even into the Cabinet. Based at Vlakplaas, a farm west of Pretoria, it was responsible for the

attacks on train commuters, the massacres launched from
Inkatha hostels and for supplying arms to Inkatha. It had also
trained Inkatha members in sabotage and assassination. It
established death squads in the KwaZulu police which murdered ANC members in KwaZulu/Natal. And it was responsible for the deaths of civil rights activists and prominent ANC
members throughout the country.

Given the scale of the third force's activity, it is hard to
believe de Klerk was ignorant of its existence since some of
his closest allies were involved. He and the Government as a
whole were still determined to destroy or at least cripple the
ANC. That way they might cling on to power even in the
democratised state which was now the price whites accepted
had to be paid for international approval and internal stability.

Endemic violence in KwaZulu/Natal between Zulu clans
had of course been a fact of life in South Africa long before
any ANC/Inkatha dispute. For 20 years Inkatha, the only
legal black political organisation in KwaZulu/Natal, was un-
challenged. Indeed during this period it was tacitly encouraged by the National Party as a political alternative to the
ANC. As a Zulu movement it was also a narrow *tribal* alternative. Although the ANC leadership had a preponderance of
Xhosas, the majority tribe, it had always been a non-tribal
movement and included Zulus, and now also Coloureds, Indians and whites. Inkatha thus became a vehicle for deliberately reincarnating tribalism which had for generations been
politically dormant in South Africa. But when the United
Democratic Front was formed in 1983, the younger, more
progressive Zulus identified with it, leaving Inkatha with its
main support among tribal traditionalists in rural areas.
Clashes erupted between the younger UDF supporters and
the older Inkatha vigilantes who were supported by the security services. These conflicts had intensified in 1987, when
the UDF made sweeping gains in the Natal midlands area
around Pietermaritzburg. Inkatha began aggressive and in-
timidatory recruitment drives, causing communities to form
defence committees to resist the recruiters, and so a cycle of
'attack, revenge, retaliation and retribution' became embed-
ded in the region's social fabric.

UDF activists and the ANC (after it was unbanned in
1990) were not slow to meet violence with violence, both in
Natal and the Witwatersrand townships. But they did not
operate with the collusion and assistance of the State's security forces, as it later transpired Inkatha did. There were a

number of incidents in Natal which police officers were later
found to have instigated and supported. From 1988 they had
sometimes also taken part in murderous attacks upon UDF
supporters – attacks which were covered up by the Government at the time.

De Klerk attempted to suggest that events prior to 1990
were water under the bridge, with the implication that they
they were a thing of the past. But overwhelming evidence
emerged that hit squads and destabilisation, together with
collusion between the security forces and Inkatha, actually
intensified *after* his negotiations with the ANC began. Political assassinations of prominent local figures averaged about
10 annually during the 1980s. This figure jumped to 28 in
1990, 60 in 1991 and 97 in 1992. Violence in Natal reached
new heights after Mandela's release, where in March 1990
some 12,000 Inkatha warriors attacked ANC communities to
the west of Pietermaritzburg, causing havoc and at least 35
deaths. Between December 1991 – when the negotiations
began in earnest – and early 1994, just before the elections,
over 11,000 were killed and many more maimed, sometimes
at the rate of 50 or 60 deaths daily.

The black community's belief that a 'third force' within
the military-security establishment was behind the violence,
in an effort to weaken the ANC and prevent it from organising and electioneering effectively, contributed to their widespread disillusionment at the collapse of CODESA 2, obliging
Mandela to respond. He had to accede to the demand for
more militancy. The ANC therefore decided to launch a
campaign of 'rolling mass action' – a series of strikes, boycotts and street demonstrations, which began on 16 June
1992, the anniversary of the 1976 Soweto uprising.

Before this could take effect, however, on the night of 17
June 1992 in Boipatong township south of Johannesburg, a
band of armed Zulus crept out of a migrant workers' hostel
and shot and hacked to death 38 people in their homes.
Residents claimed police had escorted the attackers and several said they had seen white men in tracksuits directing the
operations. Tapes from the police central control room that
day were destroyed and British experts who were later called
in were scathing about the inadequacy of the police investigation. When de Klerk tried to make a conciliatory visit to
Boipatong three days later a hostile crowd forced him to
leave and two hours later police fired on the still seething
crowd, killing at least three and wounding many more.

Soon afterwards Mandela announced the ANC's formal

withdrawal from negotiations, listing 14 demands the Government must meet before talks could resume. The most critical ones were an end to 'the regime's campaign of terror' against the ANC, the implementation of an earlier agreement to secure the migrant workers' hostels and a halt to the carrying of so-called 'traditional weapons' by Inkatha members (spears, clubs and machetes). The Government rejected these demands and what was described as a 'war of memoranda' ensued.

Boipatong strengthened the ANC's militant wing. One of the ANC's main complaints was that it was unable to organise and hold meetings in the 'self-governing' homelands, where such activity was prohibited by the local rulers while de Klerk was meanwhile pushing ahead with the building of his anti-ANC alliances. The ANC leaders accepted a suggestion by the militants to hold a mass demonstration in the Ciskei Bantustan. This went ahead on 7 September after de Klerk refused a request that the territory's military ruler Oupa Gqozo be removed and replaced by an interim administration with free political activity. A crowd of 80,000 marched on the Ciskei capital Bisho, just outside King William's Town in the Eastern Cape. When a column led by Ronnie Kasrils tried to bypass a line of black Ciskei soldiers officered by white South Africans, the soldiers opened fire. Twenty-eight marchers were killed and over 200 wounded.

The shock of Bisho reverberated through the nation and, because the demonstration had been their initiative, discredited the militants within the ANC. The balance of influence now swung back towards the negotiators. A week after the massacre Mandela reduced the ANC's 14 demands to 3: the release of 200 disputed political prisoners, the effective securing of 18 migrant workers' hostels in the Witwatersrand area identified by a United Nations' mission as a focus of violence, and a ban on carrying 'traditional weapons'. De Klerk reacted positively by inviting Mandela to join him at a summit meeting to find a way to end the violence.

Though relations between the ANC and the Government had been deteriorating at the top, they had been progressing at the next rung down. From June to December, with negotiations officially suspended, the two chief negotiators of Working Group 2 had continued meeting one on one, unnoticed, several times a week, trying to pick up the pieces. The old guard Gerrit Viljoen had retired after CODESA 2 and Roelf Meyer, one of a group of upwardly mobile young Afrikaner politicians, was appointed in his place as head of the Government's negotiating team. He and Cyril Ramaphosa had built a high level of mutual trust and an intuitive understanding of each other.

These meetings took place at a time when a subtle change in attitudes was occurring in both camps. In the Government camp the group of young Afrikaners faced the reality that their futures and career prospects lay in what would inevitably be a non-racial South Africa. The necessity to come to terms with the ANC seemed much more realistic than trying to build an anti-ANC alliance with Buthelezi and Inkatha (which was in any case losing support among Zulus). The older members of the de Klerk Cabinet were preoccupied with justifying their past activities and ensuring against too much change. But after Bisho the younger ministers gained the ascendancy.

And in the ANC a similar change was taking place, with some of the moderates exploring how they could bridge the gap between power sharing and majority rule. The lead came rather unexpectedly from Joe Slovo, now chairman of the Communist Party and a hate figure for whites, whom de Klerk had earlier tried to exclude from the Groote Schuur summit. In August he suggested a 'sunset clause' that would provide for compulsory power sharing for a fixed number of years then fall away, together with a general amnesty and an offer of security to the predominantly white civil service to prevent it obstructing change. The ANC built on Slovo's ideas and presented a proposal for a 'government of national unity and reconciliation' for three to five years, together with giving civil servants, police and military personnel guarantees that they could keep their jobs. A Mandela/de Klerk summit on 26 September 1992 ended with a record of understanding that committed the two sides to resume multi-party negotiations. But Buthelezi, whose behaviour now became increasingly mercurial and egotistical, saw the agreement as the government rejecting him and striking a coalition deal with the ANC. So he broke off relations with de Klerk.

The ANC and the Government had two further meetings, in December and January 1993. On 6 March a new Negotiating Council was convened at the World Trade Centre in Johannesburg, with 26 parties participating. The ANC and the Government progressed towards agreement, carrying most of the negotiating parties with them. Ramaphosa and Meyer were prominent in sorting out the sticking points. Once again Buthelezi pulled Inkatha out of the negotiations, forming an alliance with the right-wing white Conservative Party and with the Ciskei and Bophuthatswana Bantustans (which

he had hitherto despised), called the Concerned South
Africans Group (COSAG).

A month after negotiations resumed Chris Hani, the
General Secretary of the Communist Party and a famous
ANC guerrilla leader and hero to the militant young 'comrades', was shot dead at his Johannesburg home by a white
gunman. After a white neighbour reported the incident, the
assassin and a leading member of the Conservative Party,
Clive Derby Lewis, were later arrested and found guilty of
the murder. Mandela defused an explosive situation by issuing a moving appeal on national television in which he
said, 'A white man full of prejudice and hate ... committed
a deed so foul that our whole nation now teeters on the
brink of disaster. But a white woman, of Afrikaner origin,
risked her life so that we may know, and bring to justice,
the assassin.'

There were further signs of extremist white resistance to a
democratic transition. On 25 June, as delegates gathered for
their morning session at the World Trade Centre, a noisy mob
of 3000 Afrikaners, some in the uniform of the extremist Afrikaner Weerstandsbeweging (AWB – Afrikaner Resistance
Movement), crashed an armoured vehicle through the plate-
glass front and rampaged through the building, vandalising it
and jostling black delegates. The police guarding the building
did nothing. A further shock occurred on 25 July at St James's
Church in Cape Town, packed with over 1000 white worship-
pers, when five masked blacks stormed in, opened fire on the
congregation and fled, leaving 12 dead and 56 injured. Nobody
acknowledged responsibility and it was suspected that it might
again have been the work of the 'third force'.

In September 1993 a Transitional Executive Council (TEC)
was set up to work in tandem with the Government to prepare
for a free and fair general election on 27 April 1994. The
negotiations survived all the provocations, with the last clause
of the constitution being adopted on 18 November 1993. The
new constitution promised Cabinet seats to minority parties
for the first five years in a Government of National Unity
(GNU) and protected the jobs of white soldiers, police and civil
servants; it assigned important powers to nine provincial governments and included an entrenched Bill of Fundamental
Rights; it agreed a new flag and a new national anthem 'Nkosi
Sikelel' iAfrika' (God Bless Africa) alongside the existing 'Die
Stem van Suid Afrika' (the Voice of South Africa); there would
be an elected House of Assembly of 400 members and a Senate
of 90 (10 from each province).

The two chambers would draft a final constitution within two years. But, as the fundamental principles were already agreed, this was not expected to differ much from the interim charter except for the coalition agreement. The latter stipulated that the GNU would consist of a coalition of all parties winning more than 5 per cent in the election, with each awarded Cabinet seats in proportion to its votes. The GNU would rule for five years after the first one person, one vote election scheduled in April 1994, until the following election in 1999. The leader of the majority party would become president and there would be two deputy presidents – one from the party coming second and one from any third party that gained more than 20 per cent of the vote, failing which it would also go to the winning party.

But not all of the original 26 participants had been party to the agreement and the ANC and the Government set out to try to bring in the COSAG parties – now including the Afrikaner Volksfront (Peoples Front), following its formation in May 1993 from the Conservative Party, the AWB and the Committee of Generals, led by Ferdi Hartzenberg, the new leader of the Conservative Party following the death of Andries Treurnicht in April 1993. The Volksfront generals under Constand Viljoen held a series of secret meetings with the ANC which served to clear the air. (Viljoen said they got on better with the ANC than with the NP.) But these remained inconclusive on the Volksfront's demand for an Afrikaner *volkstaat* (peoples state).

Then in March 1994 there was a dramatic turning point that broke the back of COSAG's resistance to the coming election and split the white right into squabbling factions again. Under the agreement reached in the Negotiating Council, all blacks living in the Bantustans had their South African citizenship restored on 1 January 1994 and the Bantustans themselves were to be absorbed into South Africa's nine provinces on election day on 27 April. But early in March the autocratic President of Bophuthatswana, Lucas Mangope, announced that he would not participate in the election and that his Government would retain the independence granted it in 1977 under the apartheid system. Within days the territory's civil servants began striking, demanding that their wages and pensions be paid out in advance of 27 April, when their homeland was due to disappear. As the police joined the strike, anarchy spread and by 9 March the place was in chaos. Mangope appealed to his allies in the

Volksfront for help, stipulating that there must be no AWB men among the Volksfront forces.

But the AWB leader Eugene Terre'Blanche, who was a member of the Volksfront executive, immediately ordered the AWB's clandestine radio station to broadcast a call for all members of his commando units to head for Bophuthatswana. Constand Viljoen arranged for the main Volksfront forces, without their arms, to move into the capital, Mmabatho and establish themselves at the airport, where the Bophuthatswana Defence Force had agreed to arm them. But the AWB men, some 600 strong, reached Mmabatho before them. They came in their farm trucks and cars armed with hunting rifles, shotguns and pistols and rampaged through the town, yelling racial abuse at the locals and taking potshots at people, killing and wounding several.

As an Afrikaans newspaper reported angrily, for these racists it was a 'kafferskietpiekniek' (kaffir-shooting picnic). They so outraged the Bophuthatswana Defence Force that it mutinied, driving through the town shouting ANC slogans and firing on the AWB raiders. By now there was no chance of the Volksfront getting arms, so they withdrew. Some of the AWB rabble lost their way and roared along, still shooting at bystanders. The last car in one group that burst firing through a police roadblock was halted by police gunfire and two wounded men fell out onto the road. With TV cameras recording the event, one of the men begged for medical help but a young policeman screamed at him: 'Who do you think you are? What are you doing in my country?' Minutes later they were both shot dead. For the white rightists this traumatic experience, shown nationwide on South African TV, had a cathartic impact and blew away the ancient myth that the white race, with its superior arms and training, could always dominate the blacks. It destroyed the folklore that whites would always fight to the last to preserve their supremacy. Here they had indeed fought – and lost, their most fanatical militarists actually gunned down by a black, live on television.

After the debacle Mangope stepped down and the South African Ambassador was installed as administrator, to be joined later by an ANC co-administrator. Ten days later the Ciskei leader Brigadier Gqozo resigned and asked the TEC to appoint an interim administration. And Constand Viljoen, with only ten minutes to go to the midnight deadline, registered a new party, the Freedom Front (FF), to participate in the election.

Unlike Mangope and Gqozo, Buthelezi had a measure of popular support in his homeland, KwaZulu. But he was very isolated – apart from Inkatha, only the Conservative Party had not registered for the election. Although the ANC and the Government went to great lengths to persuade him to participate, they eventually decided to go ahead without Inkatha, turning their attention instead to how to hold an election in a hostile KwaZulu/Natal. A state of emergency was declared in Natal and troops began moving in. After a secret Inkatha military training camp was disrupted, Buthelezi asked for international mediation. Mandela and de Klerk agreed, but when Buthelezi insisted that the election date itself must be part of the mediation agenda, they demurred and the mediators returned home.

Eventually, only a week before the first of the three election days, the Inkatha leader finally agreed to take part. Eighty million ballot papers had already been printed, with the names of 18 participating parties in the national and provincial elections. Eighty million separate stickers would have to be printed and attached to the bottom of the ballot papers, and a special session of Parliament would have to be called on 25 April to pass legislation permitting Inkatha's late registration. It was agreed to do both and Inkatha was in. So South Africa was ready at last for her first ever non-racial, one person, one vote election. The dream which had sustained generations of struggle, but which seemed so impossible, was at last in sight.

9 VICTORY

The last time I had seen Poen Ah Dong and Aubrey Apples was when they waved us a tearful goodbye into exile at Pretoria railway station in March 1966 when I was 16. Now aged 44, tears were shed again after I flew in as an international parliamentary observer a few days before the election. At Poen Ah Dong's house in the Coloured township of Eersterust outside Pretoria, all the children and grandchildren were lined up to greet me. Some proudly bore the names of my mother and father.

It wasn't at all like my secret visit in December 1989. Then there had been fear on the flight over and anxiety throughout the visit. Now there was hope and excitement. The day was bright and clear as I was driven straight from Jan Smuts airport by the Welsh political journalist Max Perkins and his television crew from Wales' HTV channel. They went ahead to knock on Poen's door and I waited until beckoned to walk in and be filmed. As I climbed out of the car I was suddenly overcome with extreme emotion and had to check myself – similar feelings were to recur in the days to come.

'Welcome home to the new South Africa', Poen greeted me warmly with a big hug. With him was Aubrey Apples, now blind, as well as scores of relatives, young and old. Among those missing were David Rathswaffo, Alban Thumbran and Poen's wife Poppie, none of whom had lived to see the new South Africa. Poen said that if he hadn't been asked to keep the meeting low key due to concern for my safety, the whole township would have turned out. It was to be the first of a series of reunions and events signifying the remarkable victory of the struggle against apartheid.

There were only a few hours to spare before I had to rejoin the team of parliamentary observers for the first briefing. So we went quickly to find our old house at The Willows which was just a few miles away. The surrounding area to the front and side had been completely altered by three decades of suburban property development. Eventually – there it was: the distinctive pair of linked *rondavels* seemed to have been preserved in time, although the grounds were markedly different and the swimming pool a great deal smarter. There was the front door which I had opened to a Security Police officer bearing my mother's banning order. The *kopje* behind had been declared a protected area and was therefore much the same. I looked up, searching for the tree branch where the stone thrown by the Security Policeman had bounced as he was chased up the hill by my father 30 years earlier. Now the bush and scrub looked innocent and fresh in the tranquillity of the morning sun.

We began filming a television interview outside the front door, having got permission from the person who answered it, without disclosing my identity. As the camera rolled a car pulled up and a woman got out and walked up the terrace steps. Concerned in case there might be a confrontation, I nevertheless continued answering questions. Then I caught her looking hard at me. It was Margaret Beerstecher who had lived in the house next door, but had since moved over to our old home. Recognising me, she called out excitedly and we talked of old times. Pretoria was full of memories and, driving back, it was absolutely extraordinary seeing Nelson Mandela posters up in the middle of the city. Mandela smiling from lamp posts in Pretoria of all places! Not for the last time I wondered: was this *really* happening?

But out there somewhere the old South Africa still lurked. A bomb planted by the white extremists of the Nazi-like AWB exploded outside the ANC's headquarters near our hotel in Johannesburg, killing and maiming ANC activists, candidates and passers-by. It happened shortly before we arrived and I carried my bags to the hotel through debris and milling crowds. Police and military were everywhere. Thankfully, however, such terrorism was not repeated: it was apartheid in rigor mortis.

After a briefing on our duties as observers, the HTV crew drove me to see Hugh Lewin, back at home after years in prison and exile, and now heading up the Institute for the Advancement of Journalism which specialised in training blacks. His home was in the comfortable suburb erected after the black township of Sophiatown had been cleared in the 1950s – an action which had provoked international protest led by Trevor Huddleston. Hugh spoke of his time in prison when he heard of the rugby tour demonstrations. The atmosphere was relaxed and optimistic. He was confident the ANC would poll better than many white pundits were forecasting. I was beginning to feel at ease, though the contrast with the South Africa we had left was almost too stark to comprehend. That evening I went on an impromptu visit to a cabaret bar in Market Square with fellow Labour MP Diane Abbott and our mutual friend, South African-born Ann Pettifor. (Diane, Britain's first black woman MP, would not have been allowed into such a venue, let alone have been allowed to vote in years past.) The audience, mixed-race and young, laughed together at the comedian, a sharp observer of the absurdities of the old South Africa.

But if the Market Square bar could have been in any modern metropolitan city, Alexandra township the next morning was an antidote to all illusions. An appalling slum covered in rotting rubbish, with dusty tracks, shanty dwellings, rudimentary sewage and little running water, it was just next to Sandton, one of the plushest suburbs in the world. A popular venue for tourists, its Sandton Sun Hotel stands upon an opulent shopping precinct with piped music, space-age lifts and artificial waterfalls. Black valet parkers, smartly turned out in red uniforms and caps, park your car, carry your bags and even clean your tennis shoes. After tending to your every need, it's home to poverty-stricken Alexandra. The local ANC organiser showed us round the township and we interviewed residents on what they thought it would be like to vote. Despite the squalor the atmosphere was infectiously buoyant.

Then it was off to the Wanderers, headquarters of South African cricket, to meet Ali Bacher. 'You were right Peter, I was wrong', he said as the cameras rolled, confirming how the 1970 tour cancellation had been a watershed. I did not remind him about the Gatting tour fiasco he had master-minded four years earlier – that seemed out of kilter with the spirit of unity and forgiveness in the newly constituted United South African Cricket Board. At the stadium there was a sign stating spectators who ran on the pitch would be prosecuted. It seemed an appropriate point for me to be filmed. Alongside Bacher's office, Khaya Majola had his. I'd first met him four years earlier in Port Elizabeth during the secret visit. He was then an outsider, a dissident in the fight for non-racial cricket who had sacrificed his career and spurned lucrative offers to become a token black. Now he was Director of Cricket Development in the townships. Assisting Khaya was Conrad Hunte, the great West Indian opening batsman of the 1960s, out on an English-sponsored coaching programme for young players in the townships. I told Conrad I'd seen him in Nottingham when we went up to the Trent Bridge Test match in 1966, and reminded him that he had written during the height of the STST campaign as a member of Moral Rearmament complaining that I was too 'militant'; he laughed in embarrassment.

Back in Pretoria that evening there was a reception at the British Embassy. The Ambassador, Sir Anthony Reeve, was modern, informal and astute – a far cry from the ex-colonial gents we knew in the early 1960s and who were obstacles to change rather than facilitators. An Afrikaner woman introduced herself from 'foreign affairs' in the South African civil service. 'It's a real privilege meeting you', she said, 'you have done so much for us'. Apparently I was no longer quite the ogre of old. The cacophony of change was becoming almost too much.

The next day, the eve of poll, the *Daily Mirror* asked to interview me. I had previously shied away from publicity because I was still worried that it might attract unwanted attention from the extreme right. Indeed, I went to some lengths before the visit to avoid being spotted on the list of observers. The *Mirror* photographer took me to the Wanderers and again to Alexandra. Then, in an impromptu move, I accompanied him to the Carlton Centre for the final press conference which Nelson Mandela was giving before the poll. The lax security worried me: if I could get in without a pass, what about somebody with malevolent intent? Mandela presided over the event with his usual saintly, benevolent authority.

At the *Mirror*'s instigation I sent a note up to the ANC's press spokesman, Carl Niehaus, whom I had met briefly amid the bomb debris outside our hotel. Would there be an opportunity to be photographed with Mandela? I was beckoned up at the end. There was a scrum with photographers clambering around him and I felt embarrassed that the *Mirror* man seemed to be most responsible for this. Then, unexpectedly, we were ushered into an ante-room and I found myself alone with Mandela as he rested after the press conference. We chatted for around ten minutes. He was tranquillity personified, saying that although he supposed he should be jumping for joy in anticipation, he could only feel a stillness. It was almost as if he too couldn't quite comprehend that this historic moment had arrived at long last. It was a privilege just being present. Everybody – from the press to his personal staff – treated him as something extremely precious: the man who held the whole country's future in his hands.

That afternoon came my first 'observer' activity with a Lesotho MP, Washington Mohele. Our taxi driver, Desmond Khoza, a professional bookkeeper who had lost his job, was a well-informed ANC supporter. At the introductions, he turned round and gave me a hard look in amazement – his face breaking out into a big smile. 'I can't believe it's you', he said, 'after all these years, how wonderful to be driving you'. He later enquired after my parents whose activities he had followed in the 1960s.

The special voting on Tuesday was for disabled or elderly citizens, and we were assigned to two plush white suburbs. It was all low-key, with everything prim and proper. A number of the women running the polling stations, surprised to recognise me, were friendly in a rather reserved way. Unknown to me, back in London, my parents were voting – for the ANC – having discovered that their old South African identity cards were acceptable. They queued up joyfully with hundreds of others outside the Methodist Central Hall in Westminster, one of three polling stations in London.

On that historic Wednesday morning, 27 April 1994, we left the hotel promptly at 6 a.m. for Orlando West and East, the homes of Sisulu and Mandela, in Soweto. From the car we could see the goldmine dumps looming in the early mist. Desmond Khoza came from Orlando so we had no difficulty finding polling stations, which would otherwise have been awkward because we were simply given lists of rather inadequate addresses – typical of the rudimentary organisation around the election.

We arrived at our first polling station at about 6.30 a.m. Although polling was only due to begin half an hour later, there were hundreds, maybe thousands already queueing up to vote, their mood calm and expectant. More were streaming in out of the morning haze as the sun lifted. Everybody was delighted to receive us and it was soon evident that the democratic niceties were being almost painfully respected; the calm seriousness with which the polling officials handled their first-ever democratic election engagingly moving.

Because Desmond was an official driver for international

observers we were able to take him in to jump the queues and vote first. He waited anxiously to have his hand stamped. Then, as he put his ballot form in the box, he turned to catch my eye, smiling, part triumphant, part astonished – before leaving the polling station with a broad grin and punching the air in excitement. Hardly able to accept that, in middle age, he had actually voted for the first time in his life, he had been worried in case his ballot paper might be snatched away at the last minute. It was the same for thousands around us in Soweto and millions across the country, many of whom queued quietly in the burning heat for many hours to exercise the democratic rights they had so long and so mercilessly been denied. After voting, an old woman – perhaps in her nineties – was led shuffling away with a smile of eternity gracing her weathered face as young men bounced confidently out in their trainers, saluting their friends. After all those years, all the bitterness, the killings, the violence, the lives wasted away in prison, here it was actually happening: constitutional apartheid being exorcised. I couldn't help metaphorically pinching myself.

However the logistical problems were immense. Some polling stations were not opening until midday because they didn't have elementary equipment like stamps, the handspray for identifying those who had voted, ballot papers and so on. I wondered whether it was deliberate in such an obvious ANC stronghold – maybe a last ditch effort at sabotage? Over in Orlando West one polling station was surrounded by outside broadcasters, radio and television, including those from the BBC. President de Klerk had just been to vote. But they were considering closing the station shortly due to a shortage of ballot papers – no doubt conveniently after, rather than before, de Klerk's media-staged appearance. At a nearby polling station we bumped into Helen Suzman clutching makeshift voting equipment: she was determined that the process should not fail.

Late into the afternoon, people were still queuing to vote outside polling churches, schools and municipal buildings. Some were still being issued with temporary voting cards in a building ironically called 'Uncle Tom Hall'. The peaceful atmosphere contrasted with the carnage and strife of the preceding years. Party monitors from the ANC and Inkatha (who might literally have been shooting at each other beforehand) stood together amicably, flanked by their old enemy, the Nationalists, all diligently democratic as they earnestly scrutinised the procedure.

In Soweto, where multiple murder and mayhem was a daily occurrence, crime and violence simply disappeared for those few days. Even the police were friendly. White policemen, sporting machine guns, welcomed me as an election observer and even allowed a memento photo among them. Happy and relaxed in the sunshine, they expressed relief that it was going peacefully as they guarded the very democratic process which was ending their brutal history of repression. The only exception was an Inkatha-dominated polling station in a hostel area in Orlando East into which Desmond as an ANC supporter was frightened to drive. There were armed Security Police who reminded me all too uncomfortably of the bad old days, looking sinister and quite out of place with the carnival atmosphere of joy and wonder infecting everybody else.

The next day we went to Alexandra township and to the white suburbs, Edenvale and Lombardy East and Rembrandt Park. It was as interesting and moving an experience in the white suburbs. Blacks and whites queued together for hours to vote, chatting for the first time as equals. Again I was welcomed – the ANC agent Shantie Naidoo couldn't believe her eyes. Nor could a grey-haired white National Party councillor, schooled in years of apartheid rule. 'Are you *the* Peter Hain?' he asked in amazement. He stuck out his hand, gave me a warm handshake and asked for my autograph. Not so many years before, he'd cheerfully have had me kneecapped. I ended up signing autographs for other whites. The new South Africa was stepping forward with a verve and excitement that was hard to believe but wondrous to behold.

However, that evening there was a dose of the same old blinkered white / South African flight from reality. It came from my cousin Peter Stocks who took me for a meal. He was hospitable and it was nice meeting again after 30 years. But it was also irritating. Unlike his daughter, Debbie, who joined us, he was expecting the Nationalists, the Democratic Party and Inkatha to do very well and the ANC to fall significantly short of a 50 per cent vote – almost the exact opposite of what transpired. Clearly whites were still alarmed and unsure. Some had hoarded great amounts of food at home in case the election provoked – who knew what?

The next day was an anticlimax because we should have been observing the counting. The chaos around the election meant that voting was extended in some areas, KwaZulu and Northern Transvaal for example. Why this prevented a start being made on counting in places like Johannesburg where voting had gone relatively smoothly, it was hard to know. The election administration had been shambolic – a sad contrast with the beautiful process of voting itself. Watching the wall-to-wall television coverage with a racial mix of presenters was another sign of dramatic change, as was the fact that I was invited into the studio to do a live SA TV interview for the first time.

Finally on the Saturday morning I travelled to observe the counting, with fellow Labour MPs Bob Hughes and Paul Boateng, to Benoni where Bob had been at school. Virtually nothing was happening when we arrived in an Indian township at 9 a.m. However we were able to see the ballot papers being unfolded for reconciliation purposes and turned upside down. It was possible to get an idea of the vote: seemingly over 90 per cent for the ANC. We then decided to go to Benoni City Hall where there were predominantly white and mixed area votes to count. By now my initial anxiety had evaporated in the euphoria and I was relaxed when people recognised me and came up to talk. One ANC agent, a Coloured woman in her sixties, who had been with Trevor Huddleston when Sophiatown had been cleared in the late 1950s, suddenly threw her arms round me and kept saying 'thank you'. Yet people like her had suffered all those years and, whatever contribution we'd made from a position of safety abroad didn't really seem to compare.

How did the white presiding officer think it would go? 'An ANC landslide.' What did he feel about that? 'No problem – actually it's a relief, having apartheid lifted off our backs.' Such equanimity from a former military policeman who had seen action in the notorious guerrilla flashpoint, the Kaprivi strip. This boded well. His courtesy and helpfulness notwithstanding, we could hardly observe any serious counting because of procedural delays and mix-ups. So we returned to the hotel and then went down to the ANC headquarters nearby, picking our way through the remaining glass and rubble from the bombing. There by pure chance we bumped into Walter Sisulu, standing around in the foyer like anybody else; the Vice-President of the ANC had lost none of his earthy humility.

My last look at the election was on television before flying out. With many results now in, the ANC was standing at 54 per cent and rising. It was an incredible lump-in-the-throat feeling to watch the citadels of white power falling as the votes piled up. Although I had no illusions that an election observer could really know what was going on, our presence was an important deterrent to any potential wrong-doing. It was a privilege to have been a tiny part of the process, to observe spellbound as all the years of struggle finally bore fruit.

The elections for both the National Assembly and nine provincial legislatures were simultaneously conducted under a proportional representation (PR) system. Each party ran a list of candidates, 200 national and 200 regional for the National Assembly, and nine separate provincial lists for each provincial legislature. Voters thus selected a *party*, not a specific candidate.

The form of PR adopted is probably the simplest possible voting system, because the citizens were able to vote wherever they were, and vote for well-known symbols and pictures of the party leaders. The list system also provided central party control over the nomination of candidates and so enabled parties to insert key officials, who stood little chance of being elected in any specific constituency, into competitive positions on the party list. It benefited ANC mobilisation of its support base and ensured the return of its senior white and Indian members, who would otherwise have no hope of being elected.

As was to be expected in the circumstances, there were irregularities and delays at many polling stations. But on the whole the proceedings were surprisingly good humoured. The Independent Electoral Commission (IEC) declared itself satisfied with the result. But there was chaos and trouble in six former 'homelands' – Transkei, Ciskei, Venda, Lebowa, Gazankulu and KwaZulu – and the IEC was inundated with complaints of irregularities. Consequently the Transitional Executive Council (TEC) decided to allow them an extra day's voting, on 29 April.

The results were announced on the 6 May, after delays caused by counting difficulties and allegations of tampering with ballot boxes, especially in the midlands and northern districts of KwaZulu-Natal. The ANC won 62.65 per cent of the votes cast and 252 seats; the NP 20.39 per cent and 82 seats; the IFP 10.54 per cent and 43 seats; the Freedom Front 2.17 per cent and 9 seats; the Democratic Party 1.73 per cent and 7 seats; the PAC 1.25 per cent and 5 seats and the small African Christian Democratic party 0.25 per cent and 2 seats. No other party polled well enough to obtain a seat. The ANC vote was overwhelmingly black (94 per cent), with 4 per cent Coloured support, 1.5 per cent Indian and only 0.5 per cent white. In contrast, although the NP's majority support was white, 30 per cent was Coloured, 14 per cent black and 7 per cent Indian. Ironically therefore the party of apartheid enjoyed proportionately most cross-racial support.

With victory in seven out of nine provinces the results were a triumph for the ANC. But the NP, IFP and FF could also take comfort from them. Though only 15 per cent of the population was white, the NP won over 20 per cent of the vote; it is probable that the NP won the Indian and Coloured communities by as large a margin as it won the white community, and it also won the Western Cape provincial district. Having rejoined the electoral process at a very late stage the IFP, essentially a KwaZulu/Natal Party, did well to win over 10 per cent of the vote nationally, as well as taking the KwaZulu/Natal province itself (though the latter was marred by so much vote-rigging that the ANC may well have been the real victor).

Even the FF's Constand Viljoen came out quite well, having achieved what he set out to do: split the white right in two (thus lessening the chance of Afrikaner anti-system violence), and put the issue of an Afrikaner *volkstaat* firmly on the agenda. Although he must have realised that a *volkstaat* was a non-starter, he appreciated that debating the issue over the five-year life of the GNU would reduce the threat of immediate and, possibly, violent secession by small enclaves of the white right in their heartlands of Northern Transvaal and the North West. The clear losers were the DP and the PAC. The former failed to break out of its suburban white base. The latter squandered a favourable position through bad leadership, bad organisation and detachment from the community. Even in the PAC heartland of the Western Cape it was beaten by the tiny African Christian Democratic Party.

No accurate population figures were available and estimates had to be made on the probable number of electors in each region in order to arrive at the turnout. On this basis it was estimated as rising from 80 per cent in KwaZulu-Natal (obviously affected by the unrest) to 92 per cent in the Northern and Eastern Cape, producing an average of 86 per cent. The IEC estimated that there were just under 21 million voters, of whom 68.5 per cent were African, 18.8 per cent white, 9.8 per cent Coloured and 2.9 per cent Indian.

The spoilt ballot paper rate varied from 0.5 per cent in the Western Cape to 1.2 per cent in the Northwest, giving a national rate of 1.0 per cent, remarkably low in a country with much illiteracy and where voting for over 80 per cent of

MAP 5   SOUTH AFRICA, MAY 1994

the population was a new and bewildering experience. This nicely confounded the age-old sneers of patronising whites who maintained blacks were too ignorant to understand how to vote.

The new Parliament was certainly the most representative in South Africa's history. But black South Africans were still disproportionately under-represented. Just over half the new National Assembly members were black (from 73 per cent of the electorate) and 27 per cent were white (15 per cent of the electorate). The Indian community had the highest representation, with 10.8 per cent of members and the Speaker from 3 per cent of the electorate. Women's representation improved dramatically to 22 per cent, almost entirely due to the ANC which had over 25 per cent of its parliamentary party as women, including the Speaker.

The first Cabinet of National Unity was announced on 11 May. The ANC with the President (Nelson Mandela) and first Deputy President (Thabo Mbeki), had 18 of the 27 ministerial portfolios and 8 of the 12 deputy positions, reflecting their share of the national vote. The NP were given the second Deputy President (F.W. de Klerk), six ministerial positions and three deputy posts, together with the Deputy Speaker. In contrast to accepted procedure elsewhere, senior portfolios were allocated to opponents of the ANC, the NP getting Finance, Provincial Affairs, Constitutional Development (Roelf Meyer) and Agriculture. The IFP secured three ministerial positions, Buthelezi getting the influential Home Affairs portfolio, and one deputy post. Both black and Coloured communities were proportionately under-represented in the Cabinet compared with Indians and whites.

The Presidential inauguration took place on 10 May 1994 in Pretoria, South Africa's administrative capital, 1000 miles to the north-west of Cape Town. There, at the grand neo-classical Government offices, the Union Buildings, which lords it over the city from its perch on the hillside of Meintjieskop, VIP dignitaries sat in the sun on the terraces that step down the hill. On the broad lawns below a multi-racial crowd of over 50,000 waited expectantly for the swearing-in of South Africa's first black President.

In addition to the heads of state who would normally be expected at such an event, among the great and good were long-standing supporters of the ANC, Cuba's Fidel Castro and Palestine's Yasser Arafat. Zulu and Xhosa praise singers – hybrids of poet laureate and court jester – jinked and extolled the new president's virtues until, at 12.16 p.m., Nelson Mandela rose:

> In the presence of those assembled here, and in full realisation of the high calling I assume as president in the service of the Republic of South Africa I, Nelson Rolihlahla Mandela, do hereby swear to be faithful to the Republic of South Africa, and do solemnly and sincerely promise ...

Towards the end of his inaugural speech, the new President declared: 'Never, never and never again shall it be that this beautiful land will again experience the oppression of one by another and suffer the indignity of being the skunk of the world.' The 4000 assembled VIPs rose spontaneously to their feet for an ovation in a moment of genuine emotion. And, as the cheering died away, across the city over the Muckleneuk Ridge, came the roar of helicopter gunships, jet fighters in acrobatic flights trailing the new South Africa flag, swooping in to salute to their first ever black Commander-in-Chief.

'MANDELA'S BOKS': the banner brandished six months later in the crowd for the South Africa–Wales rugby international at Cardiff Arms Park said it all. For my parents and me, present as guests, it was a thrill to see Chester Williams, the black Springbok winger, scoring tries for his country.

A week before, on the eve of the Swansea match, I joined the new Sports Minister, Steve Tshwete, at the top table. In 1969, when I had been organising to disrupt the Springbok tour, he had been organising rugby matches as a political prisoner with Nelson Mandela on Robben Island. I also found myself a guest of honour at dinners welcoming the South Africans at my home ground in Neath, The Gnoll, savouring the moment with Arthob Petersen, Coloured executive committee member of the new, united South African Rugby Football Union. (A year later, on 15 November 1995, the Springbok captain, Francois Pienaar, shook my hand enthusiastically at an official reception for his victorious team in the Embassy building outside which we had held so many protests and vigils.)

At the same time, while the South Africans had embraced the new, non-racial rugby era, for a good few of their Welsh, Scottish and English hosts, the Springboks' return was, after an indecent interlude, 'business as usual'. They had been just as happy to welcome the old racist South Africa, and seemed not to have absorbed the lesson of history: that apartheid would not have been defeated without uncompromising opposition, including rugby isolation. My old opponent Wilf Wooller was unrepentant: 'That bastard Peter Hain – thank God he's a socialist', he said at a pre-match reception in Cardiff. Amidst the celebrations, I took the opportunity to remind British rugby that, by failing to take a stand early enough, it helped ensure that generations of young black and Coloured rugby players never had the chance to play for their country. There was a debt to redeem: to ensure that young blacks in the poverty-stricken townships got the facilities and the opportunities to play and to tour – unlike their fathers, grandfathers and great-grandfathers.

On such occasions, the moments to savour continued to pile up for all anti-apartheid activists as we greeted each other in amazement. In July 1994, I had been invited to Lord's by Ali Bacher as a guest of the visiting South African team for the first Test since 1965 and couldn't help celebrating South Africa's win. A few weeks before I had volunteered to welcome them at the airport. The following year, in July 1995, the first ever tour by the Soweto cricket club took place. One of their matches was in South Wales, in the Neath valley, a few miles down from my home, against Ynysygerwn, one of the leading village clubs in the country, which had made me their patron. The tourists were to say afterwards that it was the highlight of a most successful tour.

Appropriately, the team of youngsters was captained by one of the leading anti-apartheid cricketers, Khaya Majola. Ali Bacher came down and I also invited Tom Cartwright (who had been replaced by Basil d'Oliveira in 1968) and who added to the sense of history coming full circle. The Mayor of Neath put on a civic reception and the day ended very late with celebrations, presentations and Khaya Majola, a big man in every sense, crying on my shoulder. Welsh songs from the Onllwyn Male Voice Choir competed with the singing from the Soweto players who had earlier performed an ANC *toi toi* and chant on the pitch as they left the field. The match was drawn on the last ball, the teams sharing 444 hard-fought runs. 'There I was wondering who I wanted to win, when Nelson Mandela swooped in and made it a draw', I quipped at the post-match presentations. It had indeed seemed like divine intervention.

A few weeks later Mandela did intervene at the World Cup rugby final between the Springboks and the New Zealanders staged in South Africa. In a masterstroke he turned up to greet the teams in a Springbok cap and jersey, uniting the whole

nation in a famous rugby victory. Even a year into his government, sport was still as potent a force for change as it had
always been in the history of the rise and fall of apartheid. So it
remained in February 1996 when, cheered on by Mandela (this
time clad in the national soccer jersey), the South African
soccer team won the African Nations Cup against the odds.
'From the moment he turned up at our hotel hours before the
match, we knew defeat was impossible', said the captain, Neil
Tovey. Mandela, a keen boxer in his youth, knew all along that
there was one thing that could unite whites and blacks: both
were mad about sport and obsessed with winning. 'Sport is not
just an activity on the beach', commented Steve Tshwete, 'it
plays a very dynamic role in building our nation'.

Another historic, though less publicised, moment occurred on
29 October 1994. At a meeting at the Trades Union Congress in London, the Anti-Apartheid Movement, for nearly 40
years the leading such group in the world, wound itself up.
　The ANC Deputy General Secretary, Cheryl Carolus, who
had flown in overnight from Johannesburg, marked the occasion with a ringing testimony to the AAM's work. Among
others, the veteran Labour MP, Joan Lestor, spoke. There
were tributes to AAM stalwarts, including Ethel de Keyser
and Abdul Minty. Bob Hughes, Labour MP for Aberdeen
North, had carried the movement's banner as its Chairman
for many crucial years. Dick Caborn, Labour MP for Sheffield
Central, had been its Treasurer, at one point helping rescue
the organisation from near bankruptcy, such was its campaigning burden. Mike Terry, Executive Secretary, had
worked tirelessly and selflessly during the critical period since
the late 1970s. In a simple ceremony, and to a standing
ovation, the three of them lifted the AAM's banner and
folded it up. It had done its job: supporting the struggle
inside; maintaining the pressure for sanctions and boycotts
outside. As Abdul Minty remarked: 'The AAM was a movement committed like few others to bringing about its own
early end.'
　We had steadfastly maintained our strategy against an
onslaught from apartheid apologists. The hypocrisy of Conservative MPs such as John Carlisle, who had shamelessly
backed the Nationalist Government and accepted generous
'freebie' trips from its front organisations, was now exposed.
It rather stuck in the craw to be present as many of these
Conservative MPs queued up to be seen with Nelson
Mandela when he visited the House of Commons, even

though they had previously denounced him as a 'terrorist'. In the early 1980s the Young Conservatives produced badges stating 'Hang Nelson Mandela' and I, among others, had angry confrontations with them at university campus meetings. But history had vindicated the AAM and all who supported it. In its place Action for Southern Africa was launched to provide support for the new country.

Christmas Day 1994: sunburning weather by 7.30 in the morning, pre-lunch drinks on the lawn and roast turkey on the verandah. It was like an action replay of my childhood.

We had never expected to return. And although I had experienced the exhilaration of the election, my parents still had a residual apprehension about going back – even to the new South Africa. But the holiday was a joy, though it did leave my parents very unsettled on their return to Britain. Together with them, my wife Pat, sons Sam and Jake, sister Sally, her partner Arthur and baby daughter Connie, we went as a group. VIP limos waited on the airport tarmac in Cape Town for a surprise welcome. Just a few miles away were the docks where, under Security Police surveillance, we had boarded the liner for Britain 29 years before.

Later, we could see the old railway tracks on the dockside where we had arrived after our Berlin corridor-type journey from Pretoria. It was hard to imagine those dark days as we lunched at the old docks, now a marina, seals lazily bobbing up and down at the quayside. Up the majestic Table Mountain by cable car we looked out over the beauty of the Cape Peninsula, surely one of the sights of the world. 'The fairest cape of all', said Francis Drake. And, yes, there beyond the Atlantic breakers, shimmering in the haze, Robben Island, where Nelson Mandela and so many others had spent the prime of their lives. It had somehow lost its grim menace with day trips and visits to his old cell a tourist attraction.

Mandela sat astride his nation almost God-like. Even whites, fearful before the elections, now worshipped him. 'Isn't *our* President wonderful', they would say. He symbolised the transformation from evil to hope. On our first evening, at a *braaivleis* at Andre Odendaal's home, we encountered a poignant tribute to Mandela's extraordinary influence. Andre, a white Afrikaner involved in the anti-apartheid struggle, whom I had first met during my 1989 secret visit, told how his mother had for several years refused to recognise his marriage to an Asian or to meet her and their mixed-race children. Then came the months after the election. Slowly the fear ebbed as

Mandela mutated from Satan to saviour. Blacks weren't going to burn her out of her farm in the Afrikaner hinterland after all. She invited his family to visit, though not yet at the farm (a mixed marriage would still shame her in the eyes of her neighbours). They should book into a hotel in the nearby town and meet in the car park. He brought her her grandson. She paused, then reached for the baby, cradling it gently as her own. Suddenly she seemed to emerge from a trance, asking to meet his wife, who had remained discreetly in their car. Now, as we enjoyed the *braai*, Grandma was upstairs babysitting – Andre's first Christmas with his mother since the marriage. But she was still apprehensive at meeting me when Andre insisted on introducing us while she hugged the baby.

It was as if a great millstone had been lifted. Whites could for the first time be themselves, at ease with the world. I was reminded of their friendliness and old-fashioned courtesy: it was always there, but obscured by complicity in the brutality of apartheid. The old South Africa we had left had been descending relentlessly into the pit of human depravity. The new one was buoyed by an infectious optimism from whites and blacks alike – though they too were caught by the same sense of wondering whether it was actually true.

It was difficult to find anybody who admitted to ever having supported apartheid. And of course most whites had just gone along with it, turning a blind eye to the misery and the oppression while enjoying the immense privileges. Over 90 per cent of whites had never visited a township, choosing not to know. But there seemed to be a desire to exorcise guilt. Some of our relatives had kept a studious distance when my parents most needed support in the dark early 1960s. Now they gave us generous hospitality, a small example of the healing process that was such a moving feature of the new country.

The dramatic change was everywhere. A Coloured car park attendant at Table Mountain enthused: 'Visitors used to say "South Africa is wonderful". Now they say "*Your* country is wonderful".' Nearly 600 miles eastward along the coast from Cape Town, past long sandy beaches and turquoise sea, lies Port Alfred on the Kowie River where my mother was born. We recalled idyllic summer holidays swimming, boating and fishing. They say 'never go back'. And Port Alfred, like the country, had changed a lot in 30 years. The yuppie marina seemed out of place. But the Kowie was as we had remembered it, especially upstream where it was protected by a nature reserve. The wide, expansive beaches remained a delight. 'It's not right.

We should never have been forced to leave all this', said my mother, tears streaming at the emotion of her return. Her parents had died there during our absence.

Also nostalgic was our return to nearby Grahamstown and the school, much the same as before the war, where she won a 'deportment girdle' for good behaviour and standing up straight. The English colonial feel of the town had been engagingly preserved. But it was startling seeing blacks and whites in the same queues in shops and banks. It was nice to be joined by black families in restaurants and pubs – and pleasantly strange to experience mixed-race swimming on previously segregated beaches (on one occasion amid a school of dolphins surfing in the waves).

We spent Christmas with Peter Brown and his family at their farm, Lion's Bush, in the Natal midlands north of Pietermaritzburg (where I'd lived as a toddler). A long-standing friend and Liberal Party veteran who had recruited my parents, Peter was celebrating his seventieth birthday as we arrived – a reminder of another talent wasted. He should have been in government, but he too was imprisoned, then successively banned from the 1960s. The peaceful atmosphere was striking: just ten miles away at Mooi River there had for years been scenes of awful carnage between Inkatha and ANC supporters. Political violence appeared to have vanished just eight months after the election.

But it was striking how the British connection had survived. Despite a creeping Americanisation, it felt almost like home to a British visitor. On the drive up from Natal to Johannesburg, we stopped at Ladysmith, scene of a famous 118-day siege during the 1899–1902 Anglo–Boer War, and found the home where we had lived for a couple of years in the early 1950s. Nearby was the site of another battle, Spioenkop (from which Liverpool football supporters named their haven at Anfield, the Kop), and to the east Rorkes Drift and Isandhlwana, of 'Zulu War' fame. In need of a swim and lunch we stopped by chance at the Inkwelo Motel below the towering Amajuba Hill – where a British defeat in 1881 ended the first Boer War – and were shown unmarked British graves. The local area is called Ingogo – Zulu for half a crown, which is what local women asked for in return for sexual favours to the British soldiers: a small mixed-race community is the result.

By late afternoon, Johannesburg was in sight, the yellow glint of its goldmine tips visible through the baking heat haze. Another group of old friends embraced us in a welcome-back party. One said how the 'stop the tour' sports protests in 1969–70 had been 'decisive' in rocking whites into accepting change. 'The government must have bitterly regretted kicking out the Hains', she chuckled. The goodwill among blacks remained remarkable. Alan Paton's warning from a black priest in *Cry the Beloved Country* – 'I have one great fear in my heart, that one day when they turn to loving they will find we are turned to hating' – seemed not to have been borne out.

The only upsetting thing was the ubiquitous wave of crime and muggings. However, another old white friend brushed this aside: 'It's just redistribution of wealth. What else do you expect with 60 per cent plus black male unemployment?' But in the plush Jo-burg suburb where we lodged with friends, every home seemed to be guarded by security gates and burglar alarms. Whites travelled only by car – and even then were vulnerable to hijacking at gunpoint. It was almost as if crime had became a means of exacting compensation from whites for the grim decades of oppression.

Although South Africa had been liberated from constitutional apartheid, the crime, poverty and destitution were much, much worse than when we lived there. Over seven million blacks – a quarter of the total black population – subsisted in squatter settlements ringing the white cities. On the Cape Flats, we were shown the latest grim squatting areas, not by accident named 'Beirut' and 'Vietnam' by their inhabitants. In Soweto we were reminded that the Cricket Club's new Elkah Stadium was the only decent cricket ground in the township, serving 25 school and 4 club teams amid a population of three million. We were welcomed there by Khaya Majola and his players and officials. The Club's Chairman, Edward Cebekulu, who had been one of the Soweto student marchers in 1976, pointed out schools that had taken part, the hostel whose workers had gone on the rampage and the memorial to Hector Petersen whose photograph dying in his brother's arms had shocked the world.

After this it was on to the Kruger National Park for a delightful few days with Jill Wentzel. On the way we stopped at the farm which she had owned with her husband Ernie (both were Liberal Party friends from our Pretoria days). Yet another who did not live to see the new South Africa, Ernie's gravestone up on the *kopje* was a tribute to his record as both legal advocate and political activist: 'Ernie – the best labourer dead – and all the sheaves to bind 1933–1986.' In the wildlife park itself, we were again reminded of what we had given up. Nwanetsi camp's isolated location on the Mozambique border gave a real feel of the primitive African bushveld: hyenas and baboons patrolling the perimeter to a cacophony of birds and Christmas beetles. My parents were spotted holding hands outside at dawn, soaking up once more the smells and sounds they loved. The experience made them admit something which – in order to avoid the limbo life of an exile – they had repressed for a quarter of a century: how sorely they missed their old homeland.

And then the *pièce de résistance*. Some of the black activists who had struggled alongside them in Pretoria, suffering much worse harassment than we did, celebrated our return. The last time we had all met was at Pretoria railway station when they waved us goodbye into exile. Poen Ah Dong and Aubrey Apples turned out with dozens of their relatives. When we knew them, they lived in shacks. Now we partied at Poen's daughter's sumptuous family home in Pretoria's exclusive Waterkloof Glen. She would never have been allowed to live in such a 'white' area in the old days, and it would have been illegal to hold such a multi-racial party where liquor was served. As Mom for the first time met her godson, Edward, whose father was David Rathswaffo, two white Afrikaners barbecued a lamb for the predominantly black guests.

At our home town, Pretoria, our old schools were much the same. At Boys High my father pointed out where, as a banned person, he had watched me play cricket from outside the school fence. Hatfield primary school honours board still bore the name P. Hain as head prefect in 1962: the gold lettering had survived even my denunciation in the media and by Government ministers in the early 1970s. At the Union Buildings my mother pointed out where she'd been spat upon by civil servants during a picket. Now all was at peace in the morning sunshine, the new flag fluttering proudly overhead. Once the seat of white oppression, it now housed Mandela's office.

The Old Synagogue, which had acted as a court when my mother had attended Mandela's trial in 1962, and where she and my sisters had met his wife Winnie, was now boarded up. But she couldn't help breaking down outside the Supreme Court where John Harris had been sentenced to death and Hugh Lewin jailed for seven years. The prison where my parents had been jailed, and where in the old days blacks were hanged at the rate of over 100 each year, was hidden behind a new, less threatening, façade. It made me wonder what all those agents of the police state who had intimidated, tortured

and killed in the name of apartheid were doing with themselves these days. Were we passing them by as we walked in
the city centre?

Only time will tell if the miracle of South Africa's transformation can be sustained into future success and stability.
Facing a life sentence of turmoil, violence and gradual collapse, the country was reprieved at the eleventh hour and it
bodes well that lessons appear to have been learnt. Even
former apartheid supporters concede that militant political
resistance, trade union agitation, boycotts and guerrilla struggle were essential to achieve change. There was no alternative but to confront whites with the necessity to abandon
their position. They would not otherwise have done so. The
free market mantra that increased trade and bridge-building
would accomplish transition was shown not merely to be
false. It was also exposed as sophistry to camouflage the
reality that those preaching it were often doing very nicely,
thank you, out of the old system.

The economy had to be brought almost to its knees by
sanctions, strikes, social instability and political resistance until white voters and the business class stared Armageddon in
the face. It was the captains of industry and high finance, so
long the main beneficiaries of apartheid, who decided the game
was up. Through their pressure, they helped create the circumstances in which the modernisers in the National Party could
first grow in influence and then take the initiative. That was
when F.W. de Klerk's moment of truth arrived. South Africa's
Gorbachev seized it with skill, determination and courage. But
even he tried to hang on until the last, so desperate to preserve
a constitutional veto for whites that he was prepared to preside
over still more ruthless political killings and violence.

It was fortunate for him – and for the whole white community – that the Opposition was not only wedded to democracy, but also highly sophisticated. For the South African
miracle is not just about whites ceding power. It is about the
extraordinary generosity shown by blacks when assuming it.
Here the ANC has again been crucial. In Mandela it had an
inspirational leader of historic stature. But underneath him it
had leaders and activists who were on the one hand astute
in the art of negotiation and compromise, and on the other
clear-sighted enough about objectives to maintain legitimacy
with their grassroots in conditions of high volatility. It is this
blend which holds the best hope for the future.

True, enormous problems remain; it could not be otherwise after the apartheid legacy. And, if not overcome, these problems could still strangle the hope that drives the new nation. Nothing will be smooth. Black Africa has hardly been a good advertisement for majority rule. The ANC's huge electoral dominance will have to be exercised with care and sensitivity if the dangers of one-party rule are to be avoided and a democracy that is genuinely pluralistic established. The new South Africa has already experienced doses of government incompetence, examples of corruption, personality clashes and policy arguments. But these are nice problems to have because they signal all the usual ups and downs of democratic politics.

With backing from the outside world, particularly through supportive trade, investment and financial relationships, South Africa could become a model democratic state in a continent stained by dictatorships and dwarfed by external debt, internal inefficiency, corruption and poverty. It could energise the Southern African subcontinent which has such huge potential, with vast natural resources, minerals and food. Given a decent chance by the international capital, currency and financial markets, it could conquer unemployment and squalor. It could also become a model *non-racial* society for the rest of the world; that would indeed be the sweetest victory of all.

Having fought to defeat the Old South Africa, I found myself an unapologetic evangelist for the New One. Every additional eleven tourists is said to create one extra job. The people are hospitable, the weather warm, the food and the wine a delight. Nowhere else in the world can such a rich variety of animals, birds and flowers, and such breathtaking variations in landscape be found, with an infrastructure that makes visiting so effortless, whether in the Mediterranean-type southern Cape, the hot humid littoral of Natal, or the dry heat of the Transvaal highveld. The country, for so long a pariah, is now at last able to reveal itself, in Alan Paton's immortal words, as 'lovely beyond any singing of it'.

SELECTED BIBLIOGRAPHY

Chapter 1: Roots

Brian Lapping, *Apartheid. A history* (London, Grafton Books, 1986).
Freda Troup, *South Africa. An Historical Introduction* (London, Penguin, 1975).

Chapter 2: Repression

Mary Benson, *Nelson Mandela, the man and the movement* (London, Penguin, 1994).
Allister Sparks, *The Mind of South Africa* (London, Heinemann, 1990).

Chapter 3: Explosion

Joseph Lelyveld, *Move Your Shadow, South Africa, Black and White* (London, Michael Joseph, 1986).
Gordon Winter, *Inside BOSS* (London, Penguin, 1981).

Chapter 4: International Protest

Peter Hain, *Don't Play with Apartheid* (London, Allen & Unwin, 1971).
Stuart Harris, *Political Football* (Melbourne, Gold Star Publications, 1972).
Tom Newnham, *Apartheid is Not a Game* (Auckland, Graphic Publications, 1975).

Chapter 5: Response

Robert Archer and Antoine Bouillon, *The South African Game* (London, Zed Press, 1982).

Joan Brickhill, *Race Against Time* (London, International Defence & Aid Fund, 1976).

Derek Humphry (ed.), *The Cricket Conspiracy* (London, National Council for Civil Liberties, 1975).

Sam Ramsamy, *Apartheid: the Real Hurdle* (London, International Defence & Aid Fund, 1982).

Donald Woods, *Asking for Trouble* (London, Victor Gollancz, 1980).

Chapter 6: Trial

Carol Ackroyd, *The Technology of Political Control* (London, Penguin, 1977).

Stephen Dorril and Robin Ramsay, *Smear!* (London, Fourth Estate, 1991).

Peter Hain, *Political Strikes* (London, Viking, 1986).

Peter Hain, *A Putney Plot?* (Nottingham, Spokesman, 1987).

David Leigh, *The Wilson Plot* (London, Heinemann, 1989).

Barrie Penrose and Roger Courtiour, *The Pencourt File* (London, Secker & Warburg, 1978).

Chapman Pincher, *Inside Story* (London, Sidgwick & Jackson, 1978)

Gordon Winter, *Inside BOSS* (London, Penguin, 1981).

Peter Wright, *Spycatcher* (Australia, Heinemann, 1987).

Chapter 7: Resistance

Alan Brooks and Jeremy Brickhill, *Whirlwind before the Storm* (London, International Defence & Aid Fund, 1979).

Stephen M. Davis, *Apartheid's Rebels, Inside South Africa's Hidden War* (New Haven, Yale University Press, 1987).

John Kane-Berman, *South Africa, The Method in the Madness* (London, Pluto Press, 1979).

Ronnie Kasrils, *Armed and Dangerous* (Oxford, Heinemann, 1993).

Chapter 8: Transition

Nelson Mandela, *Long Walk to Freedom* (London, Little Brown, 1994).

Allister Sparks, *To-morrow is Another Country* (Johannesburg, Struick Books, 1994).

Chapter 9: Victory

Andrew Reynolds (ed.), *Election '94 South Africa* (Cape Town, David Philip, 1994).

INDEX